Mickey Cochrane

Mickey Cochrane

The Life of a Baseball Hall of Fame Catcher

by
CHARLIE BEVIS

WITH A FOREWORD BY
Sara Cochrane Bollman

McFarland & Company, Inc., Publishers
Jefferson, North Carolina and London

Front cover: A familiar target for pitchers Lefty Grove in 1931 and Schoolboy Rowe in 1934 en route to American League record tying 16-game winning streaks (Urban Archives, Temple University, Philadelphia, Pennsylvania).

Frontispiece: Practice swing as #3 hitter in Connie Mack's batting order, a table setter for A's sluggers Al Simmons and Jimmie Foxx (National Baseball Library & Archive, Cooperstown, New York).

British Library Cataloguing-in-Publication data are available

Library of Congress Cataloguing-in-Publication Data

Bevis, Charlie, 1954–
    Mickey Cochrane : the life of a Baseball Hall of Fame catcher / by Charlie Bevis ; with a foreword by Sara Cochrane Bollman.
       p.   cm.
    Includes bibliographical references (p.   ) and index.
    ISBN 0-7864-0516-3 (softcover : 50# alkaline paper) ∞
    1. Cochrane, Mickey, 1903–1962. 2. Baseball players — United States — Biography. I. Title.
GV865.C62B48   1998
796.357'092 — dc21
[B]   98-13679
                                                                                                                                                  CIP

©1998 Charlie Bevis. All rights reserved

No part of this book may be reproduced or transmitted in any form or by any means, electronic or mechanical, including photocopying or recording, or by any information storage and retrieval system, without permission in writing from the publisher.

Manufactured in the United States of America

McFarland & Company, Inc., Publishers
   Box 611, Jefferson, North Carolina 28640

To my father,
who instilled in me a passion for
the game of baseball and its history

Contents

	Foreword by Sara Cochrane Bollman	1
	Preface	3
1	Driven Hero of the Motor City	5
2	Fire Starter	10
3	Kid Stuff	20
4	Minor Name Change	29
5	Sigh by Cy	38
6	No Scorn on the Cobb	43
7	Center Stage	51
8	All A's on Baseball's Report Card	59
9	Catcher on Another Plane	68
10	Picnic Grove	78
11	Assault by Pepper	84
12	Battling Japan on the Diamond: Part I	92
13	Mack the Knife	97
14	Taking a Ruth-less Job	103
15	Rowe-ing to Victory	110
16	Suffering from Dizzy Spells	120
17	Top of the Hill in a Depression	127
18	Watch Out for that Bump	137
19	All Fired Up	146

20	Battling Japan on the Diamond: Part II	153
21	Ranch Dressing in Salad Days	160
22	Greatest Receiver, TV or Radio Days	175
	Notes	183
	Bibliography	199
	Index	201

Foreword

Because I didn't make my entrance into this world until 1939, I never got to see my dad play except in one or two "old-timers" games. I have enjoyed reading Charlie Bevis' history of Daddy's baseball career. He has done an extensive amount of research and presented the material in an entertaining style.

Aside from his obvious athletic ability, Daddy was a complex person. He fought depression and alcohol dependence and finally cancer—the one fight he didn't win. He genuinely liked people and trusted them, probably too easily. He knew how to draw out the best in others. Sometimes he used gentle encouragement; sometimes he used anger, both his and theirs. He had a great sense of humor and was a wonderful storyteller. I wish pocket tape recorders had been around in the days when Daddy retold anecdotes from his extraordinary life.

He believed that you should enjoy and experience all life has to offer. "You only go around once, so make it the best you can," he would say. He practiced what he preached. We all have the same challenge—to live well and die well. Gordon Stanley "Mickey" Cochrane did both.

Sara Cochrane Bollman
Spring 1998

Preface

The seed that would grow into this biography was planted the day before my eighth birthday. That's when the lead sports story in the local newspaper concerned the death of a Hall of Fame baseball player who had grown up in the town where we lived.

"Who's Mickey Cochrane?" I asked my father.

My dad told me he had known the Cochrane family while he was growing up and that Mickey's father used to run the old movie theater in the center of town where I went on many Saturday afternoons. My dad also explained that he was younger than Mickey, but that he had played ball with Mickey's younger brother Archie, who now ran a car dealership in Billings, Montana, called Archie Cochrane Ford. Lastly, my dad remembered parades and banquets the town held when Cochrane played in the World Series back in the Great Depression.

In 1965 we visited the Hall of Fame in Cooperstown, New York, to see Cochrane's plaque, and my appetite was whetted to know more about this person who grew up in our small town and played baseball so well. Who were these Philadelphia Athletics?

As I grew older, I picked up some old baseball cards of Cochrane, and a few pictures here and there. I read what I could of his exploits, what little I could find. After college I got more interested in writing baseball history and wrote a few articles for SABR journals and baseball magazines. My corporate business career started to plateau in the early nineties. Why not write a book? And what better topic than the under-appreciated Mickey Cochrane?

Contemporary research material in newspaper and magazine articles of the day was used whenever possible to build the foundation of this biography. Many thanks to the staff of the library at the National Baseball Hall of Fame in Cooperstown, especially Bill Deane when he was there. The staff in the microtext area of the Boston Public Library was always very helpful about retrieving for me innumerable microfilms for *The Sporting News* and *Brockton Enterprise* from the back room, along with dusty boxes of Boston and New York newspapers.

The Urban Archives at Temple University in Philadelphia was an invaluable resource for access to its newspaper clipping morgue containing articles about Cochrane that had appeared in various now defunct Philadelphia newspapers. Assistance in retrieving *Baseball Magazine* articles came from the efforts of the Amateur Athletic Foundation of Los Angeles. Access to Detroit and Philadelphia newspaper microfilm came primarily at the Library of Congress in Washington, D.C., and the Free Library of Philadelphia. Side trips on business in Portland, Oregon, and Fort Myers, Florida, allowed me to gain research material on these relatively brief stops in Cochrane's life.

Thanks to Mary Cochrane and her family, especially daughter Sara, for their assistance in providing background and illumination. I initially located them through a blind letter to Archie Cochrane Ford in Montana, a lead my father Harold Bevis had given me 30 years earlier. My dad never saw any of the fruits of what he planted in me about Mickey Cochrane, however, because he died in 1971 from Lou Gehrig's disease.

And lastly, thanks to my wife Kathie and our children Scott and Kelly for putting up with my obsession for getting Cochrane's story researched and written. As has been said many times by many writers, it couldn't have been done without your support.

- 1 -

Driven Hero of the Motor City

Two steely eyes embedded in a dirt-encrusted face glared toward Stan Hack astride third base for the Chicago Cubs.

With a mask perched atop its black matted hair, the head turned slowly to peer icily at Tommy Bridges standing on the mound. Only the thumping of ball meeting the mitt of the angry Detroit catcher broke the shocked silence of the Navin Field throng eyeing the 3–3 score on the right field scoreboard.

Mickey Cochrane was not happy with how the top of the ninth inning had started off in Game 6 of the 1935 World Series. A triple by Hack had sailed over Gee Walker's head all the way to the center field flagpole. Cochrane zipped the ball back to Bridges.

Nothing needed to be said to his pitcher, as Cochrane's infectious drive to win seemingly merged by osmosis with Bridges' desire to excel. It was motivation by example, with the Tigers up three games to two on the verge of World Series victory for the first time in the 34-year history of the Detroit franchise.

This inning would become a monument to the baseball skills of both Cochrane and Bridges. Ten more pitches would be thrown, nine of them strikes, with no further runners reaching base.

Cochrane drew the mask down and assumed his crouch behind home plate as Cub shortstop Billy Jurges stepped into the batter's box. He was retired on three straight strikes, waving his bat at the final serve which broke low over the outside corner of the plate.

As Cub pitcher Larry French came up next, Cochrane peered quizzically at him through the iron bars of his mask, wondering why Cub manager Charlie Grimm wasn't pinch hitting for him when a fly ball would put them ahead.

After French swung and missed at the first two pitches, Cochrane decided to have Bridges throw another curve ball to go for the strikeout. French barely made contact with Bridges' delivery as the ball was topped out towards the mound.

Yanking the mask off, Cochrane positioned himself for a possible play on Hack at the plate. Bridges pounced on the dribbler, however, and immediately looked to the runner at third base.

Hack had come a few steps down the third base line but quickly realized it would be a fruitless venture. He would be out by several feet, and crashing into Cochrane in an attempt to jar loose the ball would be foolhardy. Cochrane stood like a rock to protect home plate from invasion by opponents.

Bridges retired French for the second out by tossing the ball to first baseman Marv Owen, substituting for slugger Hank Greenberg, who had broken his wrist in Game 2 of the Series.

Six pitches, six strikes, two outs followed Hack's triple. Rather than becoming rankled, Bridges bore down. Cochrane knew how to handle his troops, what it took for each player to generate his best effort. His quiet, get-tough approach with Bridges seemed to be paying off.

Cub leadoff hitter Augie Galan was next, and Cochrane continued with Bridges' strength, the curve ball, or "hook," as he liked to call it. Bridges, however, was too pumped up. He held onto the ball too tightly and tried to throw it too hard. The pitch hit the dirt two feet in front of the plate — a potential wild pitch.

Cochrane didn't panic. He needed to intercept the misdirected pitch from proceeding to the backstop, which would easily allow Hack to score the go-ahead run for Chicago. But this pitch was going to be tough to catch.

"There was only one thing I could do, get down on my knees and try somehow to block it. Luckily I came up with it," Cochrane recalled modestly, leaving Hack glowering at him from third base.

Billy Herman was on deck; he had had three hits already that day and had knocked in all three Chicago runs. If Galan reached base, there was a good chance Herman would blow the whole game open.

Bridges calmed down and proceeded to get two strikes on Galan before he hit the 1–2 pitch solidly. It went more high than far, however, and landed in Goose Goslin's glove in left field for the third out of the inning. The cheers of the crowd rocked the stands as the Tigers ran off the field having averted possible disaster.

"When I think back to the 1935 World Series," Herman recalled later in life, "all I can see is Hack standing on third base, waiting for somebody to drive him in. Seems he stood there for hours and hours."

Cochrane needed to turn briefly into full-time manager during this interlude in the action. In his chameleon role as player-manager, he seemed to flip easily back and forth between roles. Shucking his chest protector on the way to the dugout, he intercepted Flea Clifton on the way in from third base and briefly encouraged him. His leadership was conveyed not in eloquent words but rather through his approach to the game on the field.

Clifton was playing only because Greenberg was injured; Cochrane had

1. Driven Hero of the Motor City

moved Owen from third base to first and inserted Clifton at third. However, going hitless in 15 at bats since Game 3 of the Series, Clifton had unfortunately lived up to his light hitting reputation.

But Cochrane hadn't hesitated to stay with Clifton here in an important tight situation, providing Flea with an extra degree of confidence as he ambled up to the plate to face French in the bottom of the 9th in the tie game. Cochrane himself shed his shin guards and grabbed a bat because he was the next batter.

Clifton battled French to a 3–2 count. With Cochrane exhorting encouragement from the on-deck circle, Clifton fouled off the next pitch but then succumbed to French, swinging and missing as French racked up his seventh strikeout of the game.

The Cubs' benchjockeys taunted Cochrane as he jogged up to the left-handed batter's box, although they would soon be quieted. Cochrane, the number two hitter in the Tiger order, realized that the first pitch would probably be the only decent one he would see, as French tried to get ahead in the count and then pitch around him, so he had better make the best of the first pitch.

Cochrane connected with the first pitch and laced a hot grounder into the hole between first baseman Phil Cavarretta and second baseman Herman, who ran to his left and dove to knock down Cochrane's hit on the outfield grass. Cochrane didn't watch the play but used his speed to simply race to first base, where he would consider further possibilities. Herman didn't attempt to throw out the speedy Cochrane as he collected his third single of the day.

Following Cochrane was second baseman Charlie Gehringer, second in a series of three left-handed hitters in the 2–3–4 spots in Cochrane's Detroit batting order.

In contrast to the mastery of the Bridges-Cochrane battery during the top half of the inning, the Cubs combination of French and Gabby Hartnett had less success in the crucial situations. French's first two pitches to Gehringer were called balls.

As the base runner on first, Cochrane took a modest lead as Cavarretta stationed himself on the base for a possible pick-off throw from French. Perhaps more importantly, Cochrane was tormenting French with verbal barbs as he tried to distract him from concentrating on getting Gehringer out at the plate.

On the 2–0 count, French came inside with a slow curve, which Gehringer jumped on to drill a line drive down the first base line. At the crack of the bat, Cochrane pushed off to head to second base, expecting Cavarretta to have moved off the bag to get into position to cover more ground at first base, but Gehringer's shot flew at the base toward the right field corner. As Mickey began to calculate whether he could score on the play or not, he heard a sound he wasn't expecting to hear: the thud of ball hitting leather. Cochrane stopped cold in his tracks. Cavarretta hadn't moved after all!

Fortunately for the Tigers, the ball handcuffed Cavarretta, hit the heel of his glove, and trickled away. Cochrane started his 90-foot trek to second base once again, this time simply hoping to make it there safely. Cavarretta recovered the ball in time to step on first base to put out Gehringer and then wheeled to throw to shortstop Jurges in an attempt to double up Cochrane.

Cavarretta didn't have the time to step to the side to get a better angle for his throw and was forced to throw straight on, directly behind Cochrane. Cavarretta's throw glanced off Cochrane's shoulder as he slid safely into second base.

Cochrane was on second base with the winning run as Goose Goslin came to bat with two outs in the bottom of the 9th. Cochrane's heart was racing. The World Series title was one hit away.

The crowd at Navin Field was going crazy, screaming, "Yea, Goose. Yea, Goose," over and over. The noise was deafening, especially from the expansive left field bleachers (which later were replaced by today's double-deck seating). The cheering drowned out even Cochrane's shouts at Goslin from second base.

Goslin was out in front of French's first pitch and hooked it into the right field stands for strike one as the crowd groaned. Reaching down, Goslin rubbed dirt on his hands, then gripped his bat and stepped back into the batter's box to face French's next delivery, which would put both Goslin and Cochrane into the history books.

French tossed a slow curve to Goslin, who connected with enough of the ball to arch a "dying quail" over second base out of the reach of Herman, Jurges, and center fielder Frank Demaree. Cochrane didn't need to see where the ball landed. There were two outs, and he was off with the crack of Goslin's bat.

Cochrane was around third base almost before the ball had struck ground as coach Del Baker frantically waved him home. Cochrane's head was down and his arms and legs were pumping for the energy to score the run to give Detroit its first-ever world championship.

"World Series money tickled Cochrane's feet and lent him speed," said one writer who described the fabled dash to glory.

Cochrane crossed home plate standing, scoring easily as Demaree's lame throw in was cut off by Cavarretta, who pocketed the ball to prevent the Tigers from taking a souvenir of their victory.

"Damn, that was so frustrating," Herman remembered. "Running after the ball that's got the World Series riding on it, knowing that you're not going to catch it and knowing that you're not going to miss it by much. It just drops on the grass and breaks your heart."

As Cochrane crossed the plate, his stern baseball persona evaporated and his personal exuberance came out. Syndicated writer Paul Gallico captured Cochrane's emotion in his newspaper column:

> It was something to see — Mickey Cochrane stabbing his spikes into the plate with the winning run and his first world's championship, and then

1. Driven Hero of the Motor City

going mad, like a young colt, leaping and cavorting about, shaking his bare, dark head.

He ran all the way back to the screen, then whirled in a mad dance of victory, hurling himself into the arms of his players, punching and thumping them, reveling to the utmost of his buoyant Irish nature in the victory for which he had fought so hard.

When Cochrane stood on second, a lone figure in white, I have never seen such will and energy from a single person. He had to come home. He willed to come home. I believe if Goslin hadn't hit he would have stolen home from second base.

When Cochrane touched home plate, all the hard work, all the pain and heartache of being the player-manager of the Detroit Tigers for two years paid off. With the Philadelphia A's, he had won World Series titles in 1929 and 1930, but this third championship was different. And it wasn't merely that he was now also the manager besides the catcher.

Cochrane was more than just a baseball hero to the city of Detroit. He became a genuine civic hero as well. His turnaround of the Tigers gave every working man in the area, even the nation, hope. If the Tigers could shed their losing ways and win a World Series, so could anyone suffering through the Great Depression turn his or her life around as well. This hope was needed when unemployment had soared to 30 percent among the autoworkers of the Detroit area.

While Cochrane had polished his intellectual skills at Boston University, also playing football and baseball there in the early 1920s, he had not had a privileged upbringing. His father had labored to provide for his family, and Cochrane himself washed dishes to get through school in order to get to this ecstatic Tiger clubhouse on October 7, 1935. The average assembly line worker at Ford could identify with Cochrane and vice versa. Being a role model would eventually become, though, a terrible burden for Cochrane to shoulder.

A police escort was required to allow Cochrane to leave Navin Field as a huge crowd still waited 45 minutes after the game was over. Thousands paraded in downtown Detroit as well amidst a blizzard of paper and a din of automobile horns and earsplitting cannon blasts while loudspeakers blared "Hold That Tiger." It was indeed a great day for Detroit baseball fans.

The 32-year-old Cochrane had played on five American League pennant-winning teams during his 11 years in the major leagues, three with the Athletics and now two with the Tigers, while never playing on a team that finished lower than third place. Since 1920, when the Yankees began their domination, only three American League players have played in five different World Series without donning the Yankee uniform for any of them. Cochrane is one of those three.

Cochrane had every expectation that this 1935 World Series victory would propel him to ever greater heights. Little did he realize that this was the zenith and that life would take him down a different path after October 7, 1935.

- 2 -

Fire Starter

Three weeks before he crossed home plate with the winning run of the 1935 World Series, Cochrane was honored by friends and neighbors in his hometown of Bridgewater, Massachusetts.

"Mickey Cochrane, ace pilot of the pennant winning Detroit Tigers, came back to his home town last night and was accorded a conqueror's welcome by his fellow townsmen, who have watched with pride and enthusiasm his marvelous climb up the ladder of athletic fame," the local newspaper, the *Brockton Enterprise*, reported.

At 6:30 P.M. on September 17, Cochrane was met at Trinity Church near the center of Bridgewater for the start of a parade around the town common; he rode in an open car on the way to a banquet at the Boyden Gym. Most of the Tiger team came with Cochrane that night, following a game that afternoon with the Red Sox in Boston, 30 miles north of Bridgewater.

"Automobile horns were sounded and the fire alarm shrieked as the parade wound its way through the center of town as Mickey, nervously puffing away on a cigaret, waved a greeting to his boyhood companions," the New Bedford *Standard-Times* wrote of the event.

Proclamations were read from the mayor of Detroit and Michigan's Governor Frank Fitzgerald. Speeches honoring Cochrane were made by former coaches and teammates, by toastmaster Judge George Alden, in whose back lot Cochrane first played baseball, and by townspeople who used Cochrane as an illustration of a small town success story. Clearly, Cochrane was a hometown hero.

How did Mickey grow into America's hero in the midst of the Great Depression by winning the 1935 World Series?

He was fiery. This word is inevitably the one adjective used to describe Mickey Cochrane. His competitive spirit and all-consuming drive dominated his baseball career. The inscription on his plaque at the Baseball Hall of Fame even begins "Fiery catcher."

2. Fire Starter

House where Cochrane grew up, 299 Pleasant Street in Bridgewater, Massachusetts (author's collection).

The fire that fueled Cochrane's energy level was stoked in the small town of Bridgewater, where immigrants John and Sadie Cochrane raised their family. Bridgewater today is a thriving suburb of Boston. Like many such communities near major urban areas, Bridgewater has been transformed over the years from the small town it was when Cochrane lived there and returned there in 1935.

A well-kept town common helps retain some of the town's New England charm, and it looks much the same as it did when Cochrane's parade wound around it back in 1935. Until recently, the common also provided the only visible link to its native son enshrined in Cooperstown. A small monument dedicated there on June 28, 1985, honors Cochrane with this inscription: "May his leadership and fierce competitive spirit be an inspiration to the youth of Bridgewater."

On April 26, 1997, nearly 50 years after being enshrined in the Baseball Hall of Fame, Cochrane was honored again by his hometown when a six-foot-high granite monument was dedicated at the town's playing fields and the baseball diamonds were christened the Mickey Cochrane Baseball Complex.

The hero of the 1935 World Series was born Gordon Stanley Cochrane on April 6, 1903. He wasn't known as Mickey in his youth; when someone called out, "Hey, Mickey!" it was always a call to his pal Mickey Costa.

Cochrane's ancestry was Scotch-Irish. His father, John Cochrane, was born in 1870 as an English citizen in the village of Dromoor near the town of Omagh in Ireland. He was one of a dozen children parented by James Cochrane and Margaret Sample, whose families no doubt emigrated from Scotland, where the Cochrane surname originated.

"This Scottish surname is usually borne in Ireland by the descendants of settlers from Scotland who brought it to Ulster in the 17th century," the book *Irish Family Names* reveals. "Cochrane is used interchangeably with Corcoran, a name of Irish origin."

The Cochranes were not a Catholic family from the green of Ireland, but rather were Orangemen from County Tyronne in Northern Ireland who belonged to the Church of England, the Anglican faith. This made it rather contemptible that Gordon would eventually be tagged with his nickname Mickey based on the belief that he was just another Irish "mick."

Understandably then, no one in the family or anyone who knew him well ever called him Mickey. Instead he became Mike in private life while being Mickey to the public. Only his parents called him Gordon as an adult.

"Grampa had this mix of an accent between New England and Scottish," Mike's daughter Sara remembered. "He'd call Dad Gordon but it'd come out sounding like Gat-on."

John Cochrane came to the United States in 1888 with his parents and siblings and soon settled in Bridgewater. John, a caretaker of a private estate for a wealthy family, became a naturalized U.S. citizen in 1892.

Two years later, in 1894, a minister at Trinity Church, where the 1935 parade began, married John Cochrane and Sarah Campbell. Trinity was an Episcopalian church, the American version of the Anglican faith. Gordon also had Scottish ancestry on his mother's side; Sarah's parents were born in Scotland. They came to America by way of Canada, where Sarah, later to be known as Sadie, was born in 1870 on Prince Edward Island.

Gordon was the fifth of seven children of John and Sadie Cochrane, most born in their home at 188 Union Street. Edith was the oldest, being seven years old at Gordon's birth in 1903, when Flora was six, Arthur was five, and Albert was three. A child was stillborn in 1907 between Gordon's birth and that in 1910 of his brother Archie, named after his maternal grandfather. Arthur died of tuberculosis when Gordon was just nine years old.

In 1908 when Gordon was five years old, his father bought a 16-acre farm about a half-mile from the Union Street house at 299 Pleasant Street and became a full-time farmer. Sadie Cochrane took in sewing to help with family finances, but the shrewd and thrifty John Cochrane appears to have saved and invested his money well. Following the end of World War I, Gordon's father became co-owner of the Princess Theatre in the center of town and ran the popular movie house for more than 20 years.

Young Gordon was not a budding farmer. He much preferred playing ball and running races with his friends, whereas his father, who had never had much

2. Fire Starter

time for frolic and had needed to work as a youngster, considered Gordon's time better spent on the family tract.

Cochrane often said that when his father handed him a hoe to use in the potato patch, he would head to the field but then duck behind a stone wall.

"I'd get to that wall and throw the hoe away, grab my glove from inside my shirt and beat it down the road to town. Most of the time I'd get away with it. My older brother would do the hoeing," he said. "But once in a while he'd get tired of doing it all and tell on me. Then I'd get home and get a licking. I used to average about one licking a week."

That road to town was Mt. Prospect Street, a distance that Cochrane traveled many times training to run. He once had distant dreams of running in the Olympics, so he would sprint every opportunity he could.

"That stretch of road at night was pitch dark and scary," Mike would recall. "Boy did that make me run like hell."

Growing up in a small rural town, Gordon naturally learned to hunt and fish, activities he would pursue for his entire life. It also helped him become friendly with the neighboring Bohr family, particularly one of the daughters, Mary, who would one day become his wife.

"Mike used to borrow our hunting dogs and go hunting across Pleasant Street," said Mary, remembering her early meetings with Mike, who was two years older than her.

"The Kid's love for shooting came naturally enough from his association with the man who later became his father-in-law, Bill Bohr, an ardent sportsman who kept a kennel of crack shooting dogs, a number of them strong in the Sir Roger de Coverly strain of blood," a 1934 *Standard-Times* newspaper article concluded. "The Kid learned to shoot up back of Ray Rhoades' house on Pleasant Street where Ray, Harrison Keith and he used to put in hours of practice with a hand trap, the boys taking turns in throwing the hardest, fastest, daisy trimming, scaling type of Blue Rocks that they could manage."

Cochrane honed his eye on trap shooting, but he may not have been a natural born tracker. "The boys tell a story at Cochrane's expense of a trip he made with his brother Bert and Harrison Keith," the *Standard-Times* article continued. "A deer had been seen in the neighborhood of the Cochrane home a few days previously and as the trio clambered over a stone wall, the Kid noticed some fresh tracks on the far side of the wall. 'Deer tracks' he exclaimed and started out to trail the animal down. Through bushes, along cow paths, and across a strip of meadow he trailed the animal, right up to the other end of the enclosure, where the object of the search was found, a big, fat and lazy pig."

Gordon loved not only hunting and fishing but all sports as a kid. But even as a 10 year old, he had an odd ambition. He wanted to be a big league manager when he grew up. "A lot of kids want to be big-league players, but I don't know of another who looked beyond that to the manager's job," Mike recalled in the 1950s. "How did I happen to think about it? Who knows? Maybe I just had to be the boss."

Flora Stuart, one of Cochrane's grade school teachers at the McElwain School, foresaw that as well. She recalled at the 1935 testimonial that "he had initiative, courage, determination, ability to direct others and was a fighter always."

The leadership fire was already burning slowly in the broad-shouldered child with the thick black hair, blue eyes, and solid jaw. His father probably unwittingly stoked it up a notch.

John Cochrane was not initially pleased with his son Gordon's choice of profession. Mike remembered his transition from the college diamond, "then into pro baseball with my father shaking his head." A December 1924 *Boston Globe* newspaper profile of Mike even had a subheadline "Cochrane's Folks in Bridgewater Were Not Enthused at Baseball Career."

In that profile John Cochrane was portrayed as one who "wouldn't stand in the way of the fulfillment of his [son's] cherished dreams and wanted him to make a success at whatever he chose to pursue." John Cochrane did want Gordon to enter business "but consented to allow the lad to try his hand at baseball."

John Cochrane did become a faithful follower of his son's baseball career. A September 18, 1935, newspaper account notes: "Thoughts wandered to the kindly-faced lady and gray-haired man at her side, Mickey's mother and father. It wasn't hard to visualize their emotions. Seated at the head table, beside their famous son, they listened to men from all sections of the country extoll the virtues and prowess of Mickey Cochrane. They had every reason to be proud of their boy."

Cochrane was an overachiever on the ball fields from the beginning. He said that he tagged along after his brother's gang of friends as a stubby-legged youngster and won the disapproval of them all. But after a while the gang became resigned to him, and adopted the attitude "I suppose we'll have to take the kid along." According to Cochrane, this is how his early nickname of "Kid" was born.

Others remember that Kid Cochrane was dubbed in more adult adventures as a 17-year-old high school "boy" playing on a local amateur basketball team with the older "men." Although he wasn't on the starting five at first, he often came off the bench to spell those players on the court. His spirit was so infective that the spectators would shout when the team was down in the score, "Put the kid in!"

By his own admission, as well as the observation of others, Kid Cochrane was a much better football player, even a better basketball player, than he was a baseball player. "I had experienced little trouble with football," Mike often said, "but baseball was a sport of another order."

2. Fire Starter

At the time Cochrane entered Bridgewater High School in the fall of 1916, there was no football team, but the school did field a baseball squad. As a 14-year-old freshman, he broke into the varsity lineup in the spring of 1917 on May 18 when the varsity defeated a team of Bridgewater High alumni 4–3 at the town's South Field diamond.

The *Brockton Enterprise* reported that "the High School team had several regulars out.... Corcoran, a substitute, played a good game at short and scored two of his team's four runs." If the writer had only known the freshman shortstop's baseball future, he might have made sure he spelled his name right. The substitute shortstop, while going 1 for 4 for the day at bat, did collect 50 percent of the team's hits off the alumni squad.

As they say, the rest is history. A week later he played second base and batted last in the order in a 7–1 loss to Abington High. But during the ensuing weeks, Cochrane progressively moved his way up in the batting order while taking over as the team's shortstop. In the season finale on June 15 at South Field, Bridgewater beat rival East Bridgewater High 6–3 as Cochrane, batting second in the order, drove in the go-ahead run in the 4th inning. Gordon S. Cochrane had arrived — the newspaper finally spelled his name correctly.

While Cochrane did exhibit a good deal of skill at the game, the baseball teams at Bridgewater High were not spectacular. America had entered World War I shortly before the 1917 baseball season began, and by 1918 many students were entering the service or were working after school to help support family in those trying times. Gordon's older brother Bert left in May 1918 for the naval reserve after playing in just one baseball game that spring. His cousin Fred would die on a French battlefield in October 1918.

With a shortage of players, Cochrane had a lock on the shortstop position for his sophomore year, although the team won only one game that year and lost several others by lopsided scores during the short New England spring.

In Bridgewater High's only victory in 1918, 8–5 over Howard High of neighboring West Bridgewater, Cochrane was a catcher for the first time, moving from shortstop to replace the team's injured catcher, Antulonis. A week later he caught the entire game in his team's 13–1 loss to Abington High, producing the unusual looking box score with the catcher as leadoff hitter going 1 for 3.

"Cochrane tried his hand at catching and found trouble in holding Dewhurst, having three passed balls," the newspaper account noted. The coach probably couldn't wait for his regular catcher to return, because Cochrane was no natural behind the plate.

The following 1919 season was another series of disappointing losses for the Bridgewater High nine. Cochrane played mostly shortstop and third base that season and took the mound several times to try to stop the opposition bats. He was a better pitcher than catcher.

"Cochrane went to the box for Bridgewater in the eighth inning and although East Bridgewater found him for two hits, they were unable to score," according to the newspaper account of a May 24 game that emphasized the positive. Bridgewater was already down 14–3 at the time Cochrane went in to pitch.

That junior year Cochrane emerged as a hitter, collecting ten hits in his first four games. A familiar newspaper refrain that year was "Cochrane starred for the losers." In the season finale on June 14, in yet another defeat, Cochrane received his first headline, "While Cochrane was hit hard — Cochrane hit homer."

When not on the baseball diamond, Cochrane played a little basketball and track for his high school. In early April of 1919, Bridgewater defeated Howard High 15–14 in double overtime for the so-called basketball championship of the three Bridgewaters. Basketball was not the run-and-gun game it is today. Back then it was a much more deliberate passing game with dribbling discouraged, and it was played on a court enclosed by a cage or net to keep the ball in play at all times. Players were often referred to as "cagers," not hoopsters.

The track team was not as organized as the other teams at Bridgewater High. It competed in no head-to-head meets, but it did participate in a few regional meets. At a multischool meet at Brockton in the spring of 1918, Cochrane and three teammates lost the relay race to the city runners from Brockton, who dominated the meet. During the fall of 1919, at what was billed as the first annual Southeastern Massachusetts High School athletic meet at the Brockton Fair, Cochrane didn't run in any track events, but he won the football punt for distance contest with a kick of 47 yards, 2 feet.

Football and Cochrane were a powerful combination. Shortly before World War I was about to conclude on Armistice Day in 1918, Bridgewater High announced the reestablishment of its school football team, after an absence of several years. Eighteen candidates went out for the eleven spots on the team, players going both ways on offense and defense in those days.

Even with an abbreviated schedule, Cochrane showed a talent for the game of football. The team lost all four of its games in 1918 and didn't score a point until its last game on Thanksgiving Day against an alumni squad. "Cochrane at quarterback showed good judgement in picking out plays and his tackling in the backfield was deadly, once stopping the speedy Kilbridge with a clean field before him," the *Brockton Enterprise* reported.

In the fall of 1919, during his senior year, Cochrane led the football team to a 5–5–1 record in his only full season of high school play. As the team's quarterback, Cochrane not only directed the offense but also ran and passed the ball in the days before the forward pass was fashionable. He played defensive back when the other team controlled the ball and was all over the field in his attempts to stop the opposition from scoring.

As if quarterbacking and tackling weren't enough, Cochrane also used his

2. Fire Starter

strong right leg to do the kicking — punts, extra points, field goals, and kickoffs. Often his kickoffs soared all the way to the other team's goal line, making them tough to catch and return for decent yardage, helping to pin the opponents back in their own territory. It was not unusual for a newspaper account to open with "From the first kickoff by Cochrane of the Bridgewater team..." and go on to describe several long kicks to the goal line.

In contrast to baseball, where Cochrane's individual efforts couldn't propel his team to victory, his contributions on the football gridiron could yield a better return for Bridgewater High. His forward pass to Copp helped lead his team to a 27–0 victory over St. Mary's High of Taunton. Two weeks later on November 8 Cochrane's two touchdown runs, including a 96-yard run, powered Bridgewater High to a 32–0 victory over Plymouth High. And to cap the season on Thanksgiving Day, in the second half Cochrane ran the ball five yards to score the only touchdown of the game as Bridgewater defeated Rockland High 6–0.

This Thanksgiving football victory would be Cochrane's last high school game. For the basketball and baseball seasons of his senior year in high school, Cochrane stepped up to a higher level of competition by playing for local amateur teams.

On the Sunday of Thanksgiving weekend, the Bridgewater Club defeated the Middleboro YMCA team 24–20 on the basketball court at Boyden Gymnasium at the Bridgewater Normal School (now Bridgewater State College) as Cochrane scored seven baskets from his left forward position. He picked up a number of kudos in newspaper accounts of the Bridgewater Club games, such as this description of his play in a February 12 game: "Cochrane, the clever high school player, was a delight to the fans. He played wonderful ball and scored two baskets."

George Hoyt, the coach of the Bridgewater Club, recalled at the 1935 Cochrane testimonial that Kid was a tough competitor from the beginning. "At first he wanted to do all the scoring and all the defensive play as well. He's the perfect athlete. He richly deserves all the fine tributes being paid to him."

"The Bridgewater Club year after year tangled with the best of them and kept well up in the race for New England amateur and professional honors with Cochrane and Pratt as star forwards," one newspaper writer wrote years later. "The Pratt-Cochrane forwards were something to make a coach open his eyes in amazement. If Cochrane was fast, so was Arthur Pratt. If Pratt was shifty, so was Kid Cochrane. Both were wonders."

One of Cochrane's early proponents of his athletic career was Charlie Hayes, who operated the local ice cream parlor. Hayes would present Cochrane with a loving cup at the 1935 testimonial, which was engraved "presented by the people of Bridgewater in recognition of his great achievements in baseball."

"We used to go to Hayes for ice cream after basketball games," Mary Cochrane remembered of her early dates with Mike; they and Charlie Hayes would discuss the outcome of the games. "When we weren't at Hayes, we'd go for walks down Bedford Street or skate on Carver's Pond."

"One thing at Charlie's store which the Kid liked particularly was that great big bowl of homecooked salted peanuts which stood conveniently open on the marble slab of the soda fountain," a writer once observed. "When Cochrane was traveling with the big league teams, Charlie used to do up great boxes of the salted peanuts and mail them to the Kid."

Mike's friendship with Hayes had one downside for historians, though.

"Charlie Hayes, former confectioner and baker in Bridgewater had the greatest collection of clippings and photos concerning the Kid in existence. They told of Kid Cochrane's achievements from his school days on," a 1934 look back at Cochrane's early days revealed. "But a fire in the block where the store was located disposed of part of the collection and the closing of the store while he was in the hospital took care of the remainder."

In the spring and summer of 1920, Cochrane played for the Bridgewater Knights of Columbus, or K of C, one of three town teams that were organized that year. Although by no means its dominant player, he was an integral member of the squad, generally playing first base and a bit of outfield.

The fact that Cochrane didn't play baseball for Bridgewater High his senior year has led to the story that Cochrane was cut from the team by the coach because he wasn't good enough. "Mike wanted to play for both Bridgewater High and the K of C team at the same time," Mary Cochrane recalled. "Coach Murray told him to not show up if his loyalty wasn't with the high school. So Mike didn't bother with him."

After graduating from Bridgewater High on June 21, one of 38 graduates, the 17-year-old Cochrane took to the ball fields of southeastern Massachusetts. The toughness of the Kid began to really come out, especially in the intratown games against the Bridgewater Ramblers and the Bridgewater Catholic Club.

In an August 14 game with the Ramblers, Cochrane drove in the only run in the Knights of Columbus 4–1 loss during the fourth inning. "With two strikes on him, Burbank tried to sneak one over for the third but the 'Kid' met it on the nose and drove it to right putting Nolan over for the Knights' only tally."

And in a Labor Day battle with the Ramblers for the championship of Bridgewater, the Knights of Columbus defeated the Ramblers 3–1 at St. John's Field in East Bridgewater before a holiday crowd of 1200 spectators. Cochrane started the winning rally in the seventh inning with a hard smash to right field, going 2 for 4 out of the sixth spot in the order.

Labor Day traditionally marks the end of the summer season in New England, as crisp cool days replace the heat of the short summer. This particular Labor Day in 1920 marked the end of Kid Cochrane's youthful days on the playing fields of Bridgewater and the beginning of a new segment of his life.

2. Fire Starter

Using the knowledge gained in his commercial course studies at Bridgewater High and the wages he earned that summer laboring at the Stanley Iron Works, Gordon headed to Boston University. While most others in Bridgewater could only hope to excel on the athletic field for the Bridgewater Knights of Columbus or Rambler teams, Kid Cochrane's intensity wouldn't settle for this. He had higher aspirations.

- 3 -

Kid Stuff

It was the Roaring Twenties, the golden age of sport. Babe Ruth transformed the game of baseball, as did Jack Dempsey boxing, Bobby Jones golf, Bill Tilden tennis, and Red Grange football.

If there had been any likelihood of earning a decent living playing football for pay, Cochrane would never have given baseball a second look. Still in its infancy in 1920, the National Football League consisted only of a few teams located in the Midwest. College football was where fan attention was centered; little interest diverted towards the fledgling professional circuit.

The 17-year-old Cochrane had a big decision to make about which college to attend. Mike's girl Mary Bohr had moved to Windsor, Vermont, with her family when her father's work took him to a shoe factory there. "My parents liked Mike and they wanted him to go to Dartmouth," Mary Cochrane recalled. Dartmouth was just up the Connecticut River from Windsor in Hanover, New Hampshire. "However, Dartmouth wouldn't let Mike play football as a freshman."

Mike had the same problem with Lehigh and other schools he considered. He was impatient and wanted to play immediately, so he choose lesser-known Boston University.

Cochrane played four years of varsity football at Boston University, starring at quarterback and halfback from his freshman days on the Commonwealth Avenue campus. Ivy League schools like Harvard and Dartmouth dominated college football in the East during the 1920s, and Boston College played a top-notch schedule of both eastern and midwestern schools.

Boston University didn't get the newspaper headlines, playing a tier below crosstown rivals Boston College and Harvard against the likes of New Hampshire State, Tufts, and Worcester Polytech. BU didn't even have its own playing field as did BC and Harvard; it played most of its games on the road and scheduled "home" games at nearby Braves Field whenever it could, which wasn't too often.

The team practiced on a vacant lot below Braves Field near the railroad yards. "The team had a coach, a schedule — and Cochrane," as one writer put it. Cochrane said they had uniforms for about 27 players "but there weren't many that matched."

Football in the twenties was a perfect outlet for Cochrane's competitiveness, which was probably accelerated by playing for such an underdog as BU. The hitting was just as hard as in today's game, but then there was only limited padding in the uniform. Leather helmets provided little protection against head injury, and there was no face mask to absorb blows to the face. The energy level needed to play the game also had to be higher than today, as the two-platoon game was years away. Players played both offense and defense.

As he had been for Bridgewater High, Cochrane was at many times a one-man show — running, throwing, catching, and tackling all over the field. It's been said that a typical practice stunt at BU was to have an 11-man squad kick off to Cochrane and have him weave his way through the pack. If he couldn't elude all the would-be tacklers and score, Cochrane would call for another kickoff. What a way to work on speed and agility. Cochrane's goal was to be tough to catch when he was running on the gridiron.

Right out of high school in the fall of 1920, Cochrane played on the BU varsity team coached by Percy Wendell. In an otherwise lackluster BU season, the freshman Cochrane scored his first collegiate touchdown on a 25-yard-pass play in BU's 28–0 shutout win over the Connecticut Aggies (now the University of Connecticut) in a rare Braves Field appearance on October 30.

Wendell played Kid at quarterback, which didn't set well with Cochrane. Later reflecting on his freshman year, he noted: "Wendell used the Harvard system, in which the quarterback never carried the ball. He was supposed to have brains. That was baloney to me."When Wendell left BU to coach at Williams College, Dr. Charles Whalen came to coach BU for Kid's next three years. "Whalen shifted me to one of the halfback posts, then I did carry the ball and plenty," Cochrane remembered. "Once in a while they carried me off the field, but I was never seriously hurt."

The 1921 season was BU's most successful with Cochrane in the backfield, as the team under Whalen compiled a 6–2 record. The season began prophetically on October 1 with its perennial loss to Boston College, but in 1921 the score was only 13–0 on BC's home turf at the Heights. BU then rattled off six victories, with consistently "the punting of Cochrane [being] one of the features of the game."

When BU stunned Tufts 8–7 on November 5 at its suburban Medford campus, Kid kicked a 75-yard punt that went out on the Tufts 4-yard line to put BU in position to score a 2-point safety, which became the eventual margin of victory. Cochrane, pictured for the first time in a Boston newspaper, also helped set up the winning touchdown by Babe Tonry with a reverse field run, as practiced many times by the railroad yards below Braves Field.

After two successful seasons on the BU football gridiron, Cochrane began to aspire to greater heights. According to newspaper accounts in January 1922, Cochrane actually transferred to Georgetown University that winter to play a higher level of football at that institution in the fall. For unknown reasons, Cochrane was back at BU to play baseball that spring.

The fall of 1922 Cochrane played not only with the BU varsity but also with the semipro Providence Steam Roller to satisfy his thirst for a better brand of football. A few years later, the Steam Roller became a franchise in the National Football League briefly. To protect his collegiate status, Cochrane played under the moniker Mickey Hickey.

"They never played him where he would stand out or get hurt," Mary Cochrane said. Mary continued to be Mike's companion, accompanying him to Rhode Island for the games. She was attending a private school outside Boston, the Dana Hall School in Wellesley, where she had persuaded her parents to send her from Vermont to be closer to Mike.

For much of Kid's junior and senior years, his aggressive play did result in injuries serious enough to keep him off the playing field. But when Cochrane did play, his exploits were memorable even though BU finished at 2–4–3 in 1922 and 1–6 in 1923.

To begin his junior year, BU tied Colby 3–3 at Waterville, Maine, on the strength of Kid's 32-yard drop-kick field goal.

Cochrane's initial injury occurred a week later before 6000 fans at Braves Field in BU's 20–6 loss to BC, as he scored the only touchdown for BU on a fourth-down 3-yard run. Under the headline "Cochrane Stars for Intown Eleven," one newspaper commented on the lack of BU blocking. "Cochrane, protected, will make a lot of difference in the BU forces. But he has not the build to stand a pummeling."

Cochrane achieved mythic status in the BU annals two weeks after the BC battle when BU tied Holy Cross 7–7 in Worcester. The *Boston Herald* headline told it all: "Cochrane Returns After Early Injury to Save Day."

Knocked unconscious in the second quarter after having run the Holy Cross ends ragged, Kid was finally aided from the field "groggy and stumbling." He returned in the second half to score BU's lone touchdown on a delayed pass from the 2-yard line and then drop kicked the extra point to tie the game. The *Boston Herald* called the game "a triumph of grit and spirit and in it, Gordon Cochrane, BU's dazzling halfback, was the main figure, materially and inspirationally." The way the comeback was orchestrated, the game could easily be dubbed a 7–7 victory for BU.

Cochrane played only briefly the next week at Brown because of a weak shoulder, but he returned again the following week at Dartmouth, the long train ride to Hanover, New Hampshire, keeping him off the practice field long enough for the shoulder to heal sufficiently.

BU lost 10–7 to Dartmouth, but it was another sentimental victory for BU over a then perennial powerhouse squad. Cochrane completed 8 of 24 passes

3. Kid Stuff

Cochrane in his football playing days at Boston University (Boston University Photo Services, Boston, Massachusetts).

for 110 yards, amazing stats in this era of the running game and cantaloupe shaped ball. The forward pass was legalized in 1906 but wasn't popularized until Notre Dame began using it in 1913. By 1922 it was still mostly used by teams in the Midwest, not in the East.

The Dartmouth game was perhaps Kid's finest hour on the football field. Dartmouth had pulled its regulars early in the game but had to rush them back on the field because, as one newspaper put it concisely, "Cochrane was all over the field on both defense and offense." As Dartmouth star Eddie Dooley was to recall years later: "He did all the work on his side. Every time you looked up, there was Cochrane's red Irish face and fighting jaw."

In yet a third tie game in 1922, a 13–13 standoff at New Hampshire State (now the University of New Hampshire), Cochrane heaved the ball to Buster Williamson for the first score on a 40-yard touchdown pass and then scored himself on a 10-yard run.

Cochrane later recounted the obstacles he faced that day at New Hampshire State. "I worked until four in the morning ushering some benefit show where a flock of movie stars put on their stuff. I missed the eight o'clock train to the game and had to find someone to drive me, arriving just in time with no lunch and no sleep."

Boston University was on the road Cochrane's entire senior year, playing only one game even in Massachusetts, a 13–0 loss at Holy Cross on October 27 which "left him in a crippled condition."

The previous week at Brown in Providence, BU lost 20–3 with BU's only score a 48-yard drop kick by Cochrane, still a school record for a field goal. The *Providence Journal* reported numerous long runs by Kid, including a 44-yard run in the third quarter on a sweeping end run, and his being injured three times, having to be carried from the field in the fourth quarter. Legend has it that Cochrane returned one more time and tackled the first Brown player he saw as he stepped on the field.

There's actually some disagreement about whether the field goal was 48 or 52 yards long, as accounts vary as to whether the kick came from the BU or Brown 48-yard line. There is no disagreement that it was kicked just five yards from the sideline, making the kicking feat that much more remarkable.

There were not many bright spots in BU's 1923 season. Following its 18–7 victory at Colby, where Kid scored on a 30-yard touchdown run with three minutes left in the game to seal the victory, BU was routed 49–0 and 61–0 by Syracuse and Rutgers. Cochrane's collegiate football career ended on muddy Yankee Stadium turf when New York University blocked one of his punts that resulted in the game's only score in the 7–0 BU loss.

Perhaps if Cochrane hadn't been injured so much and if BU had played a heftier schedule, Cochrane might have gained All-American status. But he was injured a great deal in 1922 and 1923, and BU didn't play enough teams of the caliber of Dartmouth and Boston College.

Whalen said many good things about Cochrane over the years. But in a December 1924 interview with the *Philadelphia Bulletin*, the physician Whalen remarked: "He is a normal young man in the matter of health, but he is abnormal when it came to athletic ability. I will be surprised if he does not fare well in major league baseball."

3. Kid Stuff 25

At the 1935 Cochrane testimonial, Whalen recounted Cochrane's exploits and called him "the most versatile athlete in America."

"I know that Cochrane is a great baseball player, but I'll always think he was an even greater football player," Whalen added. "If he had gone to Harvard, Dartmouth, Princeton or some other big university, he would today be one of football's immortals."

Once football season was over, Kid played basketball at BU and with the Bridgewater Club during the winter of 1921. He once played the Original Celtics team, the best professional club at the time, "the champions of the known world." Bridgewater lost 56–39 as Kid scored eight points. According to the local newspaper, Cochrane and Connell "without a doubt were Bridgewater's stars."

Kid also participated his freshman and sophomore years in collegiate boxing for BU, which was a varsity sport back in the 1920s. He boxed in the heavyweight division, although he weighed in at just 160 pounds. He got on the squad when he heard that the regular BU heavyweight was disabled just before a meet with the University of Maine.

"Cochrane heard about the vacancy and although he never had had a glove on, volunteered his services and went to Orono, Maine," one writer recounted the situation. "There he outboxed the Maine intercollegiate champion in three rounds and clearly earned the verdict over an adversary to whom he had given away twenty pounds."

Kid often told about his biggest bout:

> We were fighting Rhode Island State and they had a heavyweight who looked like he went around 300 pounds. We had no real heavyweight, so they put me in with him. He must have been two feet taller and as soon as I saw him I figured I was gone.
> Sure enough, he clipped me early and knocked me down. While I was taking the count of nine, I said to myself "I'll take one good crack at this guy before I go out." I started to swing from the floor, the wildest possible, and it caught him right behind the ear. He went down like a log.

Also boxing for BU was Charlie Farrell, who went on to acting fame in Hollywood. Farrell's most popular movie was the 1929 musical *Sunny Side Up* with Janet Gaynor. John Cochrane undoubtedly showed that film often at the Princess Theatre back in Bridgewater.

Cochrane could never get the better of Farrell in the ring, though. Farrell once told Grantland Rice, "If Mickey had ever landed one there wouldn't have been much left to the fight. For he could punch with a heavyweight. And I don't think I ever saw such fine ring spirit. He was always charging in swinging, always on the aggressive side. Defense never held any interest for him."

Cochrane also played some ice hockey for BU "on the steel runners where he showed the same uncanny instinct which he had displayed in other branches of sport. He was a hard man to elude."

Kid's biggest exploits on frozen water though occurred back home on January 27, 1923, at Carver's Pond in Bridgewater. Frank Burrill, an 18-year-old, was trying out new skates and according to newspaper accounts, "decided to try out the new ice which had formed near the ice house after the first crop was harvested a few days before." Burrill fell through the thin ice, and "Cochrane crept onto the thin ice on his stomach, with others holding his legs and in this manner Burrill was reached and pulled onto firm ice."

Cochrane was no pampered athlete; he worked his way through BU. He waited tables and washed dishes in a basement cafeteria, ushered fights and shows and was occasionally a bouncer at dances. He lived in a moderate way at the Lambda Chi Alpha fraternity house and took the train when he needed to go home to Bridgewater.

Majoring in business administration, Cochrane also had an interest in the arts, somewhat contrary to his rough and tumble image as an athlete. Kid played saxophone in a dance band at a variety of BU social events. He also had a bit of the Thespian in him, rubbed off from Farrell, and he acted in several Shakespearian plays. And he acquired a love for dancing.

Football may have been Kid Cochrane's passion, but baseball was to be his mealticket.

BU's proximity to both Braves Field and Fenway Park brought Cochrane close to the big names of baseball. The visiting teams stayed at the Brunswick Hotel, where Cochrane could observe the players in their time off the playing field while he labored across the street from the hotel.

In 1928, Cochrane recalled that while working at his restaurant job, he thought to himself: "See those lucky stiffs on the Brunswick steps? Nothing to do but play baseball while I am here washing dishes. Some day I'm going to sit over there and look over here and watch some other guy washing cups and saucers, knives and forks. Yes, sir."

Cochrane decided it was a pleasant way to live. A man with his tenacity looking for a pleasant way to live? Undoubtedly, baseball for pay was more linked to "the lure of security" that he obliquely referred to in his book *Baseball The Fan's Game*. He couldn't make enough to marry his sweetheart Mary Bohr and support a family by playing semipro football for the Providence Steam Roller, but he could make enough by playing baseball.

But baseball didn't come as easy as football. As Cochrane later said: "They couldn't decide whether I was an acrobat or a shortstop at BU. It was not versatility which shifted me around the diamond. The managers and coaches were anxious to find a place where I would be less likely to get hurt, where I could remain with the least damage to the team until it came my turn to bat. For I was a pretty good hitter."

3. Kid Stuff 27

Cochrane played two seasons with the BU baseball team, his sophomore and junior years in 1922 and 1923. In the spring of 1922, Cochrane started out in left field and almost immediately showed that he was going to bring some of his football talent to the baseball diamond. In a 7–0 loss to Holy Cross at Worcester, Cochrane led off the game with a single, was sacrificed to second, and then tried to score on a single to right, but "Cochrane was nipped just as he tried to hurl himself into a tally." Holy Cross pitcher Harold Gill yielded not one further BU hit that afternoon.

Cochrane's football backfield mate Buster Williamson was BU's regular catcher in the spring of 1922. Despite protestations by Cochrane later in life that he rarely played catcher before arriving in the minor leagues, Cochrane caught quite often for BU. It seems Williamson had Kid's flare for getting injured.

With Williamson hurt in an April 27 game at Tufts Oval, Cochrane took a turn behind the plate in the 8–0 BU loss. He also started the next game at Boston College, allowing three passed balls in the 17–2 lopsided loss to BC.

On a road trip to Vermont to play several schools, Williamson split the index finger of his right hand to the bone in a game at the University of Vermont. The wound required five stitches to close and forced Williamson to miss the remainder of the season. Cochrane caught the last few games of the Vermont trip and then the final two games, one a "home" game at Tech Field across the Charles River in Cambridge at what is now MIT.

"The catcher got hurt and somebody had to catch," Cochrane recalled. "So the coach asked me and I was afraid to say no. That's how I came to catch as a college player."

Cochrane was a consistent player for BU, getting at least one hit in each game for BU, usually batting cleanup or fifth in the order. He showed some power, hitting home runs in a 10–5 loss at Norwich on the Vermont road trip and in the 6–4 "home" victory over the Massachusetts Aggies.

In the spring of 1923, Kid continued his consistent play for BU in a rain-shortened schedule, playing a number of different positions—shortstop, third base, first base, left field, and catcher. He even pitched one game in relief, the fourth hurler for BU in a Patriots Day loss to Boston College, 17–2, as Clarence DeMars won another Boston Marathon.

While BU athletes got to use Braves Field sparingly for football, they never got to use it for baseball and played virtually all their games on the road. Batting cleanup for BU in 1923, Kid helped lead the team to several victories over smaller schools like Lowell Textile 7–4 and Middlebury 4–3, but as in football, the team came up short against stiffer competition, losing to Harvard 6–3 and Brown 3–2.

Both seasons Cochrane hit around .300 for BU, good but not spectacular and not what you would expect of a future major league ballplayer, much less a future Hall of Famer.

It didn't look as if the gifted football player would light up the baseball world, although Cochrane was the catcher once again in his last game for Boston University on May 22. Four days later on May 26 he was playing minor league baseball.

- 4 -

Minor Name Change

The three summer vacations during Cochrane's BU years were largely filled with baseball. Cochrane was almost always silent, though, about his 1921 and 1922 summer activities. A 1931 article in the *Sporting News* was one of the few times that Cochrane revealed anything about those two summers.

In the summer of 1921 following his freshman year, Cochrane attended ROTC training camp at Plattsburgh, New York, and said he then worked six weeks as a bus boy at a hotel at Old Orchard, Maine, to pay tuition for his sophomore year.

Kid may have also played a few games back home that summer. Cape Cod League publicity material notes that "Hall of Famers such as Pie Traynor, Mickey Cochrane and Red Rolfe played here before embarking on illustrious professional careers" and the league has "a long and proud history dating back to 1885."

As it turns out, the Cape League didn't actually commence play until 1923, although teams from Cape towns did exist before then. There was not a Cochrane on any Cape team then, though he may have played on a Bridgewater-area team against a Cape team under an assumed name to avert "ringer" status.

The 1931 article confirms clippings in a Cochrane scrapbook which indicated he played baseball in the summer of 1922 with an amateur team at Saranac Lake in upstate New York. Nestled in the Adirondack Mountains, Saranac Lake had a team in the local "hotel league" that was loosely organized among resort towns in the area.

Almost every account of Cochrane's Saranac Lake experience indicates he played there only briefly in 1923 before the team folded. This appears to be completely false. Oddly, Cochrane virtually never mentioned the coach of the Saranac Lake team, Dan Sullivan, who recruited a number of New England college players over the years for summer league teams.

Newspaper clippings in the Cochrane scrapbook show that he played right field, shortstop, and some catcher for Saranac Lake and that the team won the championship of the Adirondack Mountains by defeating Plattsburgh 12–9.

Why would Cochrane be so secretive about this seemingly happy baseball experience? The answer appears to lie with Sullivan.

"Cochrane once played for Dirty Dan Sullivan," recalled a former major league player who played collegiate ball in the 1930s while Cochrane played with Detroit. "Dirty Dan would do anything to win a game, I mean anything. He was nasty. I heard a story that a player once took a called third strike to end the game with the tying run on base. Sullivan chased that player around the field waving a bat at him he was so mad they lost. That player didn't screw up again."

At the 1935 Cochrane testimonial, Sullivan called Cochrane "a coach's dream: spirit, personality, fight, drive and ability to think fast." Instead of recalling Cochrane's great feats, Sullivan told of the "green youngster" and his need to sharpen his batting eye by having neighborhood youngsters pitch batting practice to him. Sullivan also related a story about being impressed with Mike's boxing with Jack Dempsey, who trained then at Saranac. According to Mary Cochrane, however, "There's no truth to the story that Mike once boxed with Dempsey there. He was smarter than to get in a ring with that man."

Cochrane likely had a bad experience playing for Sullivan in 1922, despite the team's success, and was looking elsewhere to play the summer of 1923. Hence when Saranac Lake teammate Joe Russell caught on with the Dover, Delaware, team in the Eastern Shore League, Cochrane decided to try it too. They both were in the Dover lineup on May 26 soon after the BU baseball season was over.

One positive aspect to the Saranac Lake experience may have been that Cochrane learned that there are limits to competitiveness on the baseball diamond. Be tough and play to win, but there's a line that shouldn't be crossed in that effort.

Dover was in its first year as a team in the Eastern Shore League, a Class D minor league, the lowest level of organized baseball but still a professional circuit.

Russell told Cochrane that Dover still needed a catcher. He decided to go for the money to pay for his senior year at BU despite his modicum of playing time behind the plate in his limited high school and college experience as well as his actual distaste for catching.

"I don't want to catch. I don't like it. I want to play somewhere in the infield or outfield," Cochrane remembers telling Russell about his Dover idea.

"I didn't want to be a catcher. It was thrust upon me, as they say in the classics. In other words, I was shoved into it," Cochrane remembered. "I was in a fever to get out from behind the plate. Oh boy, I was terrible back there."

"It was the one position that I actually despised," Cochrane would aver.

Jiggs Donahue, the Dover manager, probably spotted Cochrane's potential as a left-handed hitter and was willing to settle for his ambition to hang in there as the regular catcher, lacking any other option. With another year of

4. Minor Name Change

eligibility at BU for football and baseball, Cochrane played under the assumed name of Frank King to protect his amateur status.

"My mother thought it was odd my writing to Mike in Delaware under a different name," remembered Mary Cochrane. "She wondered what was going on."

A business administration major at BU and would-be shrewd negotiator, Cochrane said that he agreed to play for Dover only if he received his release at the close of the season. Not expecting anything of him, the Dover owners readily agreed.

"I was fast and I could hit, but if I thought I was a catcher the local baseball scribe pulled me up short," Cochrane has said. "All too often there appeared in his reports of the game a line which went something like this: 'King, the Dover catcher, missed his usual number of foul flies.'"

Cochrane found foul flies tough to catch. "I was terrible, foul balls were dropping all around me," he once said. "I couldn't catch the blamed things. Sometimes they almost hit me on the head. I was having a helluva time."

"Once a couple of the team directors told Donohue to fire me," Cochrane added. "'Fire him, hell,' Jiggs replied, 'If he goes, I go too.'" Donohue added that Cochrane would learn to catch if he had to beat it into him and that the directors wouldn't be sorry they kept Cochrane.

A former major leaguer himself, Donohue could make good on his promise to turn Cochrane into a decent catcher. Donohue played in the majors for three seasons as a catcher for the Boston Braves and briefly with the 1910 Philadelphia Athletics. (He was not the Jiggs Donohue who was the first baseman on the Chicago White Sox "Hitless Wonders" team.)

The determination in Cochrane got turned up a notch by the Dover directors' apparent lack of confidence in his abilities, counteracted by Donohue's complete confidence in his potential. Calling upon his practice habits running kickoffs back near the railroad yards behind Braves Field, Cochrane decided he had better find someone to help him practice catching foul flies. Enter Brown University pitcher Frank Knight, a Dover teammate.

"In payment for warming him up and helping him develop a new curve, Frank agreed to hit foul fungos to me," Cochrane has said. "We went to Dover Park a couple of hours every morning for weeks. He would hit the flies for an hour and then I would warm him up."

"Knight has always claimed that he made a great catcher out of me and a rotten pitcher out of himself," Cochrane would joke.

Those hours of tedious, tiresome practice taught Cochrane one of the necessary skills of a catcher. For a while he battled the foul flies "as if catching them were a matter of life or death." He also played the plate as if he were on the football field, blocking runners from scoring and making forceful tags on runners who dared to attempt to slide by him.

In 62 games for the Dover team, "Frank King" batted .327, good enough for tenth in the league. His fielding at catcher was marginal; he led the league's catchers in errors with 13 and at .957 he had the second lowest fielding percentage.

The Dover Dobbins won the Eastern Shore League title in 1923, their maiden season in the eight-team league, winning 24 of their last 26 games to fend off the teams from Cambridge, Maryland, and Laurel, Delaware. Actually only seven teams were around at the finish as Milford, Delaware, folded under pressure from the league for playing "class" ballplayers.

Coming into the final weekend of the season, Dover received an offer of $1500 cash from the St. Louis Cardinals for that awkward catcher named King, and the owners offered to split the price with Cochrane. Thinking that he could make a better deal on his own, Cochrane reminded the Dover owners that he played under the condition that he become a free agent at the end of the season. But the Dover officials refused to budge on the 50/50 split of the Cardinal offer.

Knowing that the Dobbins needed to win two of their last three games to take the pennant, Cochrane met with the club officers and issued an ultimatum as augustly as he dared.

"We're about to start this doubleheader and we have to win one game to clinch the pennant," Cochrane recalled. "Write out my release right now, or I won't catch and you'll have to use an outfielder or a pitcher behind the plate."

Cochrane got his release, and Dover went on to win the Eastern Shore League title. Dover also won the Five-State Series against the Martinsburg, West Virginia, Blue Sox who were the winners of the Blue Ridge League, considered the best of the Class D leagues at the time.

The Dover Dobbins were a heavy hitting, light fielding, good pitching team that compiled a 53–24 regular season record. They lost the first two games to Martinsburg, which was managed by Earle Mack, son of Philadelphia Athletics manager Connie Mack. But Dover then went on to take four straight games over the Blue Sox to cop the championship before Cochrane needed to return north to Boston University for his senior year. Connie Mack attended at least the first game of the Five-State Series to get a glimpse of the tough-nosed Dover catcher, and he undoubtedly received reports from Earle on the other games.

"The series was marred by a dispute between catcher King of Dover and umpire Sipple of the Blue Ridge," the *Sporting News* reported. "Prompt action of the arbiter in settling the dispute by chasing the offender and fining his kicking teammates put an end to a squabble that might have wrecked the series. Manager Donohue took King's place in the game."

Cochrane expounded on this incident later in his career. "The ump called me out on a third strike that bounced off the plate. I took a swing at him and he put me out of the game with a $25 fine. The fans at Dover took up a collection in the stands the next day and they handed me $35 — I paid the fine and made 10 bucks!"

Looking at the incident more soberly at another time in an interview with the *Sporting News* publisher J. G. Taylor Spink, Cochrane said, "It was one of the darkest chapters of my life." This was another baseball experience early on that taught Cochrane the need to regulate his competitive nature if he wanted to succeed on the baseball diamond.

Tom Turner, a scout for the Portland Beavers of the Pacific Coast League, eventually secured Cochrane's services through an agreement dated September 1, 1923, written on Hotel Richardson stationary:

> Portland Baseball Club signs catcher Gordon Cochrane for season 1924 salary $325.00 per month and transportation both ways.
>
> Thomas L. Turner
>
> $1000 signing bonus
> Cochrane agrees to report 3/1/24

The transaction was reported in the *Sporting News* on October 4, 1923, along with Portland's purchase of shortstop Stanley Benton of Williamsport in the New York-Penn League. "I couldn't turn it down," Cochrane recalled later. "It looked like a pile. I was hungry and couldn't eat a degree. So I quit college in February and went to Portland."

"Mike never got his degree from BU and thankfully, he never needed it," Mary Cochrane has said.

Cochrane seemingly played his senior year of football at BU the fall of 1923 as a professional. When he agreed to Turner's deal that September, he crossed the amateur/professional line he had carefully avoided by playing under the alias Frank King. BU football coach Doc Whalen helped boost Cochrane's baseball career though.

"'Do you want to be a good ball player or a great ball player?'" Cochrane fondly remembered Whalen asking him. "The question sounded silly at first, but it made a profound impression. It set me thinking. Did I have it in me to be a great ball player? Up to that time I hadn't given the matter serious thought. But if Doc was convinced I had it in me to climb, then I decided with myself that I would never be satisfied until I had reached the peak at my position."

Cochrane was only one step from the major leagues, with a new name unfamiliar to his relatives and friends back in Bridgewater. Cochrane had said they called him Kid in college, to which Turner countered "won't do."

"Tell you what, you're from Boston" Cochrane recalled Turner saying to him. Despite Cochrane's protests that he was not from Boston, but Bridgewater, Massachusetts, Turner said: "You're from Boston as far as Portland is concerned. In fact, you're a Boston Irishman named Mickey Cochrane." So Gordon "Kid" Cochrane left Boston University for the Pacific Coast League as Mickey Cochrane.

Cochrane always focused attention on the "transportation both ways" portion of the agreement, contending that he was still doubtful of those tough-to-catch foul pops and wanted his way paid back East just in case. He also said there was an implied "for two" aspect of the agreement, a second train ticket for his bride-to-be Mary Bohr, his sweetheart from Bridgewater. They were married in Sacramento in March 1924 near Portland's preseason training site of Stockton.

"We couldn't get married in Massachusetts since Mike wasn't 21 yet," Mary Cochrane recalled, "so we planned to get married in California. However, my mother found the wedding rings, so my father decided that my mother should accompany me to California."

"My parents consented to the marriage since they thought Portland would be a bad influence on a bachelor," Mary added. "My parents liked Mike, but they were concerned with the saloons and pool parlors out West. You know, women and drinking and the like."

The Pacific Coast League played 200 game seasons back then, beginning in early April and lasting to mid–October. Playing a seven-game series over the course of each week provided ample opportunity for Portland manager Duke Kenworthy to spot his young catcher into games, alternating Cochrane with veteran catchers Tom Daly, a former major leaguer, and Wray Query.

Despite his own doubts about his catching ability, Cochrane displayed talent with his bat from the start. In an April 1 intrasquad practice game between the "regulars" and the "lambs," "Mickey Cochrane led the onslaught of the young sheep with a single, a double and two tremendous triples in four times at bat" in the lambs' 9–8 victory.

This preseason loss by the regulars to the newcomers was to be a harbinger of things to come. Portland opened the season by losing its first five games to the San Francisco Seals, but in the first game of the Sunday doubleheader to wrap up the series in San Francisco, Portland finally tasted victory. In the second game of the doubleheader, Cochrane played his first professional game in which his real name appeared in the box score. Mickey went 3 for 5 in the Beavers' 5–4 loss to the Seals.

Mickey played sporadically for Portland the first couple of months of the 1924 season, as the Beavers took on PCL rivals Los Angeles Angels, Oakland Oaks, Sacramento Senators, Salt Lake City Bees, Seattle Indians, and the Vernon Tigers (who would later become the Hollywood Stars).

When Cochrane did play, he hit well as the Beavers' third-string catcher, usually going 2 for 3 or 1 for 4. At Oakland on May 24, he went 3 for 3 in a 7–6 loss in 10 innings to the Oaks. He was still a little shaky behind the plate as catcher, as he was also charged with two errors in that loss to the Oaks.

"Manager Kenworthy is working Mickey Cochrane more and more and local fans are realizing why such glowing reports of the youngster came up from the training camp," the *Sporting News* reported that June. "Mickey is probably the fastest man in the club in a straightaway dash, is really leading the club in hitting, and has a lot of style to his receiving. By next year at least he will be recognized as one of the best catchers in the circuit and the most promising for a future major league career."

4. Minor Name Change

That July the Beavers were called a "one-a-week club,"—that was their number of victories in a week. On July 29 the team was mired in last place with a 48–65 record, having lost 18 of its last 21 games. Kenworthy was ousted as manager, and third baseman Frank Brazill, only 25 years old, was installed as player-manager.

Cochrane was already hitting .321 at this juncture of the season in his part-time role, 33 hits in 103 at bats. In an article on the managerial change with a subhead "Cochrane Has Future," the *Sporting News* prophetically noted that Mickey "has given ample demonstration of the fact that he is the best young catcher seen in the PCL in years. His speed and ability to throw has caused comment all over the circuit and Mickey will undoubtedly be the first string catcher next year, unless the local management decides to let him go to the majors."

Mickey gave credit for his continued advancement as a catcher to Daly, a fellow Massachusetts native from Cambridge. Cochrane said after the 1924 season that instead of having to battle with Daly for a catching spot, he found Tommy only too glad to help him in any way he could. Like Jiggs Donahue before him, and others to follow him, Daly took Cochrane under his wing, and as one writer noted in 1924, "taught the youngster a good deal about playing the diamond game as professionals play it."

At Cochrane's 1935 testimonial, Portland's catcher from the previous season, Jack Onslow, also claimed some credit by joking, "I was on my way out of ball playing when Cochrane arrived and my departure really gave Mickey his chance to become a great catcher."

Brazill made Cochrane the Beavers' number one catcher in early August. Mickey promptly went on a 23-consecutive-game hitting streak that lasted until September 10, when he was then leading Portland in batting with a .366 average. The hitting streak started on August 6 with a 2 for 3 outing against Salt Lake City pitcher Rudy Kallio. And in the nightcap of the August 10 doubleheader, Cochrane went 3 for 3 with a home run off Kallio in a 13-6 victory.

"They had silver showers in Portland, where fans showed their appreciation by throwing silver dollars and 50 cent pieces on the field. I picked up $36 one afternoon for hitting a 3-run homer," Cochrane once related, perhaps remembering that blast off Kallio.

In an August 17 loss to Oakland, the hard-charging Cochrane had only one hit, but according to the Portland *Oregonian*, "in the fifth inning Cochrane doubled and scored on Wolfe's single to center by jumping over the catcher and landing fairly on the plate to elude the tag." That Oaks catcher was Del Baker, who would coach for Cochrane at Detroit twelve years later.

Despite Mickey's punch, Portland never made it higher than fifth place, and by mid-September the team was playing out the string. The city and its newspapers were concentrating on the college football season, not the Beavers' baseball exploits.

Portland took its relaxed attitude on a train ride to Salt Lake City, Utah, for a seven-game series packed into five days from September 17 to 21. Salt Lake City had one of the smallest stadiums in the PCL, and in the rarefied air of the mountains, baseballs really took off during the Bees games. The team hit .327 in 1924 with 194 home runs, Lefty O'Doul and Duffy Lewis both batting .392 to lead the PCL that season. The PCL as a league batted .298 in 1924, riding the surge of Babe Ruth–style free swinging as the game of baseball was changing from its former bunt-and-run style to a power hitters game.

In the first four games of the series, the teams averaged 35 hits between them as Salt Lake City took three of the four games. Hitting reached its heights in the September 20 contest as Portland banged out 34 hits in an 18–8 victory. Cochrane went 4 for 6 in that game, topped only by Emmett McCann's 7 for 7 game. Mickey hit one home run, while Brazill and Jim Poole had two roundtrippers apiece.

It was a long season for Cochrane, his first real professional test. Despite the fire, he undoubtedly tired down the stretch, finishing up at .333 for the seventh place Beavers, down from a high of .368 on September 14. The Seattle Indians had clinched the PCL title at Portland's Vaughn Street Grounds on October 19 with a 12–4 victory over the Beavers, who finished with an 88–110 record for the 1924 season. It was the only team Cochrane would play on as a professional that had less than a .500 winning percentage.

Mickey had exactly 100 hits in 300 at bats in 99 games for the Beavers. He collected 7 home runs, 5 triples and 8 doubles along with 56 RBI's Hand a single stolen base. Fielding-wise he was charged with 14 errors in 341 chances for a not-so-great .959 average. He would get better in this category in the future.

"When I found out I could hit the pitching out there on the Coast I felt I could hit them in the big leagues," Cochrane reflected years later. "But I wasn't much satisfied with catching."

The biggest news of the Beavers' 1924 season was the sale of the club right after the season ended by its owner W. H. Klepper. The sale facilitated the elevation of one Mickey Cochrane to the Philadelphia Athletics club in the American League.

Legend has it that either the Shibe family, the primary owners of the Philadelphia ball club, or Connie Mack purchased the Portland club just to obtain the rights to Cochrane. The biggest problem with this legend is that back in 1924 major league clubs were prohibited from owning minor league teams and thus creating a farm system. But dollars did change hands to preserve Cochrane's services for the A's.

Actually it was Tom Turner, the scout who had signed Cochrane, who purchased the team from Klepper, with financial assistance from Philadelphia. As part of the transaction, Turner agreed to make Cochrane available to the A's for an official purchase price of $50,000.

Mack always said that he purchased a "controlling interest" in the Portland club, never that he bought the club. The euphemism was even used more than 25 years later in Mack's autobiography, where he wrote, "I got Mickey Cochrane by purchasing an interest in the Portland club for $132,000 and $50,000 cash for his services."

Little remembered is that besides the $50,000, five major league players were also transferred from the A's roster to Portland: Denny Burns, Bob Hasty, Harry Riconda, Charley Howland, and Ed Sherling. Only Riconda ever saw the majors again, in sporadic duty with four National League teams over four years.

Asked many years later if Cochrane was worth the almost $200,000 price tag, Mack exclaimed "Worth it!? He was worth ten times that much. More than any other player, he was responsible for the three pennants we won in 1929, 1930 and 1931."

At the time, commentary was not so prescient, as is illustrated by this 1925 example: "While Mack has every confidence that Cochrane would make good, nevertheless he is a gamble. Fewer catchers make good from the kickoff than pitchers, infielders and outfielders. They have to do something else besides play. They have to think. The whole game revolves around them. It is the history of baseball that a young catcher loses many a game for a club before he acquires the brains, poise and skill to run the ball game. The young catcher is the biggest gamble in baseball and many are rejected before a jewel is found."

There were two births that winter. Gordon Jr. was born to Mike and Mary Cochrane. The second birth was his dad's major league baseball career. This young catcher would become a jewel.

- 5 -

Sigh by Cy

Cochrane was one of four future Hall of Fame players who were in the very early stages of their careers in 1925. Al Simmons, Lefty Grove, and Jimmie Foxx were also youngsters on that club. The four would form the nucleus of the 1929–31 championship A's teams.

Simmons, the foot-in-the-bucket swinger, was in his second year with the A's and played center field. Grove was a rookie like Cochrane, but more highly regarded given his fabulous pitching career with the Baltimore Orioles of the International League. Foxx was only 17 years old, but already showing great potential at the bat.

At this stage of his career, Foxx was a catcher competing with Cochrane for a backup spot behind Cy Perkins, who had been the A's regular catcher for the past five years. Headlines like "Mack Keen About Kid Catchers" were not uncommon. All three catchers would go north with the team for Opening Day at Shibe Park against the Boston Red Sox on April 14. "Fox [sic] and Cochrane form the reserve catching strength," one newspaper noted.

Little known is that Cochrane actually held out briefly before reporting to the A's spring training camp at Fort Myers, Florida. After signing his 1925 contract, the cocky Cochrane demanded in a letter to Mack a portion of the $50,000 paid to Portland for his services. After Commissioner Landis began to talk about a suspension, Cochrane reconsidered.

"I understand Connie Mack isn't at fault. I blame it on Turner," Cochrane told reporters in Philadelphia before he boarded a train for Florida. "You can't censure me for demanding a portion of the purchase money. However, I will give the Athletics my best services and I hope to be a regular catcher after I get used to big league ways."

Cochrane was an instant hit at Fort Myers, with a February 24 headline stating, "Cochrane's Homer with Three On Features A's First Day of Training."

"Cochrane propelled Stokes' first pitch up into the skies in centre field and circled the bases like a rabbit," the *Philadelphia Bulletin* reported. "Before the five and a half innings were over, Cochrane had infused enough

5. Sigh by Cy

pep into his team to bat out a 9–8 victory" after being behind 6–0 after three innings.

Batting was one thing, but catching was another, as Mack later recalled:

> I liked him on the train, he listened so eagerly. But was I in for a shock at camp. After the polished Perkins, Mickey was awful! He was crude at receiving the ball. His stance and crouch were both wrong. And on foul balls he was simply pathetic. Still he was a natural hitter.
>
> But after five days in the Athletics' camp I wasn't sure he would even make a relief catcher. I nearly put him in the outfield!

Said Cochrane, "I couldn't convince Mack that I was a major league catcher. I knew I didn't look like one, but that was because I was scared finding myself in a major league camp and I was trying so hard it hurt."

"One morning I found him catching flies knocked out to him by kids," Mack remembered. "After practice he had rookies hitting them. That night he was in my room asking questions. By the time we left camp, I knew my worries were over. A misfit in February, he was a star in April."

"When I first saw him he didn't look quite ready," said Perkins, the man whom Cochrane replaced. "He had a lot to learn about catching. He made himself great by sheer hard work."

With white elephants emblazoning their uniforms, the A's took the first three games of the season against the Red Sox. With rookie Grove on the mound in the opener and Perkins behind the plate, the A's came back from a 6–0 deficit to win 9–8 in 10 innings.

The Cochrane legends started that April 14 first game. Cochrane always told the story that in the eighth inning he saw Rudy Kallio pitching for the Red Sox. Since he had hit Kallio quite well in the PCL, he exclaimed, "I can hit that guy." Mack took him up on it and had him pinch hit for Perkins. Cochrane drove in the game winning run. Perkins then lamented with a sigh, "Well, there goes my job," as Cochrane buckled up his shinguards to catch the 9th for the A's.

It's a good story, but the facts are a bit mixed up. Mack sent Cochrane up to pinch hit for the light-hitting Perkins in the 8th against Boston pitcher Ted Wingfield, and Cochrane grounded out to Bill Rogell at second base to end the A's 4-run rally. Mickey did take the field in the top of the 9th and having somewhat mastered those foul pops at Dover and Portland, went right to the grandstand to nab Rogell's foul fly.

Cochrane did make his first major league hit in the 10th, a single to left field off Kallio with Jim Poole on second base. It should have been the game winning hit except that as the newspapers noted, it was "a vicious single, hit so hard that Poole held third base." Poole did score on Sammy Hale's dribbler down the third base line to win Cochrane's first game in the majors.

"It hurt me to hear Perkins say that his job was lost," Cochrane recalled later, although he did say Perkins did it with a smile as if he knew his days were numbered anyway. "Yet, I couldn't help feeling glad too. I wasn't scared anymore. I knew that once I got in there, nobody would get me out."

Cochrane did start the next three games against the Red Sox, catching Sam Gray on the 15th, Ed Rommel on the 16th, and Grove on the 17th. Batting eighth in the order, Mickey's batting heroics continued with an RBI-single on the 16th to tie the score 3–3 en route to a 7–3 win. Cochrane faced Walter Johnson of the Senators for the first time on April 18 and went 2 for 2 against the fireballing future Hall of Famer. Perkins' days as number one catcher indeed seemed to be over.

Mickey exhibited a number of errors at catcher in these early games, being called for catcher's interference, allowing one passed ball, making a bad throw trying to pick off a runner at second. Yet he showed some brilliance also, blocking the plate in the tenth inning of the Red Sox opener at Fenway Park on April 22 to stop fellow catcher Val Picinich from scoring on a fly to right field which would have won the game. Instead the A's won in 11 innings 6–5.

Foxx remembered that while the A's were in Boston that April, Cochrane was missing at breakfast the first morning at the Brunswick Hotel. After finishing his breakfast, Foxx went outside the hotel and "there was Cochrane sitting in the biggest chair on the hotel steps, smoking a big cigar and muttering 'I told 'em, I told 'em.'" Cochrane had fulfilled his desire formed as an undergraduate at BU to be a big league ballplayer lingering around the Brunswick Hotel.

Boston University students and graduates honored Cochrane on April 23 with a band present on the field; they awarded him a traveling bag with lots of stuff to put in it.

Wins over the Red Sox, who were destined to finish last in 1925, propelled the A's towards their first successful season since 1914. By May 8, Philadelphia was in first place, which they would hold for nearly two months through the end of June. The increasing fan interest in the A's during 1925 made the decision to doubledeck Shibe Park and add bleachers for the 1925 season look prophetic.

It was the first time in over a decade that the A's had been in first place. Mack's teams had been pretty dismal the past several years, following the dismantling of the championship teams of 1910, 1911, 1913, and 1914 after the stars wanted too much money to continue playing in Philadelphia. The A's finished in last place seven straight years from 1915 to 1921. Since that time the team had gradually worked its way up the American League standings one place a year, finishing in fifth place in 1924 after spending a good part of the season in last place.

Mack's rebuilding effort paid early dividends in 1925, and Cochrane was a huge part of that effort. Mickey hit three home runs in a 20–4 victory at St. Louis on May 22 to tie the American League record, taking advantage of the short 354-foot distance to the right center field bleachers before a twenty-foot

5. *Sigh by Cy*

screen was erected in 1930. He hit the first two homers off Milt Gaston into the Sportsman Park bleachers in 95-degree heat and hit the third one off George Blaeholder onto Grand Boulevard behind right field. Blaeholder was pitching in just his second major league game.

Symbolizing this youthful outlook was the A's 17–15 win over the Indians on June 15. A high-scoring affair it was, but hidden in the final score is the fact that the A's were down 15–4 going into the 8th. They didn't give up and rallied for 13 runs, a record comeback, presenting rookie Tom Glass with his only major league victory in the process.

Mike, Mary, and Gordon Jr. took up residence in an apartment at 2736 North 22d Street, just off Lehigh Avenue, little more than one block from Shibe Park in the heart of the North Penn community. Many of the A's players lived in the neighborhood then dominated by Irish and Italian families. Al Simmons, like many of the single players, boarded with residents. He roomed behind right field on North 20th Street and became good friends with the Cochranes.

Defending American League champion Washington battled the A's for the league's top spot and regained it on June 30 when Johnson shut out the A's 7–0. The A's and Senators traded first place throughout July before the A's held onto it for most of August, at one time being five games up on the Senators.

When leadoff hitter Max Bishop was injured in early July, Cochrane volunteered for the role. "Now a catcher in the leadoff position was something new, even for Connie, and at first the idea didn't go over so well with him," a *Baseball Magazine* article related. "For nearly a month until Max Bishop got back into the game about August 1, 'Cochrane, c' was the first line in the Athletics' box score. And his hitting thrived upon it."

But then the roof caved in. The A's left Philadelphia three games up in first place, but looking at a 17-game road trip to the western cities in the American League.

In St. Louis the A's lost three in a row to the Browns, all by one run, including a heartbreaking 9–8 decision. The A's had rallied to score six runs in the top of the 9th to go up 8–6, but then yielded three in the bottom of the 9th to lose.

The A's won two of three at Chicago, but then proceeded to drop their next ten games in Cleveland, Detroit, Washington, and New York. The ignominy then was to drop a Labor Day doubleheader at Shibe Park to the Senators 2–1 and 7–6 to run the losing streak to 12 games and virtually erase all pennant hopes for the 1925 season.

Philadelphia finished in second place with a 88–64 mark, eight and a half games behind Washington and comfortably ahead of the third place St. Louis Browns.

Cochrane batted .331 in his first year of major league play, good for 18th in the official league statistics, and he hit six homers and had 55 RBI's. His outstanding play earned him the sole catcher slot on *The Sporting News* major league all-star team, the 22-year-old getting the nod over Muddy Ruel of the champion Senators and Gabby Hartnett of the National League Chicago Cubs.

There was no Rookie of the Year Award in those days. A Society of American Baseball Research poll of its members in 1986 for pre-1949 Rookie of the Year selections gave the 1925 award to Yankee outfielder Earl Combs, who hit .342 for the seventh place New York team. Cochrane placed second in the voting, and a Yankee first baseman named Gehrig finished third in the balloting.

As Grantland Rice wrote in an October story in *Collier's*, "Gordon Cochrane is one of the most brilliant young catchers that ever broke into baseball. Cochrane is young — but how he can catch!"

- 6 -

No Scorn on the Cobb

After spending the winter chopping wood back in Bridgewater, Cochrane headed to the A's spring training site in Fort Myers ready to take on the 1926 season. Cochrane had kept in physical shape over the winter leveling trees for $3 a cord in the Bridgewater forests, while trap shooting had helped keep his batting eye sharp. A picture in the *Boston Globe* showed John Cochrane assisting his son in trap shooting practice by releasing the clays from a hand-held trap, a sign he was beginning to approve of his son's occupation.

Unlike other players who needed the spring to shed excess pounds put on through a winter's worth of inactivity, Cochrane was ready to go from day one.

Back then teams weren't permitted to play spring games against teams within their own league. So the A's preseason schedule was heavily laden with games against minor league competition training near then-isolated Fort Myers. Eight games were scheduled with the Baltimore Orioles in nearby Punta Gorda and Terry Park in Fort Myers, and the Buffalo Bisons were competition at Palmetto up the coast a bit towards Tampa, "a six hour drive by motor car through the jungles," as one writer put it.

In 1926 the A's were lucky to get in two games with the New York Giants training at Sarasota (which they lost) and two games with the Phillies at Bradenton (which they won). Both sites were about 75 miles north of Fort Myers, a considerable distance to travel in the days when I-75 was still two generations away from existence.

Following their Florida schedule, the A's worked their way north, defeating the Rochester Royals 9–2 at Waycross, Georgia, and routing Richmond 14–5 in Virginia before heading to Philadelphia for their annual City Series with the neighboring National League Phillies.

The A's split the four games in Philadelphia in a rain-shortened series curtailed by one game, the games shifting between Shibe Park and Phillies Park, which were only ten blocks apart down Lehigh Avenue in North Philadelphia.

The success of the 1925 team did not carry over to the start of the 1926 season for the A's; they lost 10 of their first 14 games to become ensconced in

Cochrane keeping in shape chopping wood during the winter of 1926 (Urban Archives, Temple University, Philadelphia, Pennsylvania).

seventh place. Things did not begin auspiciously as Johnson bested Rommel 1–0 in a 15-inning opening day match-up at Griffith Stadium. Despite Cochrane's off-season conditioning, he went 0 for 6 versus the Big Train.

The Yankees were the big story of 1926. New York led virtually wire-to-wire to take the American League pennant once again following a two-year period when Washington was the top club. The A's made a run at Miller Huggins' team, winning nine straight in early May and then taking a doubleheader from the Yanks on May 28 to stop New York's own 16-game winning streak.

Grove, on his way to becoming a dominant pitcher in the A.L., beat the Yanks 2–1 in the first game of that May 28 doubleheader. Cochrane, maturing as a catcher, snuffed out a double steal in the 1st with runners on first and third, nailing Gehrig at second base on a blazing throw to shortstop Galloway to end the inning. Mickey was still learning the position, however; his throwing error in the 7th allowed the only New York run to score.

In the A's 6–5 victory in the second game of the May 28 doubleheader, Cochrane hit a first inning home run off Urban Shocker to get the A's off to a good start. The A's took 3 of 4 games to move into second place, but it would be the closest they would get to the Yankees in 1926.

"The Athletics were not the great ball club they had been when Cochrane and one or two others carried them along against the great odds of indifferent pitching [last year]," the *Spaulding Official Base Ball Guide* commented with regard to the 1926 season. "Mack knew before the season was six weeks old that he was not getting what he had expected from his players."

The A's did win 14 of 18 games in early July before Cochrane was put out of commission on July 17 when one of Grove's pitches split his throwing hand. He was expected to be out of action for three weeks.

Perkins, with a renewed lease on life at catcher, didn't respond to the challenge, as one reporter noted. "With Cochrane hurt and the field virtually to himself, Perkins suddenly stopped batting," after hitting over .300 for the first part of the season. "Cochrane's injury has been felt." The A's pennant hopes were completely dashed as they lost seven straight games with Cochrane out of the lineup. He came back to play on July 28.

The injury did spark Cochrane into working on ways to catch without exposing his hands to potential injury; he became famous long before Johnny Bench for one-handed catching.

Kid Gleason had joined the A's as a coach for the 1926 season. Gleason along with Perkins was instrumental in aiding Cochrane with his catching style. Another A's coach, Ira Thomas, who had caught for Mack's teams the previous decade, was also on hand to assist Cochrane. Gleason helped break Cochrane of his habit of dropping to his knees to receive a pitch.

Mack asked Perkins to work with Cochrane, and he worked tirelessly with him to make him into a first-class catcher. "It's no wonder Mike didn't know how to catch," Perkins said later in life. "He didn't know how to stand or to shift. Mike worked on throwing from down low until he was blue in that tomato face instead of red." Perkins taught Cochrane fundamentals of stance and positioning that Donahue and Daly hadn't already imparted to him at the minor league level. Cochrane also had short fingers, so he had to work harder at gripping the ball right than did the long-fingered Perkins.

"The way it worked out I took over his catching job, but we remained friends through the remainder of my life in baseball, co-workers much of the time," Cochrane recalled of Perkins, who also hailed from Massachusetts, the town of Gloucester. "I caught two hours of batting practice every day and the first thing I knew the tricks of receiving suddenly came to me in natural movements."

"I taught him all I knew," Perkins joked. "At least I didn't hurt him."

One of the biggest contributions from Perkins was making Cochrane a one-handed catcher, to protect his fingers from getting banged up. "Mastering it protected my fingers through twelve and a half major league races," Cochrane wrote. "That is, to stop the pitched ball always with the gloved hand, holding your right hand with the finger tips folded against the heel of the hand and the thumb laid along the side of the hand. After a time it becomes natural not to open the unprotected hand until the ball is in the glove."

Cochrane had many fewer of the knots or gnarls in his finger joints that were the badge of courage of most other catchers.

> One of the New York papers ran a full page of pictures of catchers' hands without identifying the owners.... It was an array of disjointed, gnarled claws, bearing witness to honorable struggles with a thousand and one foul tips. One pair, however, displayed ... fingers that might have belonged to Vladimir Horowitz. Yes, they were Cochrane's. ... Black Mike had soft, sure hands, but there was nothing else soft about him.

When former Red Sox manager John McNamara was asked in the spring of 1988 about his first baseball glove, the often crusty McNamara gleamed during his response. "My uncle gave it to me when I was about six. It was his. He got a new one and he gave his old one to me. It was a catcher's mitt. I think it was a Mickey Cochrane model. It went everywhere with me. Even to bed."

Cochrane found that it was tough to catch; he took a lot of physical punishment in his postgraduate course in catching with Perkins. Cochrane had a wide assortment of pitchers to handle in his early days with the A's.

"Grove had speed ... and more speed. The tougher the hitter, the faster he pitched," Cochrane said of the impatient southpaw. "In the beginning he was very wild. Catching him was like catching bullets from a rifleman with bad aim."

Walberg wasn't as fast as Grove, but he had a great curve ball. His big problem was lack of self-confidence. Stories about conversations between Cochrane and Walberg on the mound abound.

"Rommel had a knuckler. Ed was the hardest to catch," Cochrane remarked about the future umpire. "Nobody knows where a knuckleball is going, including the pitcher. But I had to follow it. I didn't do too badly."

Then there was Jack Quinn, an over-40 spitball pitcher who was grandfathered to throw the illegal pitch when it was outlawed in 1920. Mickey pampered neither veteran nor rookie. Once when Quinn was pitching a shutout, Cochrane kept calling for fastballs and Quinn called him to the mound to inquire about when he was going to call his bread and butter pitch. "When those zeros change on the scoreboard, I'll call the spitter," Cochrane told Quinn because his strategy was to cross up the opposing batters, who kept looking for the spitter and never saw it.

Cochrane had a different set of signals for each pitcher. "What would be tough for some fellows to get are easy for the other fellows and the other way around."

"I used to call all the pitches from the bench," Mack related after Cochrane's career ended. "But when Mickey came along I met a young fellow who wasn't afraid to tell me I was wrong. Mickey would shake off my sign and do as he pleased. In all the years he caught for me, he wasn't wrong more than a couple of times. There weren't many people who knew he could run a team and plot strategy after he had been catching regularly for only two years. He knew the batters as well as I did."

The A's finished in third place in 1926 with a 83–67 record, six games behind New York and three games behind second place Cleveland. In a sophomore swoon, Cochrane's batting dipped to a .273 average.

A new player on the A's in 1927 would have a monumental impact on Cochrane's life — Ty Cobb. Mack signed the Georgia Peach when the Tigers released him after 22 years in Detroit because of his linkage to a gambling scandal.

Cochrane seemed to absorb all the positive intensity that Cobb brought to the game while acquiring none of Cobb's nastiness, which led virtually everyone to detest Cobb as a person.

"Ty Cobb was endowed by nature with dazzling speed of foot and a good batting eye. These did not make him the greatest player baseball ever produced," F. C. Lane wrote in a 1930 *Baseball Magazine* article. "It was not hands or feet so much as grit and determination and a restless, never satisfied ambition that drove Cobb to the pinnacle of player greatness. Cochrane has much the same mental equipment, without Cobb's unfortunate tendency to make enemies. Mickey has only friends in baseball."

While Donahue, Daly, and Perkins had assisted Cochrane in learning the baseball trade of catcher, Cobb seemed to fill the role of baseball mentor to Cochrane. That spark in Cochrane really caught fire under the tutelage of Cobb.

"Cobb was like a father to Mike," Mary Cochrane has said of their relationship. And Mike himself said, "He was a little crusty at times, but he gave me some fine advice and was an inspiration to me in every way."

Indeed, Cochrane was one of the very few ballplayers who got along with Cobb. One writer went so far as to say "some like Mickey Cochrane worshipped him." At Cobb's death in 1961, Mike was one of but three baseball people who bothered to attend his funeral, such was the distaste Cobb left behind.

Cobb worked with Cochrane because he saw a high-level of competitive spirit in the young catcher. In a 1936 article "The Boss Tiger," Cobb described Cochrane's intensity:

> As a rival, when the Tigers had met the A's, I had known him for a fighter, a hustler, a strong-willed youth with a mind that worked in split seconds and with no regard whatever for names, reputations or flashing spikes on the base lines.
>
> But I had to be on the same team with him to learn the true extent of Cochrane's competitive urge. I remember, for instance, an evening in St. Louis.
>
> We had lost a tough ball game to the Browns that afternoon — a game we never should have lost. Lickings like that were always hard for me to take. But a shower helped cool me off and I had regained most of my composure before I got back to the hotel. I was sitting in my room when the door burst open and in charged Cochrane.
>
> He was wearing a cap, which he tore from his head and threw on the floor. He jumped up and down on the headpiece while he let out a blast at the loss of the ball game.
>
> Cochrane had been seething since the end of the game. His rage had been penned up inside. Now, able to let go without being seen and criticized by outsiders, he put on one of the greatest examples of what it means to be a "hard loser" that I've ever seen. And I've been around for a long time, and done some hard losing myself.

Cobb's influence on Cochrane helped turn Mike into baseball's greatest catcher. Besides enhancing his fierce competitive spirit, Cobb passed down to Cochrane a number of his inner baseball secrets. "Cobb was probably the first ballplayer who understood and practiced psychological warfare in the nth degree," Paul Gallico wrote in his book *Golden People*.

It was Cobb, the base stealing king, who understood that he was stealing on the pitcher, not the catcher. A Cobb biographer wrote that Cobb once told Cochrane when he got the jump on the pitcher, he could have been slower and still in most cases Cochrane himself couldn't have stopped him with a cannon.

Cobb also picked up patterns in catchers and undoubtedly suggested to Mike that he not lapse into that bad habit. Cobb could call the pitches based just on his experience in watching the opposing catcher over the years.

Besides the on-field aspect of their relationship, Cobb took Mike under his wing off the field too in pursuit of Cobb's other passion — money. Cobb, a millionaire at his death, had invested wisely in the stock market over the years, being most famous for his astute buying of Coca Cola stock. Cobb's financial acumen was shared with Cochrane, who went on to be recognized as one of the game's more financially savvy players.

6. No Scorn on the Cobb

During his two-year stint with the Athletics, Cobb leased a house in Cynwyd, a Philadelphia suburb on its famous Mainline. Following the 1927 season, Mike would move his family from Bridgewater to an apartment at Bala and City Line Avenues in Philadelphia, near Cobb's house in Cynwyd. The Cochranes would soon have their own house in that town.

The Murder's Row lineup of the Yankees dominated the American League in 1927, despite Cobb's presence in the A's lineup as right fielder. He led the A's to their best won-loss record in the three years Cochrane had played for Mack. The A's finished with a 91–63 record before sparse crowds at Shibe Park during a long home stand that ended the season, there being no suspense to the pennant race because the Yankees finished 19 games in front of the A's.

It was the year Ruth hit 60 home runs, Gehrig collected 175 RBI's, and the Yankees won 110 games on the way to a .714 winning percentage mark. And the Yanks feasted on the A's early, defeating Grove 8–3 on Opening Day at Yankee Stadium and winning three of four games in that series. The fourth game wound up a tie. Ruth would hit homer #57 on September 27 off Grove, a bases-filled blast with Cochrane behind the plate frustrated at the ball not winding up in his mitt.

Cobb's style of play had an immediate impact on the A's. On April 19 at Griffith Stadium, Cobb stole home with two outs and the bases loaded with Al Crowder on the mound. "Crowder had apparently been concentrating on Cochrane at bat when Cobb took off for the plate and scored with his famous fade-away slide on the front end of a triple steal."

"Simmons, Lamar, Hale and Gordon Cochrane are playing the best ball of their careers because Ty is keeping them on their toes," *The Sporting News* wrote in May.

Their efforts wouldn't be enough though to catch the Yankees, so Mack began experimenting with 19-year-old Foxx at first base versus left-handed pitchers in early June, trying to find a place for his bat in the lineup. "Were the Athletics not provided with two top rank catchers in Cochrane and Perkins, Foxx would be used behind the plate, but he has had to confine his services for the most part to pinch hitting," *The Sporting News* told its readers in June.

Cochrane himself was often platooned against left-handers, with Perkins taking on the receiving chores. Otherwise, the A's would have had seven future Hall of Famers in their lineup on June 10 with Simmons, Cobb, and Zack Wheat in the outfield, Grove on the mound, Foxx at first base, and Eddie Collins at second base.

Cochrane recovered from his 1926 hitting difficulties, using a two-week streak from July 13 to July 28 in which he hit .500 with 20 hits in 40 at bats to propel him on to a .338 season average.

While clearly the A's number one catcher, generally hitting out of the fifth or sixth spot in the batting order, the want-to-win Cochrane still didn't have Mack's total confidence in all situations. That appears to have spurred Cochrane on.

On July 12 in a 8–5 White Sox victory at Comiskey Park, Mack pinch hit Bill Lamar for Cochrane in the top of the 7th after Mickey had gone hitless in three tries against Sarge Connally. The next day Cochrane went 4 for 5 against Ted Lyons and following a rain-out went 2 for 3 in each game of a July 15 doubleheader.

Cochrane concluded his .500 streak on July 28 with a 3 for 4 performance in a 5–2 loss to Detroit at Shibe Park, but only after Mack benched him the day before when left-handed Earl Whitehill pitched for the Tigers. Mack preferred to have the right-handed-hitter Perkins catch for the A's.

Cochrane gave Cobb credit for his hitting success. "Get out in front of every pitch," Cochrane said Cobb advised him. "Always swing looking for a fast ball. If you are set for speed, there will be time to hit a curve and lots of time to set yourself for a change of pace or slow ball."

Cochrane finished fourth in the balloting for American League Most Valuable Player in 1927, collecting 18 votes.

Cobb gave the A's some baseball insight, but his greatest legacy may have been getting the A's players into the stock market with his financial advice only a few years before it crashed. As one writer put it, Mack "proceeded to win three pennants in a row with a team of busted investors." Cobb's encouragement to invest indirectly helped create a team of hungry ballplayers eager to win that World Series check to pay off their debts.

Cochrane once wrote that "the best team I ever played with, was the Philadelphia Athletics of 1929, 30 and 31." Not only did they want to win, they needed to win.

- 7 -

Center Stage

The 1928 season started rather quietly for Cochrane, who wintered with his family in Philadelphia for the first time. Mike tried to capitalize on his newfound fame that winter by being a salesman for the Roberts Nash Motor Company. He also got in some golf at the Merion links and some indoor exercise at the Penn Athletic Club.

Cochrane, Perkins, and Foxx were Mack's catchers when the A's headed north from Fort Myers. Mickey was not yet a dominant catcher. He was still getting little respect in some quarters, *The Sporting News* 1928 roster listing him batting and throwing left-handed. Mack also played Foxx at catcher against left-handed pitchers, playing the better odds of a right-handed batter Foxx versus the lefty Cochrane.

Losing the first two games of the season didn't get the A's off to an outstanding start, despite the debut of their new uniforms. Mack discarded the White Elephant that had symbolized the A's since 1918 in favor of restoring the traditional gothic "A" that Athletic teams had worn all the way back to 1859.

Despite winning 13 of 14 games in one stretch during May, the A's quickly fell behind the Yankees, who were setting the pace in the American League once again.

A long June road trip didn't aid the A's in making any progress on New York, which was eight games up on Philadelphia by the end of June, even though one observer reported, "Cochrane and Foxx are catching commendably and batting hard." It looked as if the Yankees were going to run away with another pennant.

Then Mack came up with the lineup that was a winning combination. He liked veteran ballplayers, but his continued use of the aging outfielders Cobb and Tris Speaker, whom he had signed over the winter after the Indians let him go, was hurting the team, as was the limited duty that heavy-hitting, second-string catcher Foxx was seeing on the field. Mack's pitching staff other than Grove was aging as well.

Mack picked up pitcher George Earnshaw from Jack Dunn's minor league

Baltimore Orioles, the same proving ground that had yielded Grove three years earlier. He wasn't going to sacrifice Cochrane as his top catcher, so he instead installed Foxx at third base. Mule Haas became the new center fielder to replace Speaker, and Bing Miller became the regular right fielder instead of Cobb. Ossie Orwoll was inserted at first base to replace Hauser.

And Cochrane turned into an inspirational leader. One of the more famous stories involved Cochrane flying into a rage as the A's seemed to be complacent and accepting defeat in a game they were losing 5–2 after the third inning with the Yankees on June 20.

"You yellow-bellied bastards," he reportedly yelled as he kicked his catching gear into the dugout and snatched his bat from the rack to lead the inning off. "You're quitting like the yellow dogs you are!" He then stalked away from a now-quiet dugout and lined a double to spark a 4-run rally and an eventual 10-5 comeback victory.

Cochrane was too fired up to win the pennant. He had injured his leg on a foul tip against the Tigers in June, but kept playing and it affected his game. "There's only one thing that will bring me around and that's rest," Cochrane told newspaper writers. "If I had rested before I could be playing now. I'm not exactly out entirely, I can still pinch hit although I can't run."

After resting Cochrane for a few games in mid-July, Mack and his reconstituted Athletics began to charge after the Yankees. Between July 17 and August 8, the A's won 17 of 18 games, including ten in a row on the road, taking four at Comiskey, four at Sportsman's Park, and two at League Park before the Indians stopped the streak. The A's took two more at Navin Field before heading back to Shibe.

The A's had just about clinched second place, as they beat the third place Browns nine times in that period, four on the road and five at Shibe in mid-July. But second place wasn't good enough for Cochrane; he had his sights set on first place, which was held by the faltering Yankees.

Despite the A's winning streak, New York's lead had only shrunk from 6 games at the end of July to 3 at the end of August, but as the *Reach Guide* recapped the 1928 season, "What seemed to be an irresistible lead on the part of New York began to melt violently. Game by game the New York margin began to crumble."

Then Mickey stirred the team up for the September run at the pennant. The A's would be at baseball's center stage once again. Against the White Sox on August 29 at Comiskey, Chicago pitcher Ted Lyons tried to score on a single to right when Cochrane blocked the plate to tag out Lyons "with a football tackle and tag while rolling on the ground."

White Sox manager Slats Blackburne was furious at the method Cochrane used to stop his star pitcher from attempting to touch home plate and stormed umpire Dan Barry from the dugout, shoving him roughly in his blast about the play. Blackburne was suspended for three games by the American League's President Barnard as the A's took the game 6–2.

7. Center Stage

Philadelphia surged forward in eager anticipation of the September 9–11 showdown with the Yankees, which would probably determine which team would go on to win the pennant.

The Yankees were in front of the A's by two games on September 6, when rain washed out both teams' scheduled games. However, that didn't stop 5000 people from waiting in line to buy the remaining reserved seats for the September 9 Sunday doubleheader. Many weren't happy when the tickets sold out early that miserable day, despite the fact that 40,000 grandstand and 20,000 bleachers tickets would become available the day of the game.

"Yankee-Athletic Ticket Rush Brings Police to Quell Riot" was the *New York Times* headline, which created even further interest in the upcoming four-game series.

Washington defeated New York twice at Yankee Stadium the next day, though, as the A's toppled the Red Sox twice at Fenway Park to instigate a flat-footed tie for first place. Then on September 8 the A's took another twinbill from Boston, while the Yankees won 6–3 over the Senators, so that Philadelphia entered Yankee Stadium the next day in first place with a slim half-game lead.

Cochrane had hauled the team into first place in a September standings. The bubble burst, however, as 85,265 fans jammed Yankee Stadium on September 9, the largest crowd to that date to witness a ballgame. Reportedly 100,000 others were turned away from the gates. New York took both ends of the doubleheader, 5–0 and 7–3 to regain first place, which they held for the remainder of the 1928 season to capture their third straight American League pennant.

"Yes, those Yanks sure did make life miserable for us Elephants last summer," Cochrane said after the season. "They were one wicked bunch of horsehide hammers — and how they could hammer when we happened along."

Cochrane was 0 for 3 in the first game as Yankee hurler George Pipgras tossed a nine hit shutout. Quinn kept the A's in the hunt as the game was scoreless through five and a half innings. Then the Yankees tallied three in the 6th and two in the 8th to triumph.

In the second game, Cochrane went 2 for 4 and began a sixth inning rally by beating out a grounder to third baseman Joe Dugan ahead of a Simmons home run into the right field bleachers that put the A's in front 3–1. The Yankees scored two off Walberg in the bottom of the 7th when Mack brought in Rommel to pitch. In the 8th the Yanks loaded the bases before Bob Meusel proceeded to launch a home run to put New York up 7–3. "We broke their hearts," Ruth bragged in the Yankee clubhouse, as the A's suffered in silence in theirs.

The Yanks took three in a row with a 5–3 victory in the next game by scoring four runs in the bottom of the 8th; a Ruth 2-run homer off Grove was the deciding blast. Cochrane had tripled in the first run of the game in the top of the 1st, part of a 3 for 4 day, to no avail.

The A's salvaged the fourth game of the series with a 4–3 win, as Bishop

Rare 1920s action picture of Cochrane taken in 1928. Few action pictures of Cochrane in an A's uniform have ever been published (Urban Archives, Temple University, Philadelphia, Pennsylvania).

homered in the top of the 9th. Mack brought Walberg in to pitch the 9th to save the game, but he walked the first batter on four pitches. Cochrane stormed out to the mound, punched Walberg in the stomach, and tramped back to his position behind the plate. Walberg then retired the next batters to preserve the one A's victory of the series.

7. Center Stage

"The direct parental approach was an effective way for Cochrane to deal with the brilliant but sometimes erratic Walberg and Walberg accepted it good naturedly," one writer commented on Cochrane's leadership style.

But Mickey could handle the pitchers. He "inspired great performances out of the mediocre and he also steadied some pitchers whose potential for greatness was sometimes obscured by their own erratic temperament."

Cochrane punched and kicked Walberg, but he took a different tack with Grove, the irascible left-hander with a great fastball. "Sometimes I was a lot madder at Cochrane than I was at the hitters," Grove once said. When Grove got into trouble, Mickey would fire insults from behind the plate to get him to add some zest to his fast ball. Lefty would then try to hurl the ball right through Cochrane, and the hitters would only suffer. More than once Grove and Cochrane needed to be separated during a confrontation at the mound.

Cochrane's techniques worked. A week after the New York showdown, the A's were back a half game behind the Yankees. They didn't give up, but one-run losses to the Indians and the Tigers the following week prevented the A's from catching the faltering Yankees, who finally clinched the pennant on September 28. The A's finished at 98–55, two and a half games behind New York, who had taken 16 of the 22 games played between the two teams.

Soon after the 1928 World Series was over, Cochrane headed to New Brunswick, Canada, on a hunting expedition with teammates Eddie Collins and Joe Bush, Sam Jones of the Senators, Benny Bengough of the Yankees, and Walter Huntzinger, who was formerly with the Giants. Bengough ironically would be supplanted the following season as starting catcher for the Yankees by rookie Bill Dickey, who played 10 games at the end of the 1928 season.

The six big leaguers were headed for a two-week moose hunting expedition at the Hopewell Lodge on the Cains River in central New Brunswick from October 17 to 31. They also got in some fishing on the Mirimachi River, a famous fishing area, before traveling into the woods.

Cochrane bagged two trophies while in the Mirimachi wilderness, one native to Canada and the other distinctly American.

The Canadian trophy was a 16-point moose that had a 44-inch antler spread. The newspapers ran a picture of Cochrane in his A's jacket standing over the downed moose. Only Cochrane and Jones shot moose on the trip, Jones' animal being slightly larger at 45 inches on a 17-point antler span. Bush and Huntzinger got deer, while Collins and Bengough came up empty.

"I never experienced such a thrill in my life as when Frank Russell, my guide, pointed out that big moose to me, as it came rushing along through the woods near the Cains River," Cochrane said from Fredericton on the way home. "That moose looked as if it had 1,000,000 horns and seemed as big as an elephant. I fired only once and over he went."

Cochrane left the head of the moose for mounting by a taxidermist in

Cochrane moose hunting in New Brunswick following 1928 season, before finding out he had been named American League MVP (Urban Archives, Temple University, Philadelphia, Pennsylvania).

New Brunswick. He also shipped some quarters of moose meat back to Boston for a banquet the following week. The meat wound up on the dinner plates of 150 Elks members of the Middleboro Lodge, the town adjacent to Bridgewater on the south, rather than serving Cochrane's hometown rooters. The Bridgewater testimonial was postponed because there wasn't enough time to fit it into Cochrane's schedule before he left for Philadelphia. Cochrane would make up for this absence the following year.

The American trophy was the American League Most Valuable Player Award. Cochrane won the MVP with 53 votes, just two better than Heinie Manush with 51 votes. Joe Judge and Tony Lazzeri finished tied for third with 27 votes.

7. Center Stage

"It was a great surprise to me. I never dreamed that I would be selected," Cochrane said in Fredericton when he received word that he had won the MVP.

One press announcement described the reason for his selection thusly: "Cochrane was ranked by members of the committee as being largely responsible for the showing of the Athletics during the closing days of the campaign. His throwing arm and ability to tag runners out at the plate placed him high in the estimation of the baseball writers."

It is this intangible "responsible for the showing of" leadership quality that led Cochrane to the 1928 MVP Award and has helped shape his image over the years. While Mickey did provide inspiration to the A's down the homestretch in their failed bid for the pennant, competition for the MVP was restricted. The rules back then did not permit repeat winners of the MVP, so the likes of Babe Ruth, Lou Gehrig, George Sisler, Walter Johnson, Roger Peckinpaugh, and George Burns were ineligible for the MVP in 1928. It led many commentators to ask the question: How can you be the best if no one can repeat?

"Cochrane deserves all the honors that his hometown can confer upon him," the *Brockton Enterprise* spouted of its local hero. "He's a credit to his native town and to the great natural game. The more Mickey Cochrane's the game produces, the greater the game will be. Go to it, Bridgewater."

The MVP Award also came with a $1000 cash payment, a check which would be displayed prominently in the newspapers before the winter of 1929 was over, leading to more than $1000 worth of negative publicity for the Athletics and the American League. Not for Cochrane though, as he was ringing up the cash register further.

Using his saxophone from college, Mike played the vaudeville stage that winter. Mike's act was to tell jokes and toot the sax while Arthur Brown sang.

Cochrane played houses in Boston, New York, Brooklyn, and Philadelphia. While the money was good, he later told Bill Duncan of the *Public Ledger*, "I feel like a fool sitting up there and playing a saxophone. Maybe if I were good at it I wouldn't mind it."

Two stories of his vaudeville days that Mike told over and over concerned the broken sax and the phone call hoax.

The broken sax was an embarrassing moment in Brooklyn. Mike's saxophone had accidentally fallen backstage, damaging several keys, but a stage hand replaced it on its stand thinking it all right. The unsuspecting Cochrane sauntered into the wings to retrieve the instrument and began to play "Take Me Out to the Ball Game." The result was radio static. After a few failed attempts, he flung the saxophone into the wings and yelled, "Well, I never could play the damned thing anyhow" and walked off to a roaring applause.

While Cochrane was playing in northeast Philadelphia, the phone call hoax occurred. Five minutes before Mike was scheduled to go on stage he received a phone call that was allegedly from a local sportswriter who told him he had been sold to the Red Sox in exchange for Ira Flagstead, Ed Morris, and

$20,000. The caller asked for a statement. Seconds later the phone outside Mike's dressing room rang again, and another purported sportswriter asked for a comment on the trade.

Cochrane believed it was true and went on stage dumbfounded. He tried to open his act with the customary swift chatter but couldn't do his jokes. He walked off the stage after telling the audience, "I've just been told I've been sold to Boston and those of you who are baseball fans know that's enough to take the heart out of anyone." Friends in the audience hurried backstage to console Mike, but then they thought about confirming the trade themselves. Upon learning the phone call was a practical joke, Mike used the incident as comic material in later acts. "I have two ambitions in life now," Cochrane said the next day. "One is to sign up with the A's and the other is to meet the fellows who made those phone calls. I'll guarantee them a season's pass in a hospital." The jokester was later learned to be Mule Haas.

This innocent gag exposed a flaw in Cochrane — his tendency to worry. This flaw would be inflamed in public in the future years.

Mike also wrote a few of his own songs, "Standing by the Window, Just Watching the Rain," "There Are No Happy Days Without You," and "Glad Days Have Turned to Sad Days" among others.

Cochrane might not have been roundly criticized for cashing in on his newfound celebrity if he had just stuck to vaudeville, using, as one sportswriter wrote, the "opportunity to make more investments in gilt-edged securities that are cramming his safety deposit vault." Being perceived as holding out for more salary because of the MVP award was his undoing, which combined with the vaudeville antics led to the abolition of the MVP award in the spring of 1929.

The vaudeville experience would pay additional dividends down the road because Cochrane gained valuable experience speaking in front of large groups.

- 8 -

All A's on Baseball's Report Card

It all came together in 1929. Mike predicted a Yankee downfall before spring training even began.

"Those Yanks are going to hit the slide this year," Cochrane was quoted in a February issue of *Baseball Magazine*. "Ruth will slow up, sure. He was feeling his age last year. He will find it tough going or I miss my guess. And as Ruth goes so will the Yanks. Some others in the New York lineup are going to feel the inroads of time and in the meanwhile along will come the Browns and the Athletics, stronger in 1929 than in the previous year both in experience and in the desire to come through."

Mike did take a while to come to agreement with Mack on a new contract for the 1929 season. Coming off his financial success in vaudeville as well as the stock market, Cochrane did a little posturing to gain some leverage with the A's management. "Catching is my business," he told Bill Dooly of the *Philadelphia Record* in early February, "and I prefer it to anything else. However, I am convinced that I am in the right in this thing and am not asking for any more than I feel I am worth and entitled to." Mike also told Dooly that he had "several offers to enter the commercial fields and may decide to give up catching." Dooly reported that a large brokerage house had offered him a three-year contract at what Mike called "tempting terms" and that another large concern was ready to sign Mike up as a salesman at a high salary.

But Cochrane returned to another season on the baseball diamond and saw newly elected President Herbert Hoover throw out the first ball on Opening Day as the A's defeated the Senators 13–4, the first of 104 victories for the A's in the 1929 regular season.

Cochrane, the 1928 MVP, was on top of his game early to lead the charge for the A's. In the season's second game, Cochrane saved the day by diving to stop Walberg's wild pitches, once barehanding one. "Cochrane never caught a better game," one reporter wrote as Mickey also threw out Buddy Myer stealing, caught a foul pop no more than ten feet in the air and had a 2-run single in the fifth inning.

There was some disruption in the Cochrane household in late April as Gordon Jr., who was recovering at the Germantown Hospital for an operation for mastoiditis, needed blood transfusions to save his life. Mike would shuttle to and from Shibe Park and the hospital until Gordon Jr. recovered.

The A's sped to the top of the American League early in the season, partly by feasting on the Washington Senators, whom they defeated in 12 of 13 games during the first two months of the season. After moving into sole possession of first place on May 14 with a 10–8 win over the Tigers, the A's proceeded to rattle off 11 straight wins from May 17 to May 26, including nine over the aforementioned Senators, to solidify a lock they would have on first place for the rest of the season. Speaking at Northeast High School twelve blocks from Shibe Park, Mike remarked: "Things never looked better for the team. With the Yankees apparently on the down grade, we have the best chance ever. I am sure that the fall will find us up front by at least ten games."

Mack's troops were overpowering their rivals in 1929. "A's have replaced the Yankees as the batting swashbucklers of baseball" and "A's employ old Yankee traits" became familiar newspaper phrases as Philadelphia was winning by lopsided scores with big innings. On May 1 they scored ten runs in one inning at Boston. Then on May 22 the A's scored 12 runs in the 5th versus the Red Sox, as Cochrane went 3 for 4 to begin a 12 for 19 streak over a five-day period to lift his .319 average up to .385 by the end of the day on May 26.

The Senators looked to finally take a victory from the A's on May 23 with an 8–0 lead but saw it evaporate when Bump Hadley yielded 8 runs to the A's in the 4th, leading to a 9–8 loss.

Cochrane went 4 for 4 with four RBI's on May 24 in a 10–3 win over the Senators. Mickey hit two singles, a double, and his first home run of the season, with two runners aboard in the 7th, off Archie Campbell of the beleaguered Senator pitching staff.

In an extra-inning affair the next day, the A's won 5–4 before taking their 11th straight victory on May 26 with a score of 4–3 when Cochrane had one the best hitting days of his career. Mickey went 5 for 5 off Braxton and Marberry, with two doubles and three singles.

The 11-game winning streak was stopped by the Red Sox with a 5–4 win on May 28. However, the A's then took another six in a row to stand with a 31–9 record on June 3, firmly ahead of the second place Browns.

Cochrane and the 21-year-old Foxx in his first full season were tearing up the American League. Mickey continued to hit at the same pace for several weeks, including back-to-back 4 for 5 and 3 for 5 days against the Indians on June 13–14 at Shibe Park, hitting .389 on June 14 to rank second in the league behind the .406 average of Foxx.

During 1929, Cochrane settled into the third spot in Mack's batting order, hitting behind second baseman Max Bishop at leadoff and center fielder Mule Haas in the number two slot while setting the plate for Simmons in cleanup and Foxx in the fifth spot. The set lineup for the next three years also had Miller and Dykes at number six and seven respectively, with the shortstop batting eight ahead of the pitcher's customary number nine position.

Both the A's and Cochrane benefited from this lineup. The league couldn't afford to pitch around Mickey with Simmons and Foxx up next. However, with Mickey now hitting consistently, the league paid as Simmons and Foxx took up the RBI opportunities presented them with Cochrane habitually on base. "Facing Cochrane was tough enough," Yankee pitcher Lefty Gomez once said. "But with Simmons and Foxx on deck it was agony."

Simmons hit .356 in 1929, edged out for the batting title by just four percentage points, and led the league in RBI's with 157. Foxx hit .354 and socked 33 homers, just one fewer than Simmons, who had 34. Cochrane at the plate was clearly a great table setter for Simmons and Foxx. Behind the plate Mickey was also steering the pitches of Lefty Grove, who had a 12–1 record by July 4 and would wind up 1929 at 20–6, leading the league in several pitching categories, strikeouts and winning percentage most notably.

The 1929 A's would be ranked as the third best team of all-time in the book *Baseball's 25 Greatest Teams* published by *The Sporting News*, behind the 1927 Yankees and the 1961 Yankees. By July 4, fans began beckoning the A's for World Series tickets, the team looked so unbeatable. However, at Boston in a 4th of July doubleheader, a hitch in the A's plans came up. Cochrane fell to avoid a pitch by Milt Gaston in the 10:15 A.M. first game, his elbow ripping into his side. He played the game out and had three doubles and a home run in a 3–1 Grove victory. After trainer Doc Ebling taped him up between games, Mickey played the afternoon game in severe pain. After going 0 for 4, Mickey bowed to Perkins, who took over at catcher at the tail end of an 8–1 win.

"Cochrane looked a little tired yesterday," Mack said the next day. "He hurt his side, however, everybody knows you can't keep Cochrane out of a ball game as long as he is able to hobble around on one foot." Cochrane made it to Chicago on the team train, but was in such extreme pain in batting practice at Comiskey Park that Mack sent him to a local hospital. X-rays revealed Cochrane had a broken rib.

Mack sent Cochrane, then fifth in the A.L. batting race with a .365 average, back to Philadelphia to recuperate while the A's finished the series with the White Sox and then went on to St. Louis to play the Browns. Mickey was expected to be out of the lineup for several weeks. He was "the one man whose place could not be filled."

"The A's today with Cochrane on the sidelines were something like an order of boiled beef with the horseradish sauce missing," James Isaminger of the *Philadelphia Inquirer* wrote of Cochrane's absence from the A's when they lost 5–4 to the White Sox.

Back in Philadelphia at his apartment on the corner of City Line and Bala Avenues, Mike was fretting over his inactivity while the A's were playing out West. Music was the one thing that soothed him. "Great stuff, music," Mike told Raymond Hill of the *Philadelphia Bulletin*. "It takes your mind off your troubles and how I need to get my mind off my side right now!" His feet beat with the tune of the phonograph record, and he hummed the soulful notes of the jazz spouting from the saxophone-filled tunes.

"This setting is driving me nuts," Mike added to Hill. "Why, when they spilled the batteries over the radio today, I couldn't believe my ears when the announcers said 'Grove and Perkins for the Athletics.' It just seems strange that I'm not in there."

Mike's right side had been heavily taped by team physician Dr. Frank Baird to protect a cracked fifth rib, and Dr. Baird prescribed sun baths to help strengthen the tissue around the rib. Mike headed to Atlantic City to enjoy the sun at the New Jersey shore.

"These numbers are red hot," Mike told Hill as he danced around his apartment to Duke Ellington's latest blues. "I can't take this phonograph with me, but I'm sure going to take the records. I'll grab a portable machine and have music served with my sun baths every day."

"This is a great place," Mike sighed of Atlantic City, "but I wish the enforced rest were over and I was with the A's again. You know I feel like it's my fault every time the boys lose a game.

Mike was spotted in the press box at Phillies Park for the July 13 Sunday game with the Pirates, and the newspapers speculated he would join the A's in Cleveland for the series with the Indians. "I won't play until Thursday," Mike said after the game. "But, of course if they need me badly, I may jump in."

When the A's arrived in Cleveland for the Indians series, Mack found Cochrane in the hotel lobby waiting for him, pleading to be used in the game that day. Mickey caught the game on July 14, starting the winning rally in a 5–3 victory as he "birched a solid single to right" off Indian pitcher Jimmy Zinn in the tenth inning. Cochrane advanced to third on Simmons' single, at which point Mack pinch ran for Mickey, fearing a close play at the plate. Walter French ran for Cochrane and scored the go-ahead run for the A's on Foxx's sacrifice fly.

Cochrane caught nearly every game thereafter until the A's clinched their first pennant with Cochrane on the roster with a 5–0 win over the White Sox on September 14. The A's finished 18 games ahead of the second place Yankees by season's end.

After hitting .369 before his July 4 injury sidelined him, Cochrane tailed off a bit upon his return and finished up with a .331 average for the season, with 95 RBI's out of the third spot in Mack's batting order. Cochrane struck out just eight times in 1929, in 606 plate appearances, just four off the American League record for fewest strikeouts in a season for a regular player. If Mickey hadn't struck out five times during the hot days of August, he might have equaled Joe Sewell's record of four strikeouts in a season. Cochrane's ratio of one strikeout per 64 at bats in 1929 ranks right up there with the all-time tough strikeout years.

"After an absence of fourteen long years, Connie Mack came back home yesterday. He came back to the idyllic scene of roses and pennants where he so long held sway. The seal was put on his seventh American League pennant yesterday," Isaminger wrote in the *Philadelphia Inquirer* of Mack's return to championship form.

Cochrane celebrated during the two weeks preceding the World Series. While in Boston to play the Red Sox, Mike was honored at a banquet in his hometown of Bridgewater on September 26 after the A's defeated the Red Sox 5–3. Cochrane was paraded through town along with all the A's (except Mack); then there was a banquet at the Town Hall where old friend Charlie Hayes presented him with a hunting rifle.

"Cochrane was visibly affected by the reception," the *Brockton Enterprise* noted. "It was some minutes before he found himself. He then proceeded to tell his friends just what a banquet in his home town meant to him."

"All I can say is that this reception overwhelms me," Mike told his hometown fans. It would pale in comparison to the one six years later.

The stock market euphoria had touched Cochrane, who along with many others had failed to anticipate that the stock market would peak on September 3, 1929. In a 1929 article in the *Public Ledger*, Bill Duncan wrote: "Cochrane is one of the many Mackmen who considers the financial page of utmost importance. He studies the various stocks as closely as he does the American League batters and, so far, has been just as successful at one as the other.

"The hobby of 'beat the market' has joined the list of hunting, golf, automobile driving and others pursued by major league ballplayers."

Cochrane was a pawn caught in a speculative boom; by 1929 the broker's office had replaced the saloon as the local meeting grounds. "Stock speculation provided a legal spirit of intoxication in a time when intoxicating spirits were prohibited by the 18th Amendment. By the fall of 1929, those who were guiding the market were driving under the influence," one historian has written. "A terrible crash, to be followed by unpleasant sobering experiences and an awful hangover were the likely results."

Cochrane, just 26 years old, was a unanimous selection to *The Sporting News* all-star team, collecting all 187 votes for the catcher position. It was the third time in his five years in the big leagues that Mickey was named to this prestigious honor. He was joined on that squad by Foxx, Simmons, and Grove.

It was a landmark year for Cochrane in catching statistics, as he led American League receivers in fielding percentage for the first time with a .983 average, making just 13 errors in 749 chances. With Grove leading the league with 170 strikeouts and Earnshaw runnerup with 149 k's, Cochrane not surprisingly led catchers with 659 putouts, far ahead of the runnerup, New York rookie catcher Bill Dickey.

Tickets for the three World Series games at Shibe Park went on sale October 4 in sets of two grandstand seats for each of the three games at a cost of $33 per set. Cochrane was one of the first in line, along with Rommel and Joe Boley; they all bought ten sets each.

Despite the Black Sox scandal in the 1919 World Series, public gambling on the World Series continued. Bookies were quoted daily in the newspapers. The *New York Times* reported before the series began: "The A's were 9 to 10 favorites on Sunday according to Broadway betting commissioners."

Seating was tight in Shibe Park, where there was space for only 36,000 fans. Viewing was also decent from the rooftops of houses on 20th Street behind right field, where residents were erecting bleachers to watch the action over the 12-foot-high fence. Fans inside and outside the park would see an exciting Series.

In the span of one week in 1929, from October 8 to October 14 to be exact, Cochrane was propelled to national attention on the baseball diamond. It wasn't so much his .400 batting average in the Series as it was how he achieved that mark against the National League champion Chicago Cubs, managed by Joe McCarthy, who would become a Cochrane nemesis in years to come as Yankee manager.

There was Cochrane's leadership behind the plate. Several legends were born in the 1929 World Series. Cochrane's performance wasn't one of them, but his play built the springboard for future fame. The Cochrane legends would come in future World Series.

At the Cubs' home ground of Wrigley Field in Game 1, Cochrane immediately served notice that he would be a tough out. In the top of the 1st, Mickey worked Cub pitcher Charlie Root for a base on balls, forcing Root to go to a 3–2 count before yielding him as a base runner. The walk didn't lead to a run, but his single to lead off the 9th did as the A's tallied two runs to take a 3–0 lead. Chicago ruined Howard Ehmke's shutout bid by scoring once in the bottom of the 9th as the A's took Game 1 by the score of 3–1.

Ehmke? The legendary story of Game 1 was this little used hurler. Ehmke's 13-strikeout performance, using his side-armed, off-speed pitches to catch the heavy-hitting Cubs off stride, established a Series record that stood for 24 years until Brooklyn's Carl Erskine whiffed 14 Yankees in the 1953 World Series. While the pitching performance was itself remarkable, especially for a 35 year old, the legend was created by Mack's surprise move to start the erstwhile workhorse in lieu of his top pitchers, Grove and Earnshaw. Ehmke had pitched just 55 innings for Mack all year.

Legend now has it that Mack's move was a shocker, being revealed only when Ehmke began to warm up on the sidelines at Wrigley. Mickey himself has said that he said to Mack, "Is *he* going to pitch?"

Actually the *New York Times* reported that day that sources had revealed that "the sagacious Connie may confound all the experts and the Cubs as well

8. All A's on Baseball's Report Card

by starting Howard Ehmke, reserving Earnshaw for the second game and not shooting his two famed left-handers Bob Grove and Rube Walberg until the series shifts to Philadelphia." The sources were probably basing their guess on the fact that Mack had dispatched Ehmke to scout the Cubs the last three weeks of the season.

Cochrane's role in Ehmke's success was not highly touted, though, being limited to a statistical footnote that Mickey had 14 putouts on the day. In addition to putouts for each of the 13 strikeouts, Mickey latched onto a foul pop off the bat of Cub third baseman Norm McMillan in the bottom of the 1st. Cochrane's knowledge of Ehmke's repertoire and ability to set up the Cubs hitters undoubtedly contributed, however, to the journeyman pitcher's success.

Strikeout #13 came with two outs in the 9th as the Cubs threatened with two runners on. Ehmke got pinch hitter Chick Tolson after telling Cochrane at the mound, "I'll strike this guy out and make him like it." Cochrane said after the game: "It was an easy game for me to catch with Ehmke doing the chucking. He threw the ball where my glove was waiting for it."

The 14 putouts established a World Series record at the time, breaking a mark set by another Philadelphia Athletic, Ira Thomas, who had 12 putouts in a 1911 World Series game when pitcher Chief Bender struck out 11 New York Giant batters.

Mickey also had an assist, cutting down Charlie Grimm in his attempt to steal second base in the 4th. In his mind it was righting an injustice because Grimm had reached first on a walk largely on the strength of a ball three that Mickey thought in the strike zone. He had wasted little breath, however, complaining about the call to umpire Bill Klem.

Cochrane also had an instrumental role in Game 2 as Philadelphia swept both opening games on its opponent's turf with a 9–3 victory in the second game. Mickey's role in Game 2 has been underappreciated because history zeroed in on home runs by Foxx and Simmons as the key hits in the game. Three times Cochrane kept rallies alive which led to the hits by Foxx and Simmons. With two outs in the 3d, Cochrane singled to right field off a Pat Malone curve ball to start a rally which was capped by a 3-run home run by Foxx to give the A's a 3–0 lead. Up again with two outs in the 4th, Mickey worked Malone for a walk to load the bases which enabled Simmons to hit a 2-run single to push the A's out to a 6–0 margin. Then in the 8th Mickey received another walk with two outs, allowing Simmons a chance to poke a 2-run homer to clinch the A's 9–3 victory.

Mickey also had another 14 putouts in Game 2, guiding the fireballing Earnshaw and Grove through 13 strikeouts. He picked up the 14th putout in the bottom of the 9th when Rogers Hornsby rather foolishly tried to score from third base on a bouncer back to the mound. Grove easily cut down Hornsby with a throw to Cochrane, who was guarding the plate.

Chicago took its only victory of the Series in Game 3 following an 18-hour train ride from Chicago to Philadelphia on the travel day. Guy Bush bested

Earnshaw 3–1, despite 10 strikeouts by the lanky right-hander on one day's rest after being knocked out of the box in the fifth inning of Game 2.

Cochrane scored the A's only run in the 5th after singling to lead off the inning. He also had another single in the 3d as he was batting .500 after three games with four hits in eight at bats. He continued his timely hitting in Game 4 by going 2 for 4, with his only extra-base hit of the Series a double to left field in the 4th, as the A's produced the highest scoring inning in World Series history with 10 runs in the bottom of the 7th to erase an 8–0 Chicago lead for a 10–8 Philadelphia win and 3–1 edge in the Series.

Having made the final out of the 6th for the A's, Cochrane had only a minor role in the pivotal seventh inning explosion. He received his sixth walk of the Series as the ninth batter in the inning and scored the tying run on Foxx's single. Much has been written about the key to the A's rally that day — Cub center fielder Hack Wilson who lost two balls in the sun, one an egregious muff of Haas' drive that went for a 3-run, inside-the-park home run.

"I remember meeting Mickey in a speakeasy after that game," Jimmy Powers wrote years later. "I recall Mickey telling a group of writers, 'I don't think you'll ever see a World Series inning to match that rally. We overcame almost impossible odds.' Few of us doubted the A's would win the next day."

After a Sunday off, Philadelphia did seal its Series victory in Game 5 on Monday in another comeback, this time in front of President Herbert Hoover, who threw out the first ball, in a 3–2 victory. The A's scored three runs in the bottom of the 9th off Cub hurler Malone, capped by Miller's game-ending double. Cochrane grounded out for the second out of the ninth, illustrative of his struggling 0 for 3 day at the plate. Mickey did draw another walk in the 7th to tie a Series record for most walks in a 5-game series with seven.

Nevertheless, Cochrane did end the Series with a .400 batting average, second best on the team right behind Dykes' 8 for 19 performance for a .421 average. Mickey also broke Muddy Ruel's record of 51 putouts in a 5-game series with his 59 putouts. He also established a mark for most chances accepted in a 5-game series with no errors. Both records still stand today.

While Cochrane was faultless batting at the plate as well as fielding behind it, he was guilty of being a bit too profane in conversations with Cub hitters. Mickey and his vitriolic teammates exchanged a brutal assault of verbal abuse with their Chicago opponents that was typical of the serious benchjockeying of the day. The exchange became too hot, however, for Commissioner Landis, who stepped in to call a truce between the teams.

In Game 5 while waiting for a Cub hitter who was taking his time getting into the batter's box, Cochrane mocked Landis by yelling loudly in a soprano voice, "Hurry up, sweetheart, we're serving tea at four o'clock!"

Landis reportedly approached Cochrane in the A's clubhouse after congratulating Mack on winning the World Series and inquired, "Where are you serving tea?" to Cochrane's embarrassment.

8. All A's on Baseball's Report Card

A writer asked Cochrane what he planned to do with his World Series money, which turned out to be $5,620.

"I'm going to put some of it away to buy a seat on the Stock Exchange. We ought to be in the World Series for about five more years," Cochrane responded. "Seriously, I am going to buy some of that stock I own on margin, outright."

The glow of the spotlight from winning the 1929 World Series would unfortunately be dampened just two weeks later on October 29 when "the speculative boom, dependent upon confidence, burst when a vast supply of shares for sale hit the market in the morning but failed to create their own demand until prices had plummeted."

October 29, 1929, was Black Tuesday, the day the stock market crashed, triggering the beginning of the Great Depression.

- 9 -

Catcher on Another Plane

The joy of winning the 1929 World Series was dampened by the dawning of the Great Depression. "For American fans, the Athletic triumph provided a glittering end to a lush baseball era," David Voigt wrote in *American Baseball*. "But as the year 1929 ended, the shock of the Wall Street failure quickly cut away incomes, jobs, and purchasing power throughout the land. It was no time to launch a baseball dynasty and this hard fact became Mack's agony."

It's not entirely clear how much Mike suffered in lost value on his stock portfolio. Notwithstanding his Cobbian schooling in financial matters, he probably took a fair hit, especially if he couldn't clear his stock margin with his World Series check as he had anticipated before the October 29 crash.

"I didn't notice that we were living any differently," Mary Cochrane replied when asked about Mike losing money in the stock market crash. "He bought me a new Packard when Joan was born." Joan Cochrane was born the summer of 1930 and joined little Gordon now age 5 in the Cochrane household. Joan would become the proverbial apple of her father's eye and a darling of Detroit as a little girl.

Belying any financial setback, the Cochrane household also moved from the City Line Avenue apartment to a house at 723 Kenmare Road in the fashionable enclave of Cynwyd in Philadelphia's fabled Main Line exclusive suburbs. Over the fireplace in the living room of the three-story brick house hung a stuffed head of the moose that Mike shot in Canada in 1928.

In a 1930 newspaper article entitled "Wife of A's Star Says She's a Jinx," the petite blond Mary Cochrane said that she loved to keep house and stayed away from her husband's games because the A's always lost when she was there.

"I like to cook and made this blue dress myself. Keeping house seems so natural to me," Mary told writer Helen Mankin. "When Mike comes home [from the games on the road] I always try to have a good dinner ready. I cook it myself and because he likes beefsteak, I have that."

"I don't go to base ball games anymore," Mary continued. "The last time I was there, two years ago, the A's lost and I felt I was the jinx. I wouldn't think of going to see them, I'll listen in on the radio."

9. Catcher on Another Plane

"In Panology of War" the *Philadelphia Inquirer* titled this photograph in April 1929, six months before the Great Depression hit the country (Urban Archives, Temple University, Philadelphia, Pennsylvania).

Mary also stayed away from Shibe Park for another reason, not just that the A's lost. "Mike didn't want me associating too much with the other players' wives," Mary recalled. "Being college educated as a ballplayer was almost unheard of in those days. A lot of players and their families were very ignorant."

Mike's soft heart combined with his financial success over the past five years allowed him to assist friends who lost money in the stock market crash.

"As far as friendship is concerned, Cochrane has no peer. If he likes you and considers you a sincere friend he'll go the limit. That doesn't mean, however, that he is a sucker for every acquaintance," Bill Duncan wrote in a 1933 retrospective. "The school of hard knocks has enabled him to separate the wheat from the chaff."

To help out Cy Perkins, who lost $50,000 and was wiped out in the crash aftermath, Cochrane put up his own stock as collateral for Perkins to obtain a loan to cover his margin call and he also cosigned a note for $25,000. Mike no doubt helped out others as well, judging by Duncan's remarks three years later.

Duncan was involved when Mike contemplated dusting off his college boxing gloves to return to the boxing arena in late 1929. Duncan arranged a challenge by vaudeville boxer/ballplayer Art Shires, and Duncan as Cochrane's manager would split the winnings with "Mickey the Mauler," as Mike would have called himself. That was before Mack stepped in to nix the idea. "Just forget it. You're a baseball catcher, not a fist catcher and I won't stand for your entering the ring against Shires or anybody else," Mack insisted.

"I'll stick to catching Grove's speed balls instead of some wild lefts from Shires," Mike told the press. "I asked a friend how he thought I'd do against Shires. He told me I'd be all right if they let me wear my catcher's mask."

Cochrane reported to prespring workouts at Hot Springs, Arkansas, motoring down from Philadelphia with stockbroker William Eagleson, probably discussing a restructuring of Mike's portfolio on the way.

Following some fun in Hot Springs, including no doubt a few sips of alcoholic potables in this renowned retreat from Prohibition, Cochrane went on to Fort Myers, where Mack was intent on not letting his A's get complacent. Six rookies would eventually make the squad going north, a signal from Mack that no one's job was totally safe, even the job of a World Series champion.

A new graybeard joined the A's for 1930, catcher Wally Schang, now 40, who had played for Mack back in the 1913-14 pennant years. Mack traded third baseman Hale to the Browns for Schang, freeing up Dykes to handle third by himself and acquiring a veteran backup for Cochrane.

"I'm ready to catch anytime the ambulance carries Cochrane away," Schang said that spring, recognizing not only his role on the team but also the probability of getting any playing time. But Schang would have a role to play in keeping the A's in the 1930 pennant race, catching 36 games.

The A's started slow but broke out of their April doldrums with two blowouts against the Tigers in Shibe Park. On May 1 the A's had 18 hits in a 19-2 triumph over Detroit, including an 8-run eighth inning. Then the next day they collected 14 hits in a 10-4 win, beginning their climb towards first place Cleveland.

On May 3, however, Cochrane was hit on the right leg with a foul tip in a game with the Browns. Never one to let up and with the A's within hailing

9. Catcher on Another Plane

distance of first place Cleveland, he aggravated the leg on May 5 when he crashed into a box seat while scrambling for a foul ball, creating a giant bruise "all the colors of the rainbow." Limping through 12 innings and a 0 for 5 day, Cochrane was finally persuaded by trainer Elbing to let up and rest for a few days.

A week and a half later on May 16 Cochrane was hurt again, this time injuring his right ankle sliding into third base against the Senators. X-rays showed that Cochrane had broken a small bone in his ankle. "It was nobody's fault but my own. I slid late. If I'd hit the dirt sooner, I wouldn't have been hurt. My spikes bit into the hard surface and I stopped with a sudden jam. I thought I'd broken my leg," Cochrane said while recuperating at his new Cynwyd home amid newspaper headlines declaring "Cochrane Lost to A's for 3 Weeks."

With Cochrane's .319 batting average, glove, and spirit parked on the sidelines, Schang took over behind the plate for Mack and capably handled the A's pitching staff while Cochrane recovered.

But Cochrane returned on May 24 in a doubleheader with the Yankees, "discarding the crutches and looking sound although favoring his right ankle slightly." Mickey went 3 for 3 with two doubles in the A's 10–6 loss, announcing his return.

What a return it was. Cochrane went on a tear as the A's began climbing from second place to challenge first place Washington. For the next five weeks, Mickey batted at a .457 clip, collecting 53 hits in 116 at bats to soar over the .400 average mark to challenge for the league lead. Cochrane hit consistently, not in streaks, getting hits in 30 of 35 games and never more than eight games in a row. Only once, against the Tigers at Navin Field on June 15–16, did he bunch two big hitting games together. Mickey had a 4 for 5 game on Sunday, June 15, in the A's 10–1 victory and came back on Monday with a 3 for 4 outing.

On June 30 after going 4 for 4, Cochrane was leading the American League with a .404 average, with Simmons in close pursuit at .394 as the A's closed in on the first place Senators, just two games off the pace while only four games ahead of third place New York.

Cochrane was flying high not only at the ballpark but also off the field that summer of 1930. Mike had fallen in love with flying in airplanes after Charles Lindbergh crossed the Atlantic in 1927, and he flew in private planes whenever an opportunity arose.

"If he could own a plane, he would," Mary Cochrane said in that 1930 newspaper interview. "He likes to ride in them, but Connie won't allow that. He is afraid to let the players go up."

Before batting 4 for 4 in that June 30 game, Mike was flying gliders that morning at the Penlyn Polo Club near Ambler. "Gee what a funny sensation it was. I went only four feet off the ground but I felt as if I were four hundred feet in the air. But it sure is the stuff," Mike told Stan Baumgartner of the *Philadelphia Inquirer*. "If the old man (Connie) would let me I would buy a

Cochrane on the golf course during 1930 spring training in Fort Myers, Florida (Urban Archives, Temple University, Philadelphia, Pennsylvania).

9. Catcher on Another Plane

plane and fly. When my catching days are over that is what I am going to do, be a pilot."

Philadelphia had a 17–7 road trip in July, catapulting ahead of the Senators into first place on July 13 with a 12–1 win over the Browns at Sportsman's Park. By the end of the road trip, the A's were six games ahead of the Senators and well on their way to the 1930 pennant. The A's finished with a 102–52 record, eight games ahead of the Senators.

Once Cochrane mastered the basic catching techniques that Perkins imparted to him, he moved on to acquire a higher level of appreciation for the catcher's role. "Confidence is a favorite theme with pitchers," Cochrane related in a 1929 *Baseball Magazine* article. "If a catcher hasn't confidence in himself, then his pitcher won't have confidence in him. And if the pitcher hasn't confidence in his own battery mate, he simply can't pitch. He shouldn't be called upon to worry about his catcher. He should feel free to put everything one has on the ball, knowing that the catcher will at least knock that ball down and stop it."

Mike often put this formula more simply: "Expect every pitch to be a wild pitch! To my mind it is the secret of good catching."

Cochrane always believed that his speed and nimbleness afoot helped improve his catching abilities, allowing him to pounce upon pitches that went astray. He kept his natural speed by limiting his squatting behind the plate. "If a catcher wants to squat all the time behind the plate it may stiffen his legs," Mike often said. "I squat behind the plate on each pitched ball but I don't stay there. I'm usually half standing up."

The psychological part of catching drained Cochrane as much as the physical part. "A catcher who is on to his job, who is trying to handle his pitchers and win ball games has so much on his mind that he really can't devote the time and attention necessary to good hitting. So I find every summer when the hot weather comes that I'm a little fagged and tired, that batting becomes more and more of an effort."

Indeed, Cochrane dipped to .375 by the end of July, but was still third in the A.L. batting race. By hitting a consistent .330 for the second half of the season, he finished at .357, fifth in the league as Simmons took the batting title with his .381 average. Cochrane's .357 average in 1930 was, however, still the best season average for a catcher in the modern era.

"The greatest catcher that ever lived is in the game today. And he wears the uniform of the Philadelphia Athletics," F. C. Lane wrote of Cochrane after the 1930 season. "Cochrane has everything a catcher should have: a good arm, natural talent as a receiver, a likeable disposition which makes him a general favorite with his own pitching staff. A conspicuous trait is his speed of foot. Hitting is purely secondary with a catcher, but the catcher who can bat like Mickey Cochrane has added vastly to his own value."

"Cochrane is the most important man in the Athletic lineup," Yankee manager Bob Shawkey said of Cochrane in 1930. "In my opinion, he made the team."

Cochrane was named to *The Sporting News* all-star team again, receiving the second highest number of votes that year behind Lefty Grove. Cochrane guided Grove to a 28–5 record as Mose Bob led the league in just about every pitching category and unofficially saved nine victories in relief. It was the fourth straight year that Grove had won at least 20 games.

The A's clinched the pennant on September 18, during a month when 39 Philadelphia banks closed as the Great Depression began to deepen. Cochrane had the misfortune to play on a great team during some of America's darkest days, when many Americans had to worry about where their next meal was coming from and couldn't afford the two cents to buy the newspaper to read how the A's were doing. Worse yet, they could hardly afford the admission to Shibe Park.

After the A's clinched the pennant, Mike found time to take in the U.S. Amateur golf tournament being played in 1930 at the Merion Golf Club near Mike's home in Cynwyd. Bobby Jones was seeking his fourth major golf championship of the year to complete the Grand Slam.

Jones, a brilliant but nervous golfer, played a practice round on September 21 and met Cochrane in the clubhouse. Mike reminded Jones that "his position seemed to be very analogous to that of a baseball team needing to win that fourth game in a row to make a clean sweep of a World Series. There was just no way in which a buildup of pressure could be avoided."

There were no surprises by Mack at the start of the 1930 World Series. He broke from the box with his aces against the National League champion St. Louis Cardinals, using Grove in Game 1 and Earnshaw in Game 2.

The Cardinals would prove to be a bit tougher than the Cubs were in the 1929 World Series. Cochrane drew a walk off Burleigh Grimes on a 3–2 pitch in the bottom of the 1st, but was thrown out stealing, Al Mancuso to Frank Frisch, as St. Louis served notice that it would be a stingy competitor.

Grimes gave up just five hits in the opener, but the A's made the most of them en route to a 5–2 victory. All five hits were for extra bases, including an eighth inning home run by Cochrane over the right field wall at Shibe.

Mickey had struck out in the 6th, but he and Grimes growled at each other as Mickey strode to the dugout. Grimes later said that following a spitter he threw Cochrane to strike him out, "I just told him if I had a bird dog pup that looked like him and didn't have no sense, I'd shoot him." Grimes then put his hand to his ear and wiggled it at him, making fun of Cochrane's somewhat oversized ears. Grimes drastically underestimated the impact on his opponent.

After making a sensational catch of Mancuso's foul fly near the A's dugout in the top of the 8th (all that practice at Dover paid off), Mickey faced Grimes

9. Catcher on Another Plane

with two outs in the bottom of that frame. "Cochrane collected revenge with interest for Mickey took a firm hold on one of Grimes' fastest shoots and sent it out of the park over the right field wall."

The pumped-up Cochrane continued his assault at the plate in the bottom of the 1st in Game 2, a game in which Earnshaw held St. Louis in check for a 6–1 victory by homering off Flint Rhem. Grimes egged on Cochrane from the dugout, yelling, "Mule Ears, Mule Ears!"

"The sensation evidently pleased him immensely, for he at once smashed another one over the barrier on his first time up today to produce another great scramble for the ball in the street bordering the park."

W. O. McGeehan commented after Game 2 about the second home run: "That ought to teach the Cardinals to lay off pointer dogs and mules. They can say what they please about Mickey Cochrane personally, but they must not be cruel to animals."

Cochrane reached on Frisch's error in the 3d, which should have been the last out of the inning, and then scored on Simmons' double in a 2-run A's rally which all but put away the Cardinals.

"And so it went — Cochrane, Simmons and Foxx. Stop these three, some amble critic recently remarked and you can stop the Athletics. It is an ingenious idea, but still in a decidedly embryonic stage. Certain is it that Rhem never came close to solving the problem."

As the Series switched to Sportsman's Park, Wild Bill Hallahan shutout the A's 5–0 in Game 3, and Jesse Haines bested Grove in a pitcher's battle 3–1 in Game 4, yielding only four hits to the A's. Cochrane walked twice off Hallahan, but otherwise his bat was quiet, as were most of the team's sticks as the Series was knotted at two games apiece.

Game 5 was scoreless through eight innings as Earnshaw and Grimes hooked up in a dandy duel. Cochrane had bounced a single over second base in the 1st off Grimes, leading to a continuation of their verbal confrontations begun in Game 1. Mickey was the leadoff batter for the A's in the top of the 9th. Grimes continued the mule ears taunt with Mickey as he stepped into the batter's box, threatening a brush-back pitch too.

"What with one witty saying and another, Grimes neglected to get enough balls over the plate and Cochrane walked, emitting loud and raucous razzberries in the direction of the pitcher's box."

Cochrane jibed Grimes on the way to first base and while holding the base as Simmons flied out. With Mickey continuing to assail Grimes verbally from first base as Jim Bottomley attempted to hold him close to the bag, Foxx stepped to the plate.

"After casting one more disdainful look at Cochrane, still prancing around first, Grimes went into his motion and threw a high, fast curve to Foxx and Foxx hit this first pitch into the left field bleachers," Drebinger reported of the hit which gave the A's a 2–0 victory and a 3–2 edge for the Series. Cochrane

Cochrane socializing with teammates Al Simmons and Cy Perkins. Cochrane (left), Simmons (third from left), Mary Cochrane is third from right, Perkins (second from right). Note champagne bucket during this time of Prohibition (*The Sporting News Archive*, St. Louis, Missouri).

had responded to the Foxx homer by "feverishly hopping up and down on first base" in celebration.

Mack came back with Earnshaw in Game 6 at Shibe Park on one day's rest. (Grove had pitched Game 4 and had relieved Earnshaw in Game 5 to gain the win.) The A's nailed the Series for Philadelphia as they scored early and often for a 7–1 victory.

In the bottom of the 1st, Cochrane knocked in the first run with a double down the right field line off Hallahan to score Dykes, and he himself scored on Miller's double. Later in the 6th, Mickey hit a sacrifice fly to center field off Cardinal reliever Jim Lindsey to score Bishop with the seventh and final run for the A's in the 1930 World Series. Philadelphia was champion again.

Mickey's .222 batting average in the Series symbolized the A's anemic hitting; the team batted a lowly .197 in stark contrast to its regular season .294 average. Testimony to the superb pitching of Grove and Earnshaw was the Cardinals' .200 team average, more than 100 points lower than its .314 regular season average.

"The Cardinal taunts and their wise cracks helped us to win the World Series," Cochrane told attendees at a Poor Richard Club luncheon where he was awarded the Poor Richard Achiever Medal. "Conditions might have been different but for some tart remarks made by Gabby Street and some personal cracks from Grimes. I know I got hot under the collar and it made me work harder and it affected the other boys the same way."

After the Series, Cochrane headed for New Brunswick on a hunting trip with Collins, Perkins, and Tris Speaker. Unlike the 1928 male-only expedition, this time everyone took their wives along for a small game hunt near the Nepiequit River. "A new experience for Mrs. Cochrane" the newspapers commented.

- 10 -

Picnic Grove

Despite the nation's difficulties, Mack signed Mike to a new contract over the winter to play with the A's. The contract was for three years at $20,000 per year, covering his services through the 1933 season. Mike seemingly was financially set for three years, perhaps the hardest three years economically for the average American in this century because of the Great Depression.

Mike took to the basketball courts again that winter, running a basketball team of fellow baseball players and taking on various comers. Cochrane and John Milligan, pitcher of the Phillies, were at forward, 6'2" Yankee pitcher Roy Sherid was the center, and minor leaguers Bill Dietrick and Bill Black were the guards. One of their big games was against a Germantown team run by 21-year-old Bucky Walters, who would one day win 198 games as a major league pitcher after playing four years at third base.

Off the baseball field, the 5'10", 180-pound Cochrane was a dapper dresser in double-breasted suits, with his hair usually parted down the middle. "Baseball's costliest suit of clothes belongs to Cochrane, the haberdashery king," one writer noted.

Mike's three-story stone and stucco house in Cynwyd, about a mile and a half from the Philadelphia city line, was close to Merion and several other golf courses, making it convenient for Mike to pursue his passion for the links.

"There haven't been too many changes to the home, other than the decor," more recent owner Bob Leibreid said after living in Cochrane's former home for more than 30 years. "We bought the property in the spring of 1961 when we moved in as newlyweds."

Mary Cochrane also took up her husband's passion of golf. "She's a good golf type," the pro at the Whitemarsh Country Club where the Cochranes were members, told the *Philadelphia Bulletin*. "She's athletically inclined, slender but strong and has a good golf form."

"I'm playing golf for amusement and exercise," Mary said. "I haven't the

10. Picnic Grove

time to go in for it seriously. Managing my home and two children keeps me pretty busy."

Washington was the site of the A's opening game of the 1931 season as President Hoover tossed out the first ball and Lefty Grove notched the win in relief. It would be the first of 31 victories for the left-hander that Cochrane would help engineer that year, easily propelling the A's to a third consecutive American League pennant.

The A's moved into first place for good on May 11 in the midst of a 17-game winning streak and never looked back, forging on to a 107–45 record for the season. Mack's team had an .800 winning percentage at Shibe Park in 1931, at one point winning 22 straight games at home, a record which stood until the 1988 Red Sox won 23 straight at Fenway. Philadelphia's home winning percentage was the second best in American League history, superseded only by the 1932 Yankees with an .802 mark.

Cochrane was not only catching Grove superbly in 1931, he was rapping out base hits with abandon as well. In the A's first six games, Mickey hit just .208, but he then embarked on the hottest streak of his career, hitting safely in 30 of 36 games. Hitting in front of Simmons and Foxx, who had phenomenal years again in 1931, Cochrane got many decent pitches to swing at and he made the most of it. He took the numeral 3 on his uniform to heart.

No one was going to stop this team, which recorded a 23–4 record for the month of May as Grove topped the league with a 10–2 record at Memorial Day and Cochrane was the league's leading hitter.

From April 21 through May 30, Cochrane made 55 hits in 120 at bats for a .458 average over the period. This propelled Mickey to the top of the American League in batting with a .414 average on May 29, his highest batting average ever achieved in a major league uniform. Mickey also had eight home runs over this period, which landed him as the number two leader on May 29 tied with Babe Ruth, who would go on to win the home run crown in 1931. Mickey had one super-hot streak from May 21 through the first game of a May 30 doubleheader, collecting 18 hits in 34 at bats for a .529 clip.

At Navin Field on May 21, Cochrane went 5 for 6 against the Tigers, tagging Tommy Bridges for a home run in the 5th to go with a double and three singles. Mickey was 1 for 4 off Red Ruffing on Sunday May 24 before 45,000 fans at Yankee Stadium before the two teams headed to Philadelphia for five more games at Shibe Park.

The A's took a doubleheader from the Yankees on May 25 to extend their winning streak to 17 straight games as Cochrane went 3 for 5 in each game. In the first game, Mickey homered in the eighth inning off Hank Johnson to lead the A's to a 4–2 victory as Grove bore down in the top of the 9th to strike out Ruth and Gehrig with the tying runs on second and third to preserve the A's win before 32,000 excited fans.

In the second game of the doubleheader, the A's scorched the Yankees for nine runs in the first inning to win easily 16–4. Mickey tripled with the bases loaded on his second at bat of the inning to keep the rally going. His 6 for 10 performance on May 25 moved Cochrane over the .400 mark for the season.

Lefty Gomez stopped the A's winning streak the next day as New York won 6–2 and slowed the hot Cochrane to a 1 for 4 day. Mickey reached George Pipgras for three hits on May 27, homering in the 1st after Bishop singled to give Philadelphia a 2–0 lead. In the 8th with the A's down 5–4, Cochrane opened the inning with a single to spark the winning rally as Miller doubled with the bases loaded to create the A's 6–5 victory.

In the final game of the Yankee series on May 28, Cochrane was 3 for 5 again as the A's needed a ninth inning rally to win 5–4. Cochrane had an infield single in the 9th, a chopper to third base to load the bases before Simmons hit a sacrifice fly to score Lefty Grove, who had doubled to open the 9th and collected the victory in relief of Walberg.

The A's played the Red Sox in Memorial Day doubleheaders, not at Fenway Park but at Braves Field on the weekend of May 30–31. Cochrane was 2 for 4 in the first game on May 30 to conclude his hot streak as Grove shutout the Red Sox 5–0. Mickey took a 0 for 5 in the second game as Ed Durham and Bob Kline shut him out.

Philadelphia beat Boston 7–4 in the opener of the Sunday May 31 doubleheader, and Cochrane went 2 for 5 despite being hit on the leg by a foul tip. In the second game, however, he strained himself running out a rolling ground ball and had to leave the game.

Cochrane sat out a few games to rest his leg and then pinch hit on June 5 in the A's 7–5 12-inning loss to the White Sox, which Grove lost in relief. Mickey returned to the lineup for three games, but he went 3 for 13 and wound up reinjuring his leg to be out for two weeks.

The A's roller coaster continued on with John Heving behind the plate, whom Mack had picked up on waivers from the Red Sox in the spring after releasing both Perkins and Schang as backup catchers.

Returning on June 23, Cochrane guided Grove through the summer on his incredible stretch of victories, which reached 16 on August 19 to tie the major league record established by Smokey Joe Wood and Walter Johnson, both in the 1912 season.

Grove would finish with a 31–4 record in 1931 to give him a combined record of 79–15 over the 1929–31 stretch, with Cochrane guiding him on the way to a league-leading 175 strikeouts.

On the strength of those 31 victories, Lefty became the recipient of the first "modern" Most Valuable Player Award, the award that had been abolished after Cochrane won it in 1928 when the baseball establishment didn't take kindly to his vaudeville and perceived holdout antics. Battery-mate Cochrane finished ninth in the 1931 MVP voting.

10. Picnic Grove

Grove's 16-game winning streak was broken in St. Louis on August 23, when Philadelphia lost 1–0 as Dick Coffman hurled a 3-hit shutout for the Browns. The only run of the game was scored in the third inning when Fred Schulte singled and came home on a "double" by Oscar Melillo. The double was by all accounts a catchable fly ball misjudged by left fielder Jim Moore, a little-used substitute playing in place of the injured Simmons, who was back in Milwaukee nursing an infected ankle.

Grove was furious at losing in this fashion. "You have Grove pitching and Cochrane catching and you lose 1-0, you're a little timid about going into that clubhouse," outfielder Doc Cramer often said.

"After that game I went in and tore the clubhouse up. Wrecked the place," Grove remembered. "Tore those steel lockers off the wall and everything else. Ripped up my uniform. Threw everything I could get my hands on: bats, balls, shoes, gloves, benches. Giving Al Simmons hell all the while. Still gets me mad when I think about it."

"No one said a word. There was no point," Cramer continued. "Next day he was all right. But I never will forget those buttons [off Grove's shirt] flying past me."

"Lefty was really a good-natured fellow when the pressure of the game was off," Cochrane commented. "He was a tough loser and, for my part, I'll take that sort of competitor any time in preference to the chap who loses with a high heart."

Cochrane went 1 for 4 in that A's loss, the first game of a doubleheader that was completed in less than an hour and a half (1:25 to be exact). More importantly, though, Heving caught the nightcap because Cochrane left the team to fly back to Philadelphia to recover from his own troubles. In St. Louis, Mike had had difficulty getting to sleep, and Mack figured that a few days rest would cure him and get him ready for the World Series.

Contributing to the problem, although it was not particularly discussed at the time, was a pitch that Cochrane took to the head a week earlier at League Park in Cleveland. Mickey had hit a home run in the fourth inning of that August 16 game when Indian pitcher George Connally nicked him in the back of the skull with a pitch on his next at bat.

"Mike dropped like a sack of cement," Cy Peterman wrote in the *Philadelphia Bulletin*. "As he lay in the dust, curled in a half circle, he never stirred and the crowd of 20,000 gasped and came to its feet like one man. Not a soul there but remembered another case like that, a decade ago, when Ray Chapman went down before Carl Mays' fast one, and never got up to bat again."

The August 16 beaning hurt Mickey at the plate when he returned, perhaps influencing his performance in the 1931 World Series. Mickey was tentative upon his return, collecting eight walks in the first four games he was back. But a four-day 10 for 16 streak in early September enabled him to salvage his .349 batting average as Mack played Cochrane sparingly the rest of the season.

The 1931 A's, already 11 games up on second place Washington when Cochrane was beaned in Cleveland, were one of the best teams in the history of baseball, as they finished 13½ games ahead of the Yankees. The huge lead also led to some signs of cockiness in the A's. At a Rotary Club luncheon in September, Cochrane said, "I don't see how the St. Louis Cardinals can knock us out of another world championship."

Cochrane finished in the top five in American League batting for the second straight year, ending at .349 for the fourth best behind Simmons, who again won the batting title, this year with his .390 clip. He did it with his own bat model this year, as the Hillerich & Bradsby Company adapted the Jimmie Foxx model to create its C-26 model for Cochrane, 35" and 37 ounces weight.

Cochrane was chosen to *The Sporting News* all-star team for the fourth consecutive year, a nearly unanimous selection with 226 of the 229 votes cast for catcher. (Jim Wilson of the Cardinals received the other 3 votes.) Grove was a unanimous selection for left-handed pitcher. Simmons and Earnshaw joined Cochrane and Grove as the A's took four of the ten slots on that all-star team.

Mickey's performance in 1931 inspired one Oklahoma father, a die-hard St. Louis Cardinal fan, to name his newborn son after him. The baby born October 20 that year would become a pretty fair ballplayer when he grew up. His name was Mickey Mantle. In his book *The Mick,* Mantle related:

> Before I was even born my dad had a name picked out. Mickey, after Mickey Cochrane, My dad practically lived and died with the Cardinals while I was growing up, so the best I can figure is that he must've singled out Cochrane because of his qualities. Brash. Fiercely competitive. A sure winner. Guess dad thought that someday I'd step into Cochrane's shoes.
>
> Baseball was a very big factor in my dad's life. It didn't matter how tired he was, he still managed to play semi-pro ball on weekends. I sat in the stands, thinking he was Pepper Martin, Mickey Cochrane and Dizzy Dean all rolled up in a single package.

Numerous Cochrane families also nicknamed their sons, and a few daughters, after the now-famous ballplayer, and a few went on to some fame of their own.

Mickey Cochran (no "e") grew up in Richmond, Vermont, and was the father of Barbara Cochran, an Olympic skier in 1972.

William "Mickey" Corcoran (pronounced like Cochrane) coached famed Super Bowl football coach Bill Parcells when Parcells was a high school basketball player in Dell River, New Jersey.

Cornelius "Mickey" Cochrane coached soccer at Johns Hopkins and Bowling Green University, where the field is named after him. "I always wonder what people will say years from now, 'What's the connection with the Detroit catcher?'" Cochrane jests.

10. *Picnic Grove*

"In tryouts for the baseball team at Fort Sam Houston, the coach asked 'What's your name?' and I replied 'Mickey Cochrane' to which he retorted 'Yeah, and I'm Ty Cobb, get out of here!'" Cornelius "Mickey" Cochrane relates.

"I was continually asked throughout my career, particularly in the 50's and 60's, if I was related to him, due to the athletic connection," Cochrane recalls. "I'll also remember the secretary at the Baseball Hall of Fame in the 70's who'd announce me to Peter Clark 'Mickey Cochrane's here — not the one you think.'"

- 11 -

Assault by Pepper

As in each of the prior two World Series, Philadelphia opened the 1931 World Series with a win in Game 1 in a 6–2 victory on October 1 over St. Louis in a rematch of the 1930 Series.

Cochrane was 2 for 3 in Game 1 at Sportsman Park and scored two runs. Mickey drew a base on balls off Cardinal hurler Paul Derringer in the 4th and scored on Foxx's single in the A's 4-run rally. He singled in the 5th and then again in the 7th, the latter time scoring on Simmons' 2-run home run to clinch the victory.

Perhaps more importantly, Cochrane guided Grove to a complete game win for the Mackmen. "For the most part Lefty employed a curve ball at such tense and critical moments as are known in the strange jargon of the diamond as the pinches and also a change of pace which, dear reader, was even more deadly in effect," John Drebinger wrote as he described in the *New York Times* the pitch selection process that Cochrane and Grove used to curb the Cardinals, who did reach Grove for 11 hits. "For it never failed to change the pace of the Cardinals, who, in plunging futilely for the plate, invariably pitched on their heads."

However, in a hint of things to come, Cardinal rookie center fielder John "Pepper" Martin went 3 for 4 off Grove and was credited with one stolen base. Martin's performance in the 1931 World Series would become a thorn in Cochrane's side for many years to come. His reputation as a ballplayer would actually suffer from fans' remembrances of Mickey being tabbed the "goat" of the 1931 World Series. In retrospect, the goat horns seem to be unfounded for the most part.

Martin's first stolen base in the sixth inning of Game 1 was questionable. Contemporary accounts typically restate the facts as "after one of his singles he stole second." Martin's single had moved Chick Hafey only from first to second base, so Martin was on the back end of a double steal, the easier part of that combination. Hafey, on the front end, drew Mickey's throw to third, which admittedly was off the mark.

11. Assault by Pepper

"Hafey stole third base, Cochrane's throw was high and Dykes had to jump for the ball," according to the *New York Times*. "While Dykes, with ball in hand, was disputing the call with Umpire McGowan, Martin dashed to second." Under current scoring rules, Martin perhaps wouldn't have been credited with a stolen base if he weren't running with the pitch coincident with the runner ahead of him.

St. Louis took Game 2 to even the Series, as Hallahan pitched a 3-hit shutout in a 2–0 victory as the teams headed back to Philadelphia. Martin was 2 for 3 at the plate off Earnshaw, scored both runs, and was credited with two more stolen bases.

Martin's stolen base #2 occurred in the second inning after he had doubled. "It was Martin who stole third base right under the nose of Mickey Cochrane, generally acclaimed as baseball's greatest catcher," one newspaper account went. The less well-read, play-by-play account revealed that "as Wilson tried to bunt but missed the ball, Martin dashed to third for a clean steal sliding to the bag head first as Cochrane's throw to Dykes came too high." Being hindered by a bunter is no sin for a catcher.

"Earnshaw may have allowed himself to become slightly careless," the newspaper account continued, "for he should have known that to move on is an inherent trait of the exuberant Cardinal outfielder. So stealing third was nothing unusual of Johnny Martin." A pitcher not holding the runner close is no sin either for a catcher.

Stolen base #3 happened in the seventh inning when Martin stole second base, again victimizing Earnshaw when not surprisingly "Cochrane's throw to Williams sailed wide of the bag," as a result of haste to make up for Earnshaw's transgression.

During the 1931 World Series, Cochrane was featured as the writer of a daily column in the *Philadelphia Bulletin*. This column gave the world a glimpse of Cochrane's thoughts about Martin, which were translated by a ghostwriter. Ghostwriters typically reported no breaking news but tried to give the column the flavor of the alleged author in thought and word. Given the lack of postgame interviews in this period, the ghostwritten columns at least provide an inkling of the thoughts of famous athletes.

"Folks, we've tried to fool him with everything in the book. We've given him fast ones, inside, outside, high and low ones and even slipped one down the middle. To-date he doesn't have a weakness. But we'll get him yet," Cochrane wrote on October 3 aboard the train back to Philadelphia after Game 2.

A Saturday travel day preceding a Sunday off day, since Sunday baseball was still prohibited in Philadelphia, gave the teams two days off. John Kieran in his column "Sports of the Times" took the opportunity to try to exonerate Cochrane publicly: "To be fair to Cochrane those base runners were given fine starts by Grove and Earnshaw, but it's in the records as an indictment against the catcher just the same."

Back in Philadelphia, Cochrane provided a hint of some of his problems when he was quoted as saying, "We gotta win. We need the money," with a sheepish grin and then muttering something about honor and winning three in a row. It was a telling sign.

Game 3 was played at Shibe Park on Monday October 5 with President Hoover in attendance, once again to the beer jeers of a crowd unhappy with Prohibition. Burleigh Grimes had a no-hitter through seven innings and wound up with a 2-hitter to best Grove and the A's 5–2. Martin did go 2 for 4, but had no stolen bases.

Cochrane was hitless again, as he was in Game 2 also, although he managed to keep the game alive in the bottom of the 9th with two outs by coaxing Grimes into a walk on a 3–2 count. As a sign of an injury-riddled Cochrane, Mack sent out Eric McNair to pinch run for Mickey. McNair scored on Simmons' subsequent home run to ruin Grimes' shutout effort, a continuation of Cochrane's retribution on Grimes which had started in the 1930 Series.

"It may be that at last we've discovered Pepper Martin's weakness," Cochrane wrote in his column the next day after holding Martin hitless in his last two at bats. "I'll know better today after we've had another chance to try out our latest theory of his weakness."

Earnshaw twirled his own superb game the next day in Game 4, with a 2-hit, 3–0 shutout. Both hits were by Martin, who also was credited with another stolen base; Frank Frisch also had a stolen base.

Earnshaw's mound habits apparently were again the cause of the two stolen bases in Game 4. Frisch had walked in the 4th on a 3–2 pitch that both Earnshaw and Cochrane protested should be strike three. "On the next pitch to Bottomley, Frisch stole second cleanly, sliding head first to the bag ahead of Cochrane's perfect throw."

Martin's stolen base #4 in the 5th "duplicated Frisch's steal of second using the head first slide and beating Cochrane's good throw."

Kieran again took up Mickey's cause in his "Sports of the Times" column. "Six stolen bases charged against Cochrane at that stage in the series, a bad record for a good catcher. But Mickey doesn't get much help in that respect when Grove and Earnshaw are pitching. The crime wave doesn't bother them."

The first words of injury also surfaced in that Kieran column. "Cochrane has been troubled with a bad leg all through the series. He spends the mornings having it baked out and his afternoons hurting it again."

Eddie Collins noted in his syndicated column, "Please don't overlook the manner in which Mickey Cochrane handled the delivery of Earnshaw and few know of the physical handicap under which Mike is working."

Hallahan held the A's in check in Game 5, as the Cardinals won 5–1 to take a 3 to 2 Series edge heading back to St. Louis. The eighth inning was a watershed for Mickey for two reasons. In the top of the inning, Martin collected

11. *Assault by Pepper*

his twelfth hit of the Series in a 3 for 4 day at the plate, but Cochrane threw Pepper out attempting to steal second base. And in the bottom of the frame, Mickey finally got a hit, his first in 12 at bats since Game 1, beating out a hard drive to Jim Bottomley at first base.

Cochrane did not have a good train ride back to St. Louis, as was conveyed in a *New York Times* headline October 9, the day of Game 6: "Cochrane is ill; Mates Concerned." The story related that Mickey "had an uncomfortable trip from Philadelphia due to an attack of indigestion which assailed him last night shortly after he retired to his Pullman berth. Cochrane vigorously asserted that he would be all right and in his regular place behind the bat and in the batting order."

Cochrane may have had indigestion, but it wasn't from anything he ate. Two things were bothering him, one related to baseball and one personal. Pepper Martin was driving him crazy, a rookie bedazzling the A's with his play, having 12 hits in 18 at bats through five games for a .667 average. He also had four stolen bases, for which Cochrane seemed to be unfairly picking up the lion's share of the blame. Martin would be shut down at the plate the remainder of the Series, but the damage had already been done.

In his October 8 column, Cochrane admitted that Waite Hoyt, the A's pitcher in Game 5, "couldn't find this youngster's weakness. He hasn't any." Backtracking on his post–Game 2 thoughts, he wrote, "You may think you've discovered one only to have him crack the same pitch for a safety the next time it's used."

Cochrane himself was not playing up to his lofty standards, and for once there seemed little he could do to stop that slide. Perhaps it also bothered Cochrane that a poor, uneducated farm boy from Oklahoma was getting the better of someone who had escaped the farm to obtain a college education and become reasonably well-off financially. Unfortunately, this was another sighting of the dark side to Cochrane, his incessant worrying and the physical reaction when he couldn't personally affect the outcome. It would eventually impact his ability to lead when not on the playing field.

Years later it was often written that Cochrane "was heavily involved in the Depression stock market of that unhappy period and there was a bad break in the market during the Series. Several urgent margin calls from his brokers were delivered to the Athletic bench. Unable to meet them, or borrow additional collateral, he saw much of his early baseball earnings go down the drain."

The stock market did take a big annual tumble in calendar year 1931, losing 43% of its value, as the ineffectual policies of President Hoover did little to lessen the impact of the Great Depression. By year-end, stocks were worth 25% of their September 1929 highpoint.

If margin calls were the issue for Cochrane, they would have occurred long before the World Series in October. During September the stock market lost over 30% of its value, as the Dow Jones Industrial Average dropped from

140.13 to 96.61 from the beginning to the end of the month. Cochrane's margin account surely would have been called during this period had he been that leveraged in the stock market.

The market continued to decline during the first two games of the World Series in St. Louis and the Saturday travel day (the stock market was open on Saturdays back then), giving rise to the possibility of a margin call being delivered to Shibe Park on Monday as the market dropped further, closing at 86.48 that day.

The real story appears to have been the closing of the Franklin Trust Company, a large Philadelphia bank, on October 5, the day of Game 3. "At midnight Monday October 5, 1931 possession of the affairs and business of the Franklin Trust Company was taken by the Secretary of Banking," the *Public Ledger* reported. "According to the Secretary the public continued to gradually withdraw their deposits and this action was particularly accentuated during the past month by the hysteria and unfavorable psychological reaction which are gripping the public."

In his "Casual Comment" column in *The Sporting News*, J. G. Taylor Spink reported soon after the World Series: "It is understood that Mule Haas, Mickey Cochrane and several others of the Athletics were [more] worried about the dough that they had tied up in the banks of Philadelphia that blew up just before the Series than anything else. Cochrane is said to have lost $80,000 and Waite Hoyt is understood to have been touched for a wad."

Mike had probably taken a conservative approach after the 1929 crash and liquidated much of his stock position and invested in interest-bearing bank accounts. In this pre–FDIC period, if a bank failed, depositors lost all their money, and banks were failing at a fair pace in 1931. In 1933, the nation's banks would close entirely for several weeks. Many banks began calling in loans sooner than expected to meet withdrawal demand from nervous depositors.

Cochrane's generosity in cosigning a $25,000 note for Perkins and others to weather the economic storm haunted him during the World Series after Franklin Trust failed. No doubt his loans were being called and his broker visited the ballpark to liquidate stock holdings to satisfy the bankers who had taken his bank accounts as collateral for the loans.

It seemed an ironic twist to comments made by Connie Mack that summer to writer Westbrook Pegler that many of the A's stars like Cochrane, Grove, Simmons, and Foxx saved more than 50 percent of their pay and World Series money. "These are smart ball players," Mack said. "They know they won't last forever and they haven't been living up to their income at all. They will all have plenty of money when they are through."

The Philadelphia newspapers covered up Cochrane's financial troubles by reporting that "Mickey is sick at heart—his faith in human nature cracked. For days he's been subject to a poison pen attack—an insidious anonymous letter writing campaign which Mickey, accustomed only to praise, has felt to the bottom of his heart."

11. *Assault by Pepper*

Cochrane was seen grumbling to himself and cussing, his face screwed up in a snarl. A number of issues were clearly bothering him, unbeknownst to the public.

Cochrane's attitude didn't seem to impact Grove, whom Mack sent to the mound in Game 6 with the A's back to the wall. Lefty came through, limiting the Cardinals to five hits in an 8–1 victory. Mickey's bat awoke slightly with an RBI-single in the A's 4-run fifth inning, a line drive that Frisch leaped to knock down but which Mickey legged out to beat his throw to Bottomley at first.

Cochrane's stamina held up through a good part of the game, although his problems may have been the cause of an error charged to him in the bottom of the 9th. Collins tried to pawn it off as part of baseball in his syndicated column the next day: "Grove was so fast at times that not only was he unhittable but Mickey Cochrane had trouble catching him, in the last inning when there was quite a shadow over home plate territory. Wally Roettger fanned and the ball got away from Cochrane who said in the clubhouse 'I never saw the ball. I don't see how they could ever hit it.'"

Mickey survived through Game 6, but he wasn't getting any rest because of his concerns and thus fell apart in Game 7 from exhaustion.

The Cardinals scored two runs in the bottom of the 1st, all centered around Cochrane. Andy High scored the first run on what the newspapers termed "a wild pitch off Cochrane's glove" which probably could have been scored a passed ball as well.

It has been said that Cochrane missed Earnshaw's ostentatious spit into the dirt near the mound—his signal to Cochrane that an illegal spitball was coming. But Mickey missed the sign and the pitch because he was preoccupied with his financial problems.

Then after Martin walked and obtained stolen base #5, the Sportsman Park crowd became uproarious, with George Watkins on third and Martin on second with Orsatti coming to bat still with no outs.

Earnshaw enticed Orsatti to swing and miss for a third strike, but the ball bounced off Cochrane's glove. As he threw to first to get Orsatti, Watkins dashed from third to beat Foxx's low return throw, "the ball scudding out of the tangle at the rubber as Watkins slid into Cochrane and both went down." A similar situation happened again in the 3d when Orsatti fanned and Cochrane dropped the third strike, but this time Mickey got Orsatti at first for the third out of the inning.

Mickey's bat was feeble in Game 7; he weakly grounded out his first three times up. Then in the 8th he hit back to Grimes, who easily retired him at first with an underhand throw and surely a few choice but unrecorded words about Cochrane's weak condition.

Grimes had shutout the A's for eight innings as the Cardinals took a 4–0 lead into the top of the 9th of Game 7. The A's did make a run for their third consecutive World Series title but came up short.

After two were out, Bing Miller singled and Jimmy Dykes and Dib Williams both worked Grimes for walks to load the bases. Doc Cramer then pinch-hit a 2-run single to close the score to 4–2, before Bill Hallahan relieved Grimes and saved the game by retiring Max Bishop, who flied out to Pepper Martin.

Cochrane wound up batting a miserable .160 for the Series with only 4 hits in 25 at bats. The $3,028 check for a loser's share of the World Series pot was to be of small consolation to him. He was getting paid for a poor performance, an idea that never sat well with Cochrane.

Mickey's tribulations with Martin's stolen bases dogged him the rest of his life. It really rankled him that the blame was placed 100% on his shoulders by most baseball fans, writers, and even his own teammates. Although he received support from the Philadelphia press following the conclusion of the Series, which implied these writers knew of his real troubles, others were not as understanding.

"Mickey failed in the series so far as results go, but in failing he showed more courage than he did in victories," Ed Pollack commented in the *Public Ledger*.

"I do not see why they make Mickey Cochrane the 'goat' of the series," the *Philadelphia Bulletin* reported of Mack's comments. "Mickey has been ailing for several months. He entered the series battered and bruised. His mental attitude was all wrong and only his grit enabled him to play through seven games."

"A report eddies through the air that Jim London had $60,000 in a local bank that closed a short time ago," Isaminger wrote in the *Philadelphia Inquirer*. "Other men in sport were also hit hard."

At the New York baseball writers' show that winter, one of the writers, wearing a Cardinal uniform, sang to the tune of "Good Night, Sweetheart":

> Good-bye, Mickey, this is Pepper Martin,
> I'm on first base and I must get startin',
> The way I feel, there's nothing I won't steal,
> So, good-bye Mickey, good-bye.

The song was a terrific hit at the dinner, but when he heard about it, "it seared Cochrane to his soul" as one writer put it. Few seemed to understand that the fault fell squarely on the arms of the Philadelphia pitchers.

"I couldn't have shot him down with a gun," Cochrane repeatedly said later with a tinge of bitterness. "How could I when the pitchers couldn't hold him on base? The best base runners will tell you they don't steal on the catcher, they steal on the pitcher. Nobody in our league ever had run on our pitchers like that, so they'd never learned to hold a runner on. The only pitcher who knew how to hold up a runner was Hoyt. Martin didn't run on him. But he wasn't in there long enough to make any difference."

11. Assault by Pepper

Said Martin later on, "Oh, everybody knows I didn't steal on Mickey. I was stealing on Grove and Earnshaw. They said I even stole Mickey's shinpads. Something about those pitchers would give me a signal: 'Go.' I never knew what it was. I ran on instinct."

"Pepper was stealing on the pitchers, most stolen bases are stolen on the pitcher," Hallahan told later. "He stole against Grove and Earnshaw because those fellows just didn't hold a runner on very well. You give a catcher like Cochrane a chance to throw you out and he's going to do it. Nobody can outrun a ball."

Perhaps what was worst for Cochrane was that his pitchers didn't back him up on this front. But Mack did. "Some of the pitchers felt he wasn't supporting them properly," Mack said years later. "Earnshaw poured salt in his wounds with a suggestion that young Joe Palmisano, rookie substitute catcher, catch him in his next game. It burned Cochrane up."

"My three championship teams had the softest pitchers in the world to steal on, but not many bases were stolen with Cochrane catching," Mack acknowledged. "The Cardinals beat Earnshaw by running wild on him, he couldn't keep men on base. Even Grove, though a left hander, had a deliberate delivery that gave the runner an edge."

"The fans don't know it was the pitchers," Mike always lamented. "They'll always remember me as the catcher Pepper Martin ran wild on."

Unfortunately, it would always be a cross for Cochrane to bear.

- 12 -

Battling Japan on the Diamond — Part I

A trip to Japan was supposed to have capped for Cochrane the celebration of a third consecutive world championship, but Pepper Martin had stepped in the way. As things turned out, the trip was probably the best tonic to ease the pain of losing the 1931 World Series.

A week after the 7th game of the Series was over, Mike and Mary Cochrane set sail from San Francisco for Japan along with a band of other distinguished ballplayers to participate in a series of U.S.-Japan exhibition baseball games. Cochrane had earlier agreed to join this tour that was being put together by Herb Hunter, a baseball promoter, and Fred Lieb, a baseball writer for *The Sporting News*, in conjunction with the *Yomouiri Shimbun*, a Tokyo newspaper that sponsored the trip.

The 1931 Japan tour is generally hailed as the first American foray across the Pacific to spur the growth of professional baseball in Japan, three years before another somewhat more publicized tour in 1934 which included Babe Ruth. There had been earlier journeys to the Far East in the 1920s that Hunter had put together, but the 1931 trip included a larger cast of the cream of the crop players.

Sotaro Suzuki, then a writer for the *Yomouiri Shimbun* and now generally credited with being the father of Japanese professional baseball, said in 1975 that the "great American team of 1931 and the later team in 1934 made such an impression on our people that it paved the way for professional baseball in Japan. It showed the Japanese people how baseball was played at the highest level and filled our players with desire to give the Americans equal competition."

The two-week journey across the ocean on the liner *Tatsuta Maru* was probably just what the doctor would have ordered for Cochrane, to relax and be removed from the ongoing discussion in the United States of the 1931 World Series. Today's 12-hour plane flight to reach this same destination would not have been nearly as beneficial.

Mike's love of plane flight was sorely tested, however, in getting to San

12. Battling Japan on the Diamond — Part I

Francisco from St. Louis to meet Mary for that ocean liner to Japan. After a train ride across Missouri to Kansas City, Mike was scheduled to board a plane for the flight to the coast along with Simmons, Grove, and Frisch. It was, however, too windy under 1930s flying conditions for the plane to take off, so they continued by train to Amarillo, Texas, and then to Albuquerque, New Mexico, before conditions were deemed safe for flying.

"What a ride it was!" Frisch remembered. "It seemed to us it was still blowing a gale and there must have been several air pockets as we flew across New Mexico and Arizona. I believe Lefty Grove was the only one who didn't get airsick. Mickey Cochrane was in the worst shape when we finally stopped at Flagstaff to refuel. After we got off the plane he threw himself on the ground and said 'They'll never get me into that damned thing again.' But we persuaded him to stay with the party and things were all right from there on."

Mike couldn't, however, completely escape the 1931 World Series. While Cochrane was sitting in a deck chair on the ocean liner, a Japanese youngster approached him and asked, "Hey, Mickey, why didn't you throw out Pepper Martin?"

"You would bring that up," Cochrane responded. "Even in the middle of the Pacific they don't seem to forget."

But the youngster then spotted Lefty Grove and shouted, "Say Lefty, why didn't you hold those runners better on the bases? Then maybe Mickey could have thrown somebody out."

A German woman nearby inquired, "Who is theese Mickey you always talk about? Ees it Meeky the Mouse?"

"Gosh, I've been called everything since the World's Series, but that's the first time they called me Mickey the Mouse," laughed Cochrane.

With Frisch along for the trip, Cochrane had to face up at times to the World Series. Frisch was complimentary in his remarks to the press: "Cochrane is a baseball hustler. Don't blame him for the loss in the '31 World Series. We played better all-around ball, but Mickey never stopped fighting." But privately Frisch continued to bait Cochrane, to the point that Lieb pleaded with Frisch to let up.

Part of the trip was a stopover in Hawaii, where the U.S. team was scheduled to play the Hawaii All-Stars. At the aloha reception the night of their arrival, Cochrane addressed the gathering. "Should the major leaguers assembled by Herbert Hunter be organized into a club, this team, with the addition of a pitcher, will be able to beat any team in both the American and National Leagues to capture the World's Series Championship," Mike said, with his now usual combination of diplomacy mixed with candidness.

What a squad it was:

C — Cochrane, Philadelphia Athletics	1B — Lou Gehrig, New York Yankees
C — Muddy Ruel, Washington Senators	2B — Frank Frisch, St. Louis Cardinals

SS — Rabbit Maranville, Boston Braves
3B — Willie Kamm, Washington Senators
IF — George Kelly, New York Giants
OF — Al Simmons, Philadelphia Athletics
OF — Lefty O'Doul, Brooklyn Dodgers
OF — Tom Oliver, Boston Red Sox
OF — Ralph Shinners, New York Giants
P — Lefty Grove, Philadelphia Athletics
P — Larry French, Pittsburgh Pirates
P — Bruce Cunningham, Boston Braves

Cochrane's wry sense of humor came through at the aloha reception, when the Hawaii coaches cornered him to squeeze him for insider tips to the A's success. As Mike had both local coaches enraptured with his inside baseball talk, Gehrig, ever the straight man, ambled by to interrupt by saying that Cochrane was giving them inaccurate information.

The U.S. team easily defeated the Hawaii team 10–0, although Cochrane went 0 for 3 at the plate. It was then on to Japan, where the squad shared ship facilities with the Japanese naval delegation returning from an international conference in London, where Japan had agreed to limit the size of her navy to 60% of that of the U.S. or Great Britain. The chief of the naval delegation and his lower-ranking officers spent many hours chatting with Cochrane, Gehrig, and Frisch, whom the officers knew were idols of the American fans. The Japanese naval officers acted like nervous teenagers around the American ballplayers.

Resplendent in their jackets emblazoned with "U S" across the front, the Americans were treated as dignitaries in Japan. Thousands greeted them at the Yokohama pier upon their arrival, and during the first four days of the tour there was one welcome after another. There were many receptions, including one at the U.S. Embassy and another with the Japanese prime minister Reijiro Wakatauki, who spent an hour and a half with the players and their wives in an informal meeting where he exhibited knowledge of the game and several of the players present, including Cochrane.

While baseball was very popular at home, the Americans were not prepared to see just how popular a game it was in Japan. One Sunday morning on an 18-mile shoreline drive to see the Buddha at Nora, the route ran through hundreds of diamonds on the sandy shore, with overlapping fields. There were hundreds of young men on bicycles in baseball uniforms; as teams would finish one game, two more would be ready to go. Another time the train pulled into Tokyo station at 6:00 A.M. as ball games were in full swing among young men before they reported to work that day.

There weren't many golfers or golf courses in Japan because of the scarcity of land, but Cochrane managed to get in a few rounds anyway with O'Doul, Ruel, and Cunningham.

"Everywhere we were lavishly entertained, which always included geisha

12. Battling Japan on the Diamond — Part I

girls," Cochrane related during the 1932 spring training following the trip. "They sing and dance, but I must say that I prefer Broadway."

While the trip was a cultural success, the American squad generally dispatched its Japanese opponents on the baseball diamond with ease. The Americans won all 17 exhibitions, many by wide margins, over college and high school level squads. Despite long odds, the Japanese fans filled the stadiums to capacity; the games drew almost half a million spectators.

"The Japs can field and they have some good pitchers, but they are all light hitters," Cochrane told Philadelphia high school students the following May. They "let loose with a lot of 'banzais' which I understand is equal to 10,000,000 cheers."

The nearest the Americans came to losing was in the second game of the tour with Waseda University. A fairly large (for a Japanese) 5' 10", 180-pound pitcher held the team in check for six innings as the score was tied 1–1. The Japanese scored four runs in the bottom of the 7th off pitcher Larry French to go in front 5–1. Gehrig had to come in to relieve because of the team's small pitching staff. The Waseda pitcher lost his stuff in the 8th, and the Americans scored seven runs to take the game 8–5 as Grove shut down the opposition for the final two innings. No doubt Cochrane hurled a barrage of words at his teammates on the bench after the team's performance in the seventh inning, not withstanding the cultural and exhibition nature of the team's tour — he was there to win too.

Gehrig, who was in the midst of his record streak of 2130 consecutive games, was hit on the right hand by a 140-pound left-hander in the team's eighth game; the pitch broke two small bones and sidelined the Iron Horse for the remainder of the tour.

The most amusing incident on the baseball diamond involved Cochrane, who had hit a 450-foot home run at Sendai in a game played in gale force winds. It wasn't entirely amusing, however, to the fan who found Mickey's drive tough to catch. He was hit in the face by Mickey's home run, which bloodied his lip and knocked out three teeth.

"The fun was how the Japanese handled the situation," Lieb recounted. "At the time there was a little disturbance in the bleacher, but the game was held up for only a few minutes. About twenty minutes later arrived First Aid, Japanese style. A pint-sized ambulance drove on the playing field and stopped behind home plate. A little doctor about five feet tall stepped out, followed by two pint-sized nurses dressed in gray and white. With the doctor leading the way, they marched single file across the entire field from home plate to pitcher's box, second base, and out to the distant bleacher. Arriving at the scene of the accident, they learned that the victim was already in the promoter's office and had received 100 yen from the management and apparently felt he had put in a good day."

In several newspaper comments that Cochrane made in 1932, it appeared that he had swallowed the Japanese war propaganda. "The people don't want war. All they want to do is protect their interests in Manchuria," Mike said. "We saw troops marching away at some of the seaports, but that was the only evidence we saw of the war. They seemed to say 'We shouldn't worry about the war. Play ball.'"

Mickey's home run was one of but two on the tour; the other was hit by A's teammate Al Simmons. Although good friends, neither probably foresaw the changes coming. They wouldn't be teammates a year later, and the Japanese wouldn't be our friends ten years later.

- 13 -

Mack the Knife

"Trip to Japan Restores Old Zip to Athletics' Catcher" the headline in *The Sporting News* read in January 1932. The Japanese excursion seemed to breathe renewed life into Mike following the frenzy of the 1931 World Series and its aftermath. "After spending the Christmas holidays with his folks in Boston, he has lost the worn, wearied, peaked look."

Mike puttered around Philadelphia playing golf with Dykes, Walberg, and Miller. He visited Foxx at his Maryland home to do some trap shooting and then Dykes at his North Carolina place to shoot billiards and some more golf before heading to Fort Myers for spring training.

Mike gained 15 pounds on the Japan trip, however, and didn't return to his usual 175-pound frame over the winter. Cochrane wasn't used to playing at 190 pounds, and it quickly worked against him.

At the outset of spring training, "the catching mainstay of the A's went into the outfield to chase balls from Eddie Rommel's fungo bat." Mickey played left field in the March 4 intrasquad game before the A's left for Miami for the first two games of the "Spring Training World Series" exhibition rematch with the Cardinals.

Mickey didn't play in the Miami games but did catch his first game of the spring on March 7 when the series resumed in Fort Myers. There were no stolen bases by Pepper Martin in that 4–2 A's victory, but "Cochrane sprained his left wrist when he fell chasing a foul near the A's bench. Although not serious, the injury will keep Mickey out of action for a few days."

Cochrane didn't return to action until the March 18 game at St. Petersburg with the Boston Braves, but Grove and Walberg needed to drive him back to Fort Myers immediately after the game to attend to Mickey's infected toe on his left foot. He was on crutches the next few days and soon was operated on at Lakeland Hospital. "The foot injury did not respond to treatment and it proved a difficult task to keep the peppery backstop in bed," the *Fort Myers News-Press* reported as Cochrane lay in the hospital when the A's finished spring training and left Fort Myers on March 28.

Cochrane was off to a bad start, and unfortunately, his troubles would be symptomatic of the A's in 1932 as they failed in their quest for a fourth straight American League championship. Cochrane was in the Opening Day lineup at Shibe Park on April 12, but the Yankees defeated the A's 12–6. New York came back to preeminence in 1932, winning the American League pennant by 13 games over the A's, who barely squeaked by the Senators into second place by one game.

On April 21, Mickey did hit a grand slam homer in the 9th off Red Ruffing at Yankee Stadium to win the game 9–6 for the A's. But after the game, Ben Chapman's stolen bases were the topic of conversation, and Mickey now took the offense in the discussion that related back to Pepper Martin's stolen bases in the 1931 World Series.

"It takes Chapman about 2.4 to 2.5 seconds to run down to second," Cochrane explained to the press. "Well, the pitchers give him a full second start. Then I got about one and a half seconds to throw the guy out. No chance to draw back and take accurate aim. Just a snap throw and I get blamed for a guy like that? Why don't the pitchers hold him on?"

The depth of the Great Depression occurred in 1932, just at the height of the fame that the Philadelphia A's should have exulted in. People stayed away from Shibe Park, and every ballpark, in droves.

Prices on the New York Stock Exchange struck rock bottom on July 8, 1932, as the Dow Jones Industrial Average, which had peaked at 452 in September 1929, slid all the way down to 58. The price of U.S. Steel stock had gone from 262 to 22, General Motors from 73 to 8.

There were 2,294 bank failures across the nation in 1931. By 1932 all prices had fallen by about a third from the 1929 level. Most experts agree that the Great Depression wasn't caused by the 1929 stock market crash but rather the implosion of the money supply combined with the collapse of world trade triggered by new U.S. tariffs. In other words, there was no money to spend.

Cochrane's $20,000 salary with the A's buoyed him against this economic backdrop, but when the average annual wage for the entire American workforce was just $1280, it was no time to be smug.

Only Foxx among the A's Big Four would have a good year as he chased Ruth's record of 60 homers, falling short by just two as he finished with 58 roundtrippers. Grove was hurt for much of June, and Simmons' batting went cold. In general the A's pitching slipped badly, evidenced by the team earned-run average skyrocketing from 3.47 in 1931 to 4.45 in 1932.

For Cochrane, who batted in the third spot in Mack's batting order ahead of Simmons in the cleanup spot, Simmons' slump was particularly detrimental as the league's pitchers pitched around Mickey as he collected 100 walks, unfortunately good for fifth best in the A.L. Mickey tried to lead the team more in hitting, slugging 23 home runs and rapping in 112 RBI's, career bests for Cochrane as he personally tried to take up the slack for the A's.

13. Mack the Knife

Home runs were a big story for the A's in 1932. The Foxx chase of Ruth's home run record combined with 35 from Simmons, 23 from Cochrane, and 18 from McNair propelled the A's to lead the A.L. in home runs with 173, the first time since 1922 that the Yankees hadn't led the league.

It may have been an unsuccessful year for the A's, but 1932 was not uneventful for Cochrane. When the A's reached their hotel in Cleveland in the early morning hours of June 7, they were greeted by an explosion that blew the roof off an apartment building across from the hotel.

"Cochrane was one of the first of the ballplayers on the scene," the *Public Ledger* reported. "For more than half an hour, despite recurring explosions, he assisted pedestrians, police and firemen in rescuing men, women and children."

Mike helped three women and a man from a second-story window with a ladder "borrowed" from a neighborhood store and then went to the assistance of a 74-year-old man who hung from a fourth-floor window, pleading for help. Cochrane and writer Cy Peterman of the *Philadelphia Bulletin* held a firemen's net on the ground below the man and implored him to jump, but he waited for extension ladders to be raised to his window. Not even Mickey Cochrane could coax him down.

"Cochrane remained at his post, perspiration dripping from his chin, until the old man was lowered to safety," Peterman wrote in a front page story. Peterman later discovered that the man had a violin under his coat and quoted him as saying, "I would have broken it. I've had it 50 years, a Stradivarius, registered and valued at $60,000. Jump with my violin? I'd stay there first."

Rain in early July forced the scheduling of three consecutive doubleheaders with the White Sox at Shibe Park for Thursday July 7 to Saturday July 9. Since Sunday ball was still banned in Philadelphia, the A's were then scheduled to travel by train to Cleveland for a game on Sunday July 10 and then head back to Philadelphia for another doubleheader on July 11, this time with the Indians.

Cochrane caught five of the six games during July 7–9. He was hitless in six at bats in Saturday's twinbill, and as Peterman wrote, "Cochrane is in the worst batting slump of his career."

Mack sent only 11 players to Cleveland for Sunday's game to save money in those depression days. He allowed Cochrane to get some rest in Philadelphia and sent the other two catchers, Heving and Madjeski, with the team, along with two pitchers, Krausse and Rommel.

It turned out that the Sunday game went 18 innings before the A's won 18–17 at League Park. Krause was knocked from the box in the first inning, and Rommel needed to pitch 17 innings in relief, yielding 29 hits off his knuckleball. Cleveland shortstop Johnny Burnett set a still-standing major league record with nine hits in the game. Foxx went 6 for 9 with three homers as he took aim at Gehrig's recent record set at Shibe five weeks earlier. The A's had 25 hits, although none were made by either catcher substituting for Cochrane.

Sunday baseball would finally be made legal late in 1933, and the first legal Sunday game at Shibe Park was played April 8, 1934.

Three weeks later the A's helped christen Cleveland's new field on July 31 in the first baseball game played at Municipal Stadium. The A's defeated the Indians 1–0 before 81,184 fans. Cochrane caught Grove's 4-hit shutout and knocked in the game's only run with a single in the eighth inning off Mel Harder to score Bishop who had walked and been sacrificed to second base.

The Grove-Cochrane combination showed tenacity in the 7th when Earl Averill and Joe Vosmik both singled to open the inning and threaten to break open the game. Mickey visited Grove on the mound, and the tandem proceeded to prevent the Indians from scoring. Grove forced Averill at third base on a bunt, then struck out Luke Sewell, and fielded a weak grounder from Bill Cissell to end the inning.

On August 5, Cochrane played his only major league game at a position other than catcher. Simmons and Miller were both hurt from injuries the previous day. Recruit Johnny Jones replaced Miller for the August 5 game in St. Louis. Simmons started the game with his hand taped, but Mack pulled him in the fourth inning.

"We were getting nowhere in the game [down by five runs] and with Simmons acting so languidly at the plate I thought I would rest him for the remainder of the day," Mack said after the A's 8–7 loss. His real intent was to try to spark Simmons back into the groove he had been in when he won the 1930 and 1931 batting titles.

Cochrane, the erstwhile collegiate outfielder who played more outfield than catcher in spring training, took Simmons' spot in left field in the 4th. He fielded no fly balls, but was said to have fielded hits cleanly.

The real damage of Mack's strategy came when the A's tied the score and went ahead in the tenth inning on relief pitcher Grove's home run. Grove allowed a single and fumbled a bunt to put two Brown runners on base with no outs. Like the July 31 Indians game, Grove bore down to strike out the next two batters and then had two strikes on Rick Ferrell.

In this case, the A's didn't escape. Heving, catching in place of Cochrane, dropped two foul tips that would have been the third strike to end the game. Ferrell then doubled to center field to win the game for the Browns.

Mack undoubtedly used the game as an example for Simmons, who hit a 2-run homer the next day to win the game for the A's 4–2.

The Great Depression had overpowered Mack. The fans stopped coming to Shibe Park, his payroll was too high, and his debts had mounted. Only 400,000 fans passed through the turnstiles at Shibe Park in 1932, almost a 50 percent decrease from the 1930 attendance mark of 720,000. Mack had to take drastic action to avoid financial difficulties, and he sold Simmons, Dykes, and Haas to the White Sox for $100,000 at the end of September to keep the Philadelphia franchise afloat. He always attributed his need to sell his stars for cash to his bankers calling in loans in the dark days for the banking industry in 1932 and 1933.

"With a heavy investment and expense of building Shibe Park and operating the costliest team in our national game, we had to borrow $700,000 from one of our banks," Mack divulged years later. "The bank officers asked us to repay the $400,000 balance as promptly as possible. They didn't like to press us, but their need for more liquid capital was pressing. The Depression curtailed our credit. Banks were calling loans. We had to sell players and try to stop the gap. That is what we did, much to our discomfort."

A biographer of Connie Mack quotes him as saying, "Having gone through the heartache of breaking up our earlier championship club, I disliked doing it again, but we had to do it to live. I do not enjoy managing a tail-end club, but in those troublesome years we were confronted with a situation beyond our control."

While it is undoubtedly true that Mack's bankers called in the $400,000 loan balance, triggering the player sales, what is left unsaid is why Mack needed to borrow $700,000 in the first place. Attendance had fallen drastically at Shibe Park, which was one of the reasons. As Mack once said, "During the four years while we were contenders (1925–28) more people passed through the turnstiles each year than when we were world champions (1929–30). Figure that out in terms of human nature." Then in 1932 only 400,000 showed up at Shibe all year, an average of about 5,000 per game for a second place team.

A larger reason for the borrowing was obliquely referred to in Mack's book *My 66 Years in the Big Leagues*. "In the early 30's we were going up when stocks were going down. The Depression was sweeping the country, millions were out of work. We were caught in the financial earthquake and, like most business houses, were forced to re-trench." Other writers were more blunt. "Rumor was Mack and/or his sons Roy and Earle had taken a bath in the stock market or in real estate."

Another reason for the selling of the A's stars involved the simple baseball economics of the 1930s: income was derived almost solely from park attendance, while expenses were the payroll and park upkeep.

"Mack believed that .600 baseball was more popular than .700," Bruce Kuklick wrote in *To Everything a Season: Shibe Park and Urban Philadelphia*. "He did not believe that a dominant team might possess such style and class that it might continue to win and draw customers. In any event, after 1929, his great team did not overwhelmingly attract Philadelphia rooters."

In essence Mack believed he could maximize profit with a good second or third place team instead of a pennant winner.

Cochrane was settling into the good life in Philadelphia despite Mack's financial problems. He was now accustomed to living a double life — he was a fiery competitor on the ball field while living a mild mannered existence off it.

One writer described Cochrane as "temperamental, insolent, pugnacious on the diamond, debonair, affable, and of altogether easy-going disposition off the field. Jazz music, aeroplanes, good clothes are hobbies — also mystery novels. Mickey will travel any distance to hear a 'hot' orchestra."

Cochrane was said to have brought the Mills Brothers into the A's clubhouse during one World Series. "They sang us right into the championship," Mike said.

Bing Miller, who spoke highly of Cochrane's days with the A's at the 1935 testimonial, recalled rooming with Cochrane on the road. "It wasn't daylight and I'd wake up and there Mickey would be looking out the window, smoking. He couldn't wait for the day to begin you see. He couldn't wait to get out to the ballpark."

Mike liked the rough and tumble of college football too, which he enjoyed watching at nearby Temple and Penn in Philadelphia. He was a regular attendee at the annual Army-Notre Dame match in New York as well.

Despite Cochrane's immersement in competitive sports, "he was a very quiet person around the house," according to Mary Cochrane. "Mike never discussed baseball at home unless something very unusual happened."

And like most ballplayers, Cochrane relaxed with a few drinks, at an establishment that served alcohol in violation of the Prohibition law. "We'd go out together — Foxx, Cochrane, myself," Doc Cramer remembered. "It's a life you have to learn to control yourself. You go out in those barrooms, you've got to be careful. Mack told us 'I don't care what you boys do after a ball game. You just better be able to play tomorrow, that's all.' We generally were."

After the season, Cochrane and Foxx took part in a barnstorming tour of major leaguers, who played in an all-star game in Los Angeles and then in Hawaii. Mike took the opportunity to renew his college friendship with Charlie Farrell, now a movie star in Hollywood.

"Farrell and Will Rogers were our hosts," Cochrane told Bill Duncan of the *Public Ledger* after the trip. "This fellow Rogers isn't as funny as people think he is. He's funnier!"

Cochrane's team played the Pacific Coast League all-stars in a night game in Los Angeles, the first and seemingly only time Mike played under the lights. Shibe Park was the first American League stadium to install lights, although the first game wasn't until May 16, 1939, two years after Cochrane's last major league game.

"I didn't like it," Mike told Duncan of night play. "For a hitter not used to the lights, it's almost impossible to hit a good change-of-pace pitch or a good low curve. I suppose you could get used to the lights, but I hope they never play night baseball in the major leagues."

"We're going to miss Al," Mike commented about Simmons. "I'll miss him personally because he's a friend of mine. He's the greatest outfielder in baseball."

Mack's carving up of the A's was just beginning.

- 14 -

Taking a Ruth-less Job

The game didn't mean a thing and virtually no one was there to notice it, but the opening game of the 1933 City Series with the Phillies would propel Mickey Cochrane into everlasting fame. It was during this cold April 1 day that Cochrane was immortalized by a photographer who caught him in mid-air leaping towards home plate to try to tag out a sliding Pinky Whitney while umpire John Quinn, quite out of position, looks to make the call.

The photograph hangs in the Baseball Hall of Fame and has been duplicated in numerous publications. Not only is it simply a great baseball picture, it also exemplifies the essence of Mickey Cochrane. He played to win at all times, even in an exhibition game during a cold spring day. That didn't matter on April 1, 1933, when Whitney was trying to score. It was Cochrane's job to prevent him from doing so, and he succeeded.

The photograph ran on the front page of the April 2 Sunday sports section of the *Philadelphia Inquirer*, with the caption "Whitney, nailed at the plate in the fourth inning, Mickey Cochrane, Mackian backstop, executing a neat flying tackle as he leaps to put the ball on the National Leaguer."

Whitney had reached third base on an outfield error by rookie Bob Johnson. It appears that umpire Quinn as well as Cochrane both thought that Hal Lee's hit would go through the shortstop hole into left field, as Cochrane had stepped several feet in front of home plate. As described by reporter James Isaminger, "in a spectacular play Higgins [at third base] shovelled up Lee's teaser and pinched Whitney at the plate."

It's still a great photo, whether Cochrane was ready or not for the rookie Higgins' perhaps impetuous throw to the plate. And it is the perfect illustration of a Doc Cramer reflection on Cochrane. "You didn't have to make a perfect throw to Cochrane. If it was out a little ways, he'd go and get it and come back and get that guy. I'll tell you, there were few things as exciting as watching somebody trying to get in there on a close play with Cochrane. Home plate

Famous "leaping tag" photo of Cochrane catching Pinky Whitney at the plate in a 1933 exhibition game at Shibe Park (National Baseball Library & Archive, Coopers-town, New York).

was his, you see. You had to take it away from him. Tough? Just the same as a piece of flint."

Americans elected Franklin Roosevelt to be President in November 1932, hoping that he would cure the ills of the Great Depression, which saw 25 percent of the total labor force jobless and all but a few banks closed in a "bank holiday," when Roosevelt took office in March 1933.

The banking crisis began in Michigan on February 14 when Governor William Comstock declared a state bank holiday. All 436 bank and trust companies in Michigan were closed for a week. When no solution was found, they stayed closed, and days later the fear spread to cause bank holidays to be declared in Indiana, Maryland, and Ohio among other states. By March 4 only a handful of banks anywhere in the country were open.

"It was an eerie, ominous time in the life of the Motor City," one historian wrote. "Detroit was almost totally without money. There was a food panic. People fortunate enough to have gone to the bank before the holiday, cleaned out grocery stores and then dollar bills vanished as well, since anyone who had hard cash hoarded it. To keep paying its bills, the city government issued its

14. Taking a Ruth-less Job

own money, $42 million worth of Detroit scrip, and for months the entire community survived on this homemade Monopoly money."

Federal deposit insurance, part of FDR's New Deal legislation, helped restore confidence in the banking system. Detroit was still primed, however, for someone to help it forget its Great Depression difficulties. Cochrane would be foist into that role by year-end.

Over the winter of 1933, Cochrane had taken greater pains to shed the pounds he had gained in the fall by working out at the Philadelphia Health Club, mindful of his overweight experience the previous spring. He reported early to Fort Myers with Jimmie Foxx and Lew Krausse, and as the *Fort Myers News-Press* reported, they "obtained their physical exertion at the Fort Myers Golf and Country Club."

Mike and several A's participated in the 1933 club championship there. In 1931, Mike had won the second flight division, but he couldn't compete in 1932 because of his injuries. This year he came back with a vengeance on March 5 to qualify for the 16-player first flight division play with a score of 75 to cop medalist honors. Foxx was just a stroke behind Cochrane.

In his first round match on March 7, Mike struggled against Mark Fletcher, needing an extra hole beyond the regulation 18 holes to defeat him in match play. The haunting experience of his deposits locked up in a closed bank during the bank holiday, which recalled the experience he had had with a bank failure in 1931, no doubt took the edge of Cochrane's golf game.

Two days later Cochrane was upset by Eric Jewett, who beat Mike two and one to oust him from the tournament. But as usual, Mike didn't go down without a fight, using his mashie club (now called a five iron) as described in the *Fort Myers News-Press*:

> Again it looked as though Cochrane would square the match on the par four sixteenth when his second was nicely on while Jewett was over and slightly to the right of the green. Jewett playing his recoveries to perfection, was not to be denied, however, and his chip back again came within inches of holing out for a birdie three....
>
> Cochrane made a beautiful effort to prolong the match on the seventeenth when he laid his mashie shot within 20 feet of the pin after a drive of approximately 280 yards. His putt for an eagle three stopped short, however, and Jewett calmly sank his 20-footer to end the match.

Mack justified the sale of his three stars to the White Sox on the availability of rookies to take their places. One day Foxx cornered Cochrane on the bench and said, "Gee, Mike, if they can get rid of Al, Donk and Jim maybe they'll get rid of us."

"Aw, forget it," Mike replied. "There were good young players coming up to take over. That young Doc Cramer is a good center fielder and he may be a great one. The college kid [Frank Higgins] can take over third for Dykes. That Lou Finney who was MVP on the Coast last year will be in left. If the old man was going to deal you or me, he'd have somebody around right? I don't see any bright young catchers or first basemen."

There was a new wrinkle in the baseball world in 1933 that was described in the classic baseball novel *The Celebrant* thusly: "In the summer of '33 the promoters brought the best of both leagues together at the Chicago World's Fair; they called the clubs All-Stars and they brought out McGraw to manage the Nationals. Connie Mack ran the Americans, with all those big fellows: Ruth, Gehrig, Foxx, Simmons, Cochrane."

Everything is correct, except the inclusion of Cochrane. It's a common misconception. As one of the best players in the game and obviously one of its premier catchers, Cochrane would have expected to be named to the American League team, especially since Mack was to be the manager and he was charged with choosing the players to square off against the other league. But Mickey was not selected as an American League All-Star in 1933.

There was a nationwide fan poll to assist Mack and McGraw in picking the teams. The fan voting for American League catcher produced these results:

Bill Dickey, New York	297,382
Mickey Cochrane, Philadelphia	174,530
Rick Ferrell, Boston	29,431
Ray Hayworth, Detroit	7,034
Luke Sewell, Washington	3,096

Mack's inclination was to go with the fans' choices, but he was stymied by one of the game's ground rules that every team must have an All-Star representative. No Boston player had inspired a torrent of votes from the fans. "There was no deviation from the fans' choices in the American League, except that Rick Ferrell was picked over Mickey Cochrane, Philadelphia, the fans' second choice, in order to give the Red Sox representation."

While Mack surely thought that Cochrane deserved to be named to the team, he had to follow a rule, so the ever-honorable Athletics manager chose the Red Sox player who finished highest in the fan poll, that being Ferrell.

"It's a tragedy that Mickey was slighted," Bill Dooly wrote. "If Ruth because of past deeds as home run king must be on the All-Star team to give it the essential color, then what about Cochrane, certainly the outstanding catcher in the majors over a period of 6 years. It's easily understood that Mack might want to save his fighting maskman the ignomy of appearing as a second-stringer on an All-Star team. I hope the dean of managers looked at it that way."

Mack crossed up everyone at the actual All-Star Game on July 6 at Comiskey Park. If he couldn't have Cochrane on the team to showcase his talent,

14. Taking a Ruth-less Job

he wouldn't let Dickey have center stage at catcher either. Ferrell was chosen to start the game for the American League and played the entire contest in the A.L.'s 4-2 victory.

There was, in fact, some logic to Mack's playing Ferrell. Left-handed Hallahan was starting the game for the National League. Ferrell was a right-handed batter while Dickey was a lefty and you always play a righty versus a lefty.

All-Star status was strictly honorary. There was no extra pay involved, so Cochrane probably welcomed the unexpected minivacation during the season to play a round of golf or two. A World Series check was vastly more important to Mike than a one-time honorary thing. (The All-Star Game was at that point considered to be just a one-game affair, a sidenote to the Chicago World's Fair.)

The A's dipped to third place for the 1933 season, with only 79 victories, the fewest wins in Cochrane's nine years with Philadelphia.

The rookies played well in place of the three departed stars, but the league again pitched around Cochrane, this year even more. He collected 106 walks during the 1933 season, second highest in the league behind Ruth. He led the American League in on base percentage with a .459 average, the only category in which he ever led the league. Even with Foxx winning the Triple Crown, it wasn't enough.

As late as August 1, the A's were still under .500, but with the Yankees and Senators dominating the American League, Philadelphia was in third place despite a losing 47–49 record. Six teams were under .500, with only three and a half games separating the third and seventh place teams.

The two-game series with the Yankees on August 2 and 3 at Yankee Stadium was Cochrane's last great matchup with the Yankees in an A's uniform. The A's won 16–3 on August 2, as Cochrane hit for the cycle in a 4 for 4 day at the plate. Mickey hit a 2-run homer off Ruffing in the first inning. In the 3d, he hit a drive into the left center valley and tried for an inside-the-park homer but got only a triple as he was thrown out at the plate. He later had a single and a double in a game "which seemed to indicate clearly enough that the Mackmen still are not to be trifled with, even if they have fallen a considerable distance from their once lordly estate."

On August 3, Grove shutout the Yankees 7–0 on a 5-hitter, the first shutout of New York in 308 games, a major league record. The Grove-Cochrane combination stood out again, as "the mightiest gunners of the Ruppert forces, Babe Ruth and Lou Gehrig, were held shackled."

In the 6th with runners on first and second with one out, Grove fanned both Ruth and Gehrig to end the inning. Then in the 8th with the bases loaded and just one out, Grove struck out Ruth and induced Gehrig to fly out to Cramer in center to expunge another potential rally. Cochrane's crafty calls and Grove's control saved the day for the A's.

The win put Philadelphia at .500 again and paved the way to its third place finish that year, restoring the A's confidence and permitting them to recover from a drop to fifth place later in August and surge ahead of Cleveland and Detroit in September to regain third place.

Cochrane might have coasted into retirement, but retirement wasn't going to be with the A's unfortunately. Mack was still in financial trouble and needed to sell even more of his stars, this time ones he had no viable replacements for, despite Cochrane's earlier statement to Foxx. This time Cochrane and Grove would have to be moved as well as several others.

As early as August there were reports that Cochrane was going to be traded to Detroit. Mack recalled later that when Tiger owner Frank Navin asked him to put a price on Cochrane, he laughed and said "Forget it, Frank, I'd never sell him."

But Mack needed money because fewer than 300,000 fans would trudge into Shibe Park in 1933 to watch the once venerable A's. Mack tried peddling his famous battery in a package for a total price of $200,000, which proved too steep for any one team. A further inquiry from Navin, however, would completely change the course of Cochrane's life.

Navin tried to get Babe Ruth from the Yankees to be the manager of the Tigers, to pump up interest among fans to improve the dwindling attendance at the Detroit ballpark. Yankee owner Jake Ruppert was only too willing to permit Navin to talk Ruth into the position to get the aging Ruth off the Yankee playing fields, where he was hurting the team and had had such serious fallings out with Lou Gehrig and manager Joe McCarthy that they didn't speak to each other.

Ruth wanted to manage, but he wanted to manage the Yankees.

At the 1933 World Series, Navin worked out a deal with New York general manager Ed Barrow for Ruth to go to Detroit as player-manager, according to a Ruth biographer. "Before he closed the deal, Navin wanted to talk to Babe and reach an agreement on the details," the biographer wrote. "He asked him to come to Detroit. But Babe and [wife] Claire were leaving for a trip to Honolulu, where Babe had several exhibitions lined up. Ruth said he'd see Navin on his return."

"You're making a mistake," Barrow told Ruth. "You'd better go see him now."

"There's plenty of time," Ruth said. "The season doesn't begin for six months. I've got these things all set in Hawaii. I'll call him when I get back."

Navin couldn't understand Ruth's attitude if Ruth really wanted a manager's job in the majors. Ruth did make several contacts with Navin through the mail from the Pacific, but he wanted a large salary and a percentage of the gate to manage the Tigers. Navin understandably cooled at the thought of giving up part of his club to what he perceived as an ingrate in Ruth.

"Here, a newspaperman stepped in and changed the course of baseball history in Detroit. H. G. Salsinger, longtime sports editor of the *Detroit News*, was

14. Taking a Ruth-less Job

a confidant of Navin. When the Tiger owner told him about Mack's offer, Salsinger advised Navin that Cochrane not only would solve his catching problem but that he also could provide the managerial leadership so badly needed in Detroit." Salsinger had sounded out Cochrane on the idea before the World Series, and Cochrane had told him, "I'd like nothing better."

Navin then asked Mack if he could get Cochrane to manage the Tigers. Mack posed the idea to Cochrane and instead of riding into the sunset as strictly a player, Mike took on the challenge of managerial leadership too.

"I saw this was Mickey's chance," Mack has said. "I owed him something extra for his loyalty, so I just couldn't stand in his way when he could better himself. That's the only reason I ever let Mickey leave me."

But Mack still wanted $100,000 for his catcher, which Navin didn't have on hand. Navin needed to borrow the cash from his partner Walter Briggs and took to calling Cochrane the "$100,000 gamble." Briggs would keep a close watch on his investment over the next few years, at times too close for Cochrane's taste.

On December 12, 1933, Mack announced the sale of Grove to the Red Sox along with Bishop and Walberg for $125,000, the sale of Cochrane to the Tigers for $100,000 and catcher Johnny Pasek, and the sale of Earnshaw and Pasek to the White Sox for $20,000 and catcher Charlie Berry, who would succeed Cochrane as the A's 1934 catcher. A Philadelphia newspaper heralded the move by saying, "Cochrane Picked Over Babe Ruth."

"I'll be happy to manage the Tigers for Mr. Navin, who impresses me as a great fellow and a man who will help me build," Cochrane remarked of his new opportunity. "He said he'd give me a chance and his record proves it, as Hughey Jennings was there for many years, Ty Cobb for six years and Bucky Harris for five. I see no reason why I can't make the grade as a manager."

Navin nearly lost his new manager three days after Cochrane's sale was reported. According to newspaper headline, "Walberg Saved Cochrane's Life."

While duck hunting with Walberg in Maryland's Deal Island, Cochrane rowed out to retrieve a wounded bird and the boat began to fill with water. As Bing Miller recalled later, "All of a sudden he was in the water. I was in a duck blind and I knew Mickey had on those heavy boots and clothes and I thought that's it, he'll never make it. Of course he did, cussing me and the ducks and the boat." Walberg waded out to assist Mike in making it to land and to make a newspaper headline.

Prohibition was repealed by the 21st Amendment to the Constitution that December, ending a 14-year period when it had been illegal to consume alcoholic beverages. Cochrane, at age 30, could finally take his first legal drink to celebrate his new job.

- 15 -

Rowe-ing to Victory

Navin thought Cochrane would do the job of leader on the diamond for the Tigers, but no one really recognized the missionary attitude he would take on in his new role. Cochrane came to Detroit in January and quickly began spreading the Tiger gospel at luncheons, banquets, social gatherings, and with the print media. He was talking up the Tigers everywhere.

"I played with the Athletics for nine years and in that time we never finished out of the first division and I do not intend to do so now," he asserted at a Kiwanis luncheon.

"I'm not foolish enough to expect a pennant the first season," Cochrane told Adcraft Club dinner guests, "and maybe not the second, but I promise you an improved team." But Mike was aiming at the top from the beginning. He was used to success in Philadelphia, and he wanted it to continue in Detroit.

Mike was polished as a speaker, but he was not a slick politician giving his listeners pabulum to absorb. He answered questions directly, but was diplomatic. His method worked. Expecting to stay only a week in Detroit, Cochrane ended up staying for three weeks and making 26 speeches at various functions before making arrangements to depart for a new spring training site, the Tigers camp in Lakeland, Florida.

"Cochrane Cracks Training Whip to Get Tigers into Fighting Trim" was the headline alerting Detroit baseball fans to their manager's style. Mike introduced 20 minutes of calisthenics in the training camp routine and emphasized basics like sliding and defense. He imposed a midnight curfew and a 9:00 A.M. wakeup call for the 3-hour practice that was to begin at 10:30. He even talked to the hotel chef about menus to benefit the players.

In short, Cochrane brought to Lakeland a very different attitude about managing the club, even before his field leadership began to be included in the equation. Detroit even changed its uniform design for the 1934 season, restoring the now famous Old English "D" on its shirts rather than the former "Detroit" letters. Another signal that it was going to be a very different Tiger ball club in 1934.

15. Rowe-ing to Victory

"Do you want to be champions or are you satisfied to hang around the second division and be laughed at?" Cochrane preached to his players during spring training, spreading a gospel of victory.

"When Cochrane joined the Tigers, his rep was a tough guy to get along with," Billy Rogell recalled. "All is wrong—one of the nicest persons I ever met. He was a baseball manager *who really liked his players*. He wanted to win."

An incident happened at Lakeland which helped set the tone for the "Cochrane administration" in 1934. There's some disagreement over exactly how it started, but a fight broke out between young first baseman Hank Greenberg and rookie pitcher Rip Sewell. Greenberg said that Sewell called him a "big Jew bastard." Sewell said that Greenberg first called him a "Southern son of a bitch" over a misunderstanding over an open window on the bus back from Bradenton after they had lost to the Cardinals 3–0.

Sewell and Greenberg fought after the bus got back to Lakeland and according to Sewell, "fought and fought and fought. Nobody tried to stop it. Why didn't Cochrane break it up? Well, I guess he figured he didn't start it. Mickey was from the old school."

The next day Cochrane sent Sewell to the minor leagues.

Greenberg put the incident in the light of Cochrane discouraging anti-Semitism. Sewell says Cochrane told him: "Rip, don't think I feel any the less about you for it, in fact I think more of you. But we've got thirty pitchers and only one first baseman. What do you think I'm going to do?"

Cochrane just wanted a cohesive Tiger team and if two guys couldn't get along together, for whatever reason, then he would do what was best for the team. The team always came first. Sewell never did pitch for Detroit again, even when Cochrane needed pitchers when his staff wilted during the summer of 1935.

Cochrane had inherited a team that had finished no higher than fifth place the previous five years under former manager Bucky Harris. It had been ten years since Detroit last had a successful team, when the Tigers took a run at the pennant during the 1922–24 stretch with one second place and two third place finishes under Cochrane's mentor with the A's in 1927–28, Ty Cobb. A pennant was a distant memory for Tiger fans in early 1934; the American League championship team of 1909 had triumphed nearly 25 years earlier. The Tigers had lost all three previous World Series appearances since their inception in 1901.

"Bucky Harris wouldn't scream at anyone. Not like Cochrane," Charlie Gehringer has said. "He'd get you and let you know what the score was. He was a super guy and we needed him so badly."

The Tigers of 1933 contained some interesting players that Cochrane thought he could mold into a successful team. The grooming of several young players helped launch Cochrane forward to a title in his first year as Detroit manager.

Veterans Gehringer and Rogell anchored the infield at second base and shortstop respectively. Greenberg at first base had power potential but had hit only 12 homers in 1933. Cochrane traded for veteran Goose Goslin to add depth to youthful Pete Fox and Gee Walker in the outfield. Marv Owen was steady at third base, although Mike considered this position the weakest of the team once he himself replaced Ray Hayworth at catcher.

Mike had tried to get young Frank Higgins from the A's to shore up third base for the Tigers, only to be rebuffed by Mack, who said, "Nothing doing, I sold you a pretty fair catcher already didn't I?" So Cochrane needed to stay with Owen.

Oh yes, Mike hired as a coach Cy Perkins, the man who had worked so hard to make Cochrane into a major league catcher with the A's. Mike wanted to help his down-on-his-luck mentor, who had hit the bottle following his financial disaster in 1930 and the death of his wife. "I was sick in the mind and Cochrane saved my job a dozen times," Perkins remembered. "I was fouling things up not only for myself but for baseball."

Detroit started the 1934 season with Cochrane's face on the cover of *Baseball Magazine*, but the team played inconsistently. Only Gehringer was hitting well, while pitcher Fred Marberry was the only moundsman throwing with any success. A second-year pitcher named Schoolboy Rowe showed some promise, but had not achieved any success in April. Cochrane threatened to ship Rowe to the minors for lack of a serious attitude, which seemed to wake him up.

Luckily no one team dominated the American League in the early going, and by early June only a seven-game spread separated the first place and last place teams. A few losses easily dropped the leading teams back several notches in the standings at this juncture of the 1934 season.

Mike tried to carry over his perfectionist attitude as a player to his managerial duties. This caused him a lot of lost sleep, as Salsinger detailed in a seven-part season retrospective in the *Detroit News* entitled "What Price a Pennant?" soon after the Tigers clinched the 1934 pennant: "Every mistake caused Cochrane new agony, every defeat cost him a night's sleep. He was filled with wild joy when Detroit won, he dropped into the pits of despair when they lost. …Not a day passed in which Cochrane did not find a dozen things to worry and fret, fume and commiserate about; most were trivial."

The Tigers lost to the Yankees in early May, as Gomez shutout the Tigers 3–0 on three hits and got beat 10–6 the next day.

"Cochrane was frantic. New York was the team he wanted to beat," Salsinger wrote. "Then in Boston, the Red Sox won 14–4 and Cochrane was hysterical that night. He cried and tore his hair." The Red Sox were usually a weak-hitting team, but not against Detroit. On May 6 before 30,000 at Fenway Park, the Red Sox jumped on Marberry to score 12 runs in the fourth inning. "If Boston can pound Marberry that way and score 12 runs in one inning, what'll the other clubs do to us?" Cochrane said to Salsinger. Boston was hitting with the signs, though, as Salsinger related. "Marberry's pitching hand was exposed while taking signals from Cochrane and he didn't put his hand in his glove until his grip was set for either curve or fastball. It should have seemed strange to Cochrane at catcher, but it didn't."

Moving on to Shibe Park for a May 10 reunion for Cochrane, the A's turned against their former teammate and his Tigers with a 5–3 victory. The strain began to show in Cochrane. Once back in the friendly confines of Navin Field, however, Mike was able to regroup and begin the Tiger charge towards the pennant. "You're a better team now than any in the American League," he shouted at the team in the dressing room. "This year's race is wide-open and no club has the chance you've got, if you drop those hang-dog expressions you've been wearing for years."

"I don't know what the hell happened, but we believed in ourselves. We started clicking," Marv Owen said, recalling Cochrane's manner early in the 1934 season.

The players didn't resent Cochrane's verbal lashings, they became propelled by them and he kept driving them, as Salsinger related in a midseason story on Cochrane.

> He is strictly unorthodox. He is moved by impulse and not by plan or design. He is turbulent when other managers are composed. He is lacking in systems while they remain systematic. He violates many of the principles but he meets practically all the demands. He has one predominating virtue and that is to reach a given point by the shortest path.
>
> As a catcher Cochrane was suspected of having a bagful of tricks; was suspected of doing wonders with pitchers; of using clairvoyant methods and conjurer's secrets in handling Philadelphia pitchers and this belief is more thorough today since the pitchers Cochrane caught to fame have not done much since they started pitching to others. Instead of making catching a complicated job, Cochrane reduced it to the simplest possible formula: If a batter couldn't hit a certain pitch, that is the ball to pitch them.
>
> Cochrane manages just as he catches. He is impulsive but he has a knack of finding the shortest path to a given point. Why is Cochrane successful? Deeply sincere and honest, frank and loyal. His enthusiasm is infectious. It is honest. He is a rare psychologist without pretending or intending to be one. Men naturally fall into his groove. He leads by example and by act rather than by word.

"Ol' Mick never let you fall asleep out there," Chief Hogsett recalled. "If Mickey would call for a fast ball and I'd cross him up, God, he'd come stormin' out halfway to the mound and fire that ball back to me. 'Wake up you big Indian s-o-b,' he'd yell."

Gehringer was having the greatest season of his career, playing more aggressively under Cochrane, batting .379 at the All-Star break with 65 RBI's. Rogell was much less erratic with Cochrane and had collected 64 RBI's at the break while hitting .306. Greenberg really bloomed under Cochrane as he contributed 63 RBI's and hit for more power. The weak-hitting Owen was batting .337, making

Cochrane happy the deal for Higgins didn't happen, while his fielding was much improved. Bridges, who had never won more than 14 games, was 10–5 at the break. Rowe had come around and was 9–4.

On June 30, Cochrane used a situation to spur the Tigers. Gee Walker, a happy-go-lucky outfielder was picked off first base twice in a game with the Browns in St. Louis. Cochrane fumed at Walker's dumb plays: "It cost us a ball game. It isn't his first offense either. I've tried talking to him, but he won't listen. I'm tired of arguing with him and it's unfair to the other players who are hustling all the time." Walker was suspended for 10 days by Cochrane, signaling a wake-up call to the Tiger team. Play tough or be gone.

"Cochrane would let you know what was what. He was smart and could handle people," Flea Clifton has said. "If you could handle people like Jo-Jo White and Gee Walker, then you've got something going there."

The results showed. The Tigers were just barely behind the first place Yankees at the All-Star break.

Cochrane himself was having a mediocre first half as a player. The weight of managing the team seemed to take its toll on Mickey at bat; he was batting .293 at the All-Star break, below Cochrane standard. His play showed in the fan balloting for the second All-Star Game, where Yankee catcher Dickey tabulated 102,686, while Cochrane had just 19,932. American League team manager Joe Cronin picked Cochrane for the squad anyway for the July 10 exhibition game at the Polo Grounds.

Cochrane pinch-ran for Dickey in the top of the sixth inning of the All-Star Game after Dickey drew a walk off Cardinal pitcher Dizzy Dean. Cochrane and Cronin attempted a double steal with Earl Averill at bat, but Averill struck out and both Cronin and Cochrane were nabbed in a run down to end the inning.

Mickey caught the serves of Indian pitcher Mel Harder the rest of the game, which the American League won 9–7. Mickey batted in the 8th, but grounded out against Dean. He had one nifty play in the field, scooping up Fred Frankhouse's bunt in the 9th and throwing him out at first base on a close play. It would be Cochrane's one and only field appearance in the All-Star Game, but he was injured on that Frankhouse play.

"My spike caught in the ground and I turned my ankle," Cochrane said after the game. "We're going to have an x-ray picture taken to find out how serious it is. I'm going to try to be in there against the Yankees," referring to the upcoming big four-game series with the Yankees at Navin Field right after the All-Star Game.

Hayworth caught the opening game of the series on July 12 before a Thursday afternoon crowd of 20,000 as Cochrane recuperated. Rowe pitched a 6-hitter and struck out 11 Yankees in a 4–2 Tiger victory which put Detroit into first place by .001 over New York.

15. Rowe-ing to Victory

Rowe had been pitching well for Cochrane and hadn't lost a game since starting a winning streak on June 15 with a 11–4 win over the Red Sox. Rowe wouldn't lose a game until late August, running up a record-tying American League mark of 16 consecutive wins.

Cochrane was catching Bridges the next day, but the Yankees defeated the Tigers 4–2 as Red Ruffing pitched New York back into first place. Two interesting events happened in this July 13 game, in which Mickey went 1 for 3 and stole a base:

1. Babe Ruth hit his 700th career home run off Bridges in the third inning, a 480-foot blast over the right field wall.
2. Lou Gehrig played in his 1426th consecutive game, but left in the second inning suffering from back problems, although he did rap out a single in the first inning.

The July 14 game was the turning point in the 1934 season for the Tigers. The Yankees had built a 9–1 lead off Tiger starter Vic Sorrell, including a 4-run first inning which saw Gehrig listed as the shortstop and batting leadoff, slap a single to right field and then give way to pinch runner Red Rolfe to preserve game #1427 of his consecutive game streak.

Before 22,500 delirious fans, the Tigers rallied for four runs in the bottom of the 9th to win 12–11 and vault back into first place, this time for the remainder of the season. With New York leading 9–4 in the fifth inning, Cochrane led the comeback charge by pinch-hitting himself for Hayworth and contributing a double in his 1 for 3 day at the plate.

As the second batter in the 9th, Mickey flied out after Owen singled to lead the inning off. After Rowe pinch-hit for Marberry and singled, Fox hit a ground rule double in the roped off area in left field to score Owen and knock Russ Van Atta from the box.

McCarthy brought in old nemesis Burleigh Grimes for the Yankees to face Walker and got him to pop up for the second out, but Goslin then hit a ground rule double to right field to tie the game. After Gehringer was walked intentionally, Rogell won the game with a single to left field to score Gehringer.

Rowe came back on two days rest to beat the Yankees the following day 8–3 to push the Tigers lead to a game and a half over New York. Cochrane had an agreement with Rowe that he would pitch until he was tired; Cochrane inquired after each inning. After the 6th, Rowe said his arm was "too heavy," and Marberry held the lead for Schoolboy. Greenberg had the key blow, a double to break a 2–2 tie.

Gehrig's back seemed fine, he went 4 for 4 for the Yankees.

Schoolboy went on to win eight games in July, including back-to-back victories against the White Sox on July 28 and 29.

The Tigers were still neck-to-neck with the Yankees when they embarked on a 14-game winning streak beginning with a 4–3 victory over the Indians in the second game of a July 31 doubleheader for Bridges' 13th win of the season. During the winning streak, Cochrane picked up off waivers Al "General" Crowder from the Senators to add some depth to the Tiger pitching staff. Marberry, who had carried the Tigers in the spring, became an ace reliever, while Crowder could fill in as a starting pitcher. Cochrane also brought in a minor leaguer Red Philips as a pitcher, and in his major league debut on August 4, Philips hurled Detroit to a 16–4 win over Chicago, one of just four wins he would experience in the majors. Eldon Auker pitched two shutouts during the 14-game winning streak; he was almost a forgotten man on the Tiger pitching staff with Bridges and Rowe doing so well.

Cochrane almost caught a no-hitter on August 3 when Rowe no-hit the White Sox for six innings before Cochrane's former A's teammate Jimmy Dykes spoiled the no-hit bid with a single in the 7th. With Detroit on the way to a 14–0 win and Rowe's 11th straight victory, Cochrane inserted Sorrell on the hill and Vic no-hit Chicago the rest of the game for a 1-hitter.

There were close calls during the streak as well. Against the Indians on August 10, Rowe needed to drive in the winning run in Detroit's 6–5 victory with a sacrifice fly in the 11th inning as Oral Hildebrand and Mel Harder kept the Tigers at bay. Then two days later Cleveland's Monte Pearson checked the Tigers through the regulation, and Detroit needed to score in the 10th for another extra-inning victory. Cochrane, who was 2 for 5 on the day, was on deck when White doubled in the winning run.

The winning streak was capped by a doubleheader victory over the Yankees on August 14 at Yankee Stadium before 77,000 fans. Yankee manager Joe McCarthy led with his ace Lefty Gomez in the opening game, but Cochrane went with Crowder rather than his ace Rowe, saving him for the second game.

"I have never believed it effective to use ace against ace," Cochrane opined. "When it comes to winning games throughout the season the percentage is against it. Why sacrifice an almost certain win for a possible low-score loss?"

The Tigers beat Gomez 9–5 in the opener, getting to him for five runs in the sixth inning. Detroit began first pitch-hitting to subdue Gomez before McCarthy could get another pitcher warmed up, a tactic that Cochrane liked to use with star pitchers, since "that's about all you can do with a pitcher of the sort that Lefty was when he can't wait out the pitcher."

Rowe defeated Ruffing in the second game 7–3 on a 4-hitter, as Cochrane sparked rallies with a triple in the 3d and a single in the eighth innings.

New York stopped the Tiger win streak the next day with a 8–2 win, but the pennant was within sight for Detroit. The Tigers, now six and a half games in front of the Yankees, were being called "the team of destiny" and the "miracle team."

Cochrane set the tone himself during the winning streak, getting 27 hits in 51 at bats for a .529 average as his bat heated up. Batting second in the order,

15. Rowe-ing to Victory

Mickey was getting good pitches to hit since the league couldn't pitch around him with Goslin and Greenberg right behind him and hitting at a good clip as well.

The teams were rained out on August 16, but Cochrane spoke on a radio broadcast that day, one of seven sponsored by Ford Dealers of America to take advantage of Cochrane's new fame. Downplaying his role in getting the Tigers motivated, Cochrane remarked over the air waves:

> I've never been able to figure out what destiny's got to do with batting and pitching averages, or with fielding and base running either. If you want to know why we're on top of the league, just look at the averages. There's no destiny or inspiration about them. They're just hard and cold facts.
>
> We make most of the breaks we get. And we make lots of them ourselves by base running. By being fast on the bases we manage to make the infielders and outfielders hurry the play and they'll [be] more likely to make an error.

Fame was beginning to haunt Cochrane now. During that rain out, he was besieged at his hotel suite by glad-handers, drinkers, curiosity seekers, and agents wanting him to endorse products. Cy Perkins had to intervene to get Cochrane some rest by getting him a room under an assumed name. "The guy can't say no. He needs some sleep," Perkins said of Cochrane as he threw up his hands in dismay.

Some of Cochrane's gaunt look was self-imposed, though, as Cy Peterman of the *Philadelphia Bulletin* wrote after an interview with Mike.

"I've got to win. There's no if's or but's about it," Cochrane told Peterman. "They'd ride me out of Detroit on a rail if I lost. It's tough to stay up there."

Concluded Peterman, "It never dawned on Mike that Detroit really owes him no end of hurrahs for the great fight he has made this year."

By mid–August thousands of Detroit fans began flooding the Tiger ticket office with World Series requests, their 25-year thirst for a championship finally in sight under Cochrane's direction. But with only 22,000 seats in Navin Field, many fans would be disappointed at not getting tickets. Some 8,000 temporary "circus seats" were installed in right center field to add some capacity, but demand for tickets was strong.

Navin worked out a deal with the city of Detroit to close off Cherry Street behind the left field wall and build 17,000 temporary bleacher seats to increase the stadium's capacity to 47,000. Goslin would have to get used to cheering behind him in left field instead of just a silent fence.

It remained to be seen how many games Rowe would win. He won his sixth game in August by defeating the Senators 4–2 on August 25 for his 16th consecutive win to equal the record that Grove had tied in 1931 with Cochrane behind the plate. Rowe drove in the winning run in the ninth inning just before rain poured down on Griffith Stadium.

The streak stopped on August 29 versus the A's at Shibe Park. Schoolboy ran out of gas as the A's knocked him out of the box in the 6th and went on to a 13–5 victory to stop Rowe's streak at 16 in a row.

"Streaks put pressure on the pitcher, Rowe's was hard on a young pitcher," Cochrane wrote. "I can honestly say I was glad the streak was broken. He was relieved of the pressure and pitched better ball for the remainder of the season. The jitters lifted from the other men and we played better baseball afterward."

Cochrane had helped Rowe convert from a thrower to a pitcher, enhancing Rowe's performance with his knowledge of the league's batters. Rowe struggled once during the streak when Hayworth was catching while Cochrane was taking a respite from playing. Mickey snatched his mask and mitt and took over the job, calming Rowe down as he allowed just one more hit and picked up the victory.

"Rowe is cold steel and Cochrane is white heat. Each supplies what the other lacks," Salsinger wrote of the battery. "Cochrane with all his fire and magnetism and Rowe with his peace and calm. Rowe is an anchored iceberg and Cochrane is a flaming volcano."

Rowe used the 16-game win streak to compile a 24–8 season mark, second best in the league behind Gomez at 26–5 for New York, and just ahead of teammate Bridges with his 22–11 record.

The Tigers pushed their lead to 7 games in mid–September in another Yankee-Tiger series as Rowe won his 24th game of the season on September 18 with a 2–0 victory. This was a week after Cochrane needed to handle the touchy issue of Greenberg playing on the Jewish holiday of Rosh Hashanah. Mickey told Greenberg only his conscience could guide him, and Greenberg decided to play, hitting two home runs to propel the Tigers to a 2–1 victory over the Red Sox.

Detroit split that four-game series with New York at Navin Field, before 121,000 fans as the city could taste the upcoming title. Pages of pictures confronted Detroit newspaper readers each evening. Columns of fulsome praise were written, adding pressure to Cochrane and his players. Cochrane's comments were often printed in boldface type, so that readers couldn't miss Mike's every word. He was featured in a late September Sunday rotogravure supplement entitled "The Man Behind the Ball."

After winning three of four games against the Browns in St. Louis in the course of two doubleheaders, the Tigers clinched the pennant on September 24 when they were idle as the Yankees lost 5–0 to the Red Sox.

"Of course I'm delighted," Cochrane remarked on clinching the pennant. "But I rather wish we could have clinched it out there on the field where we have been fighting all season to win the pennant."

Cochrane seemed to be able to push all the right buttons on the Tigers. They finished with a 101–53 record, seven games ahead of the second place New York and 16 games ahead of third place Cleveland.

Four Tigers had 100 RBI seasons — the G-Men Goslin, Gehringer, and Greenberg, along with Rogell, who had the best season of his career.

15. Rowe-ing to Victory

The Tigers led the American League in batting with a .300, average and no other team was close. At one point in the season, all Detroit regulars were hitting over .300, and with Rowe pitching, everyone in the lineup would be hitting above .300.

Cochrane himself finished at .320, while finishing in the league's top five in on-base percentage. Gehringer topped the team at .356 in second place in the league behind Gehrig, who, despite his back problems, actually won the Triple Crown, leading the A.L. in batting, homers, and RBI's. It was Cochrane, however, who was awarded the Most Valuable Player Award, collecting 65 votes. Gehrig finished fifth in the balloting, behind Gehringer, Gomez, and Rowe.

"Despite the Triple Crown, Lou was bypassed when it came time to name the league's most valuable player," a Gehrig biographer sniped. "Mickey Cochrane was selected. That Cochrane was the playing manager of the pennant-winning Tigers was, without a doubt, the decisive influence, for the writers determinedly believed their own stories about inspirational value and intangibles of leadership."

This is an unintentional compliment for Cochrane. While it is true that Cochrane went out of his way to court the sporting press, and Gehrig was cast in the shadow of Ruth with the Yankees, the MVP is not a player of the year award but rather goes to a player who exhibited the most "value" to his team's regular season finish. Not many would doubt that Cochrane fit that bill in 1934.

- 16 -

Suffering from Dizzy Spells

Around mid-September when it became obvious that the Tigers would capture the American League pennant, reporters began asking Cochrane who he would name as pitcher for Game 1 of the World Series slated to open at Navin Field on Wednesday October 3.

"That's easy, Rowe," Cochrane announced. "I don't care who the other manager picks. Why if we used any but our best we'd be in the position of conceding the game and the Tigers aren't conceding anything."

Mike expected, however, that the New York Giants would win the National League pennant at that point. The Giants collapsed in the stretch drive, and the St. Louis Cardinals, now managed by one of Mike's 1931 tormentors, Frank Frisch, became the National League champs. Their ace pitchers were the Dean brothers, Dizzy, who won 30 games, and Paul, who had won 19 games. Frisch would undoubtedly go with Dizzy in Game 1.

Cochrane began to second-guess himself on his earlier remarks about using Rowe in Game 1. The player side of Cochrane overshadowed his management outlook vis-à-vis facing the formidable Dizzy Dean. Mike was not a strength versus strength kind of guy.

The Cardinals were installed as early betting favorites, and Cochrane remarked: "We'll see about that. We're not afraid of the Deans." But he was.

And the celebrating started early for the Tigers, as they were honored September 29 at a testimonial banquet where the players received expensive gifts. Cochrane also received an $800 refrigerator, a $500 radio, and several cars as the Tiger manager.

Non-baseball pressure was unintentionally being applied, as expressed at the banquet by Packard Motor Car Company president Alvan Macauley: "The Tigers have been an inspiration not only to this community but to this whole country. It was their never-say-die, refuse-to-be-licked spirit that brought them through and that is the spirit Detroit needs and America needs today."

Tough words to live up to when about 18 percent of Michigan citizens were on relief, including many former autoworkers.

16. Suffering from Dizzy Spells

"Thank you for these laurel wreaths of victory," Cochrane spoke at the banquet. "Too much of the credit has been given to me. It belongs equally on the shoulders of these other stalwart lads. No one man, but all of them, playing as a smooth-working unit, made this possible, this happy night of celebration possible."

Cochrane was figuratively and literally the toast of Detroit. City taverns were serving special Tiger drinks, including "Old Master" in honor of Cochrane, comprised of Bacardi rum, grapefruit juice and apricot brandy.

Mike was spotted partying the next night at the Detroit Athletic Club, "rolling his eyes and shrugging his shoulders to the lilt of the tunes" doing the carioca on the dance floor. Joining the band, he grabbed a saxophone and, ironically, played "Don't Blame Me" to the delight of the crowd.

Two days before the opening of the 1934 World Series, it was the player partying, not the manager. A spotlight picked Mike up on the dance floor, and he yelled out, "Bring on the Deans. I say to hell with them!"

Citing chilly weather, Rowe's youth, and (years later) the element of surprise Mack had used in the 1929 World Series, Cochrane started late season arrival Crowder in Game 1.

Dizzy jumped on Cochrane almost immediately. Dean wandered over to watch Crowder warm up on the sidelines and shouted to Cochrane, "Mickey, the General ain't got nothin. You better go find Schoolboy and get him ready."

Cochrane's reply: "Go to hell, Diz."

On a postgame radio interview, Dizzy ribbed Cochrane again when asked his thoughts of Crowder pitching instead of Rowe. "I think he used great judgment because he figured if I was at my best, no one could beat me. I don't blame Mickey but I would've been tickled to death if he started Schoolboy."

The choice of Crowder as Game 1 pitcher to avoid a Rowe vs. Dean matchup wasn't successful. Dizzy shut down the Tiger offense, and the Tiger defense committed five errors in the first three innings as St. Louis won 8–3.

Cochrane helped to set up Detroit's first run in the 3d when he singled to left on a 3–2 pitch to advance White to second base, after Dizzy had thrown repeatedly to first to try to pick off White. Gehringer then singled home White to narrow the score to 3–1 at the time. But Game 1, the first World Series game to be broadcast nationwide through the $100,000 sponsorship of the Ford Motor Company, belonged to the St. Louis Cardinals.

"The boys were a little nervous," Cochrane said philosophically after the game. "I'll give them Rowe tomorrow and we'll see what they can do with him."

Detroit came very close to dropping both of the first two Series games at home; the Tigers were losing 2–1 heading into the bottom of the 9th in Game 2 before rallying to tie. The Tigers squandered a chance to win when Walker was picked off first base with one out in the 9th with Cochrane at bat. Mickey, distraught at another Walker blunder, then struck out to send the game into extra innings.

Game 2 was the beginning of a long painful Series for Cochrane. In the third inning, Cochrane blocked the plate to stop Ducky Medwick from scoring on Joe Collins' single for the third out of the inning. Ordinarily Cochrane was a rock guarding the plate, but Medwick realized that Goslin's throw would beat him by several steps, so he crashed feet first into Cochrane to knock him down and in the process injured Mickey's right leg with two deep spike wounds.

Cochrane limped to the dugout and then strolled to the batter's box in the bottom of the 3d, where he drew a walk. Seemingly he was better when he steamed around to third base on Gehringer's single, but he was still not 100 percent well. Greenberg struck out to strand Mickey at third.

Rowe pitched the entire 12-inning contest in Game 2, as Detroit finally won when Goslin singled in the 12th for a 3–2 win. Schoolboy hurled brilliantly for Cochrane. After yielding two early Cardinal runs, he pitched no-hit ball for seven innings and gave up only one hit in the last nine innings.

The *Detroit Free Press* was inspired to verse to describe Mickey's play in Game 2 with a poem entitled "They Shall Not Pass." Its middle verses described Cochrane thusly:

> Then up spake Mike the Cochrane,
> The Captain of the Plate,
> To every man upon this earth
> Death cometh soon or late.
>
> And how can man die better
> Then facing fearful odds —
> And he braved the spikes of Medwick
> For the honor of the gods.

The Series moved to St. Louis for the next three games. Detroit dropped Game 3 by a 4–1 score when Bridges didn't make it through the 5th and Paul Dean took the mound for the Cardinals.

Cochrane's bat was quiet through the first three games. He got a single in four at bats in Game 1 but went hitless in seven at bats in the next two games. Just to be on the safe side, however, Paul Dean dusted Cochrane on his first pitch to him in the first inning of Game 3 to keep Mickey honest, a photo that made page one of the *Detroit News* the next day.

Detroit awoke from its three game slumber in Game 4, winning 10–4 as Auker cruised to the victory. "You guys are a great team," Cochrane was said to have snapped at the Tigers after Game 3. "You are in a pig's eye."

"Cochrane's tongue-lashing aroused his players for the fourth game," Fred Lieb wrote in his book *Detroit Tigers*. "Like a college coach goading his young football charges with sarcasm and ridicule, Mickey got his players fighting mad and they ripped into Frisch's pitchers for 13 hits."

16. Suffering from Dizzy Spells

Opposing player-managers Cochrane and Frank Frisch shake hands during 1934 World Series (Urban Archives, Temple University, Philadelphia, Pennsylvania).

Cochrane was involved in starting both the initial and game-winning rallies in Game 4 despite having a hand-sized bruise on his upper leg to go with his spike wounds from Medwick.

In the 3rd, Mickey doubled off Dazzy Vance's first pitch. Vance proceeded to walk both Gehringer and Goslin to load the bases, when Rogell singled to score Cochrane to begin a 3–run rally to put Detroit ahead 3–1.

After White walked in the 8th, Mickey dropped down a sacrifice bunt on Bill Walker's first serve. Walker wheeled to cut off White at second base but overthrew Leo Durocher into center field. Gehringer sacrificed White and Cochrane over a base, and Rogell came through again with another single to spark a 5-run rally to sew up the 10–4 victory and tie the Series at two games apiece.

The Tiger infield had turned three double plays to support Auker and would have had a fourth had pinch runner Dizzy Dean been able to elude Rogell's relay throw to first base in the 4th. Dean, running for Spud Davis who had singled, dashed to second on Pepper Martin's grounder to Gehringer, but didn't slide. Rogell's peg to Greenberg hit Dean square in the forehead and knocked him out cold.

Dean was carried from the field and taken to a hospital, prompting Dean to later utter a classic Deanism, "They x-rayed my head and didn't find anything." In true Gas House Gang spirit, the first words Dean was said to have spoken upon awaking were, "Did they get Pepper at first?"

In an unorthodox move, Cochrane came back with Bridges on one-day rest in Game 5 "on the theory that Bridges nursed a deep grudge when chased (he lasted only four innings in Game 3) and gets revenge by coming back off the ropes."

Bridges pitched a 7-hitter as Detroit broke the Series tie by winning 3-1 over Dizzy Dean to set the stage for the Tigers to win the World Series by only having to win one game of two at Navin Field.

The best part of the Game 5 win for Cochrane was beating Dizzy Dean on his home turf at Sportsman's Park. As one sportswriter put it, "Cochrane had a grin the size of The Grand Canyon when Orsatti forced Collins at second base to end the game."

"They were a happy pack of Tigers who returned to Detroit after the fifth game. Everybody said it was in the bag." Lieb recounted. "Cochrane had to warn some of his happy players against over confidence."

"This isn't over yet. We got to keep bearing down," Cochrane cautioned his players.

"But we licked the big guy," Goose Goslin said, referring to Dizzy Dean. "We can't lose now."

On the verge of their first ever World Series title, with odds slanted in their favor, the Tigers couldn't pull it off. Cochrane had his well-rested ace Rowe set for Game 6, set to vindicate his strategy not to pitch Rowe versus Dean in Game 1.

As Cochrane later related, just before game time he found Schoolboy dunking his pitching hand in a basin of hot water, a sheepish look on his face.

"What's the matter?" Cochrane inquired.

Grinning apologetically, Rowe replied, "I slammed a door on my hand," and held up his hand that was all puffy.

"You what!" Cochrane roared.

As Cochrane's logic went, "How can you believe a door will slam on a guy's hand when a whole town is praying for victory and a team is playing for $50,000 and more? These things just don't happen — at least they shouldn't."

Rowe was outdueled by Paul Dean in Game 6 as the Cardinals won 4–3. The Tigers gamely fought back to tie the game twice before St. Louis went ahead for good in the 7th.

Cochrane was injured again in the third inning, when he slid into first base to beat Collins' throw to Dean covering first, allowing White to score the Tiger's first run of the game. He injured his knee on the play, the same leg Medwick had hurt in Game 2. The game was held up for five minutes before Mickey limped off the field on the arms of Perkins and Clifton.

16. Suffering from Dizzy Spells

It may have been the margin of victory for St. Louis. In the 6th with Cochrane on second and Gehringer on first with the Tigers down by one run, Goslin laid down a sacrifice bunt. Bill DeLancey picked up the ball and threw to third base to nip lead-runner Cochrane, as umpire Brick Owens called him out. It was a very close play and later photographs showed that Cochrane had most likely beaten the throw to the bag. Greenberg did single to score Gehringer with the tying run, but it would have put Detroit ahead if the call on Cochrane had gone the other way.

"I've been waiting 35 years to see Detroit win a World's Championship and here we have one within our grasp and that umpire blows it for us," Frank Navin said bitterly after the game, an unusual display of emotion for the poker-faced Tiger owner.

Cochrane was really put on the shelf in the 9th when he blocked the plate to stop Ernie Orsatti from scoring on an infield grounder. Orsatti crashed into Cochrane and knocked him down, but Mickey held onto the ball, even though that same leg was badly injured again. He was taken to a hospital, but x-rays showed no broken bones.

"Look, I'm not the kind of guy to beef," Cochrane said following the game, "but if they want to play that way, I'll get rough myself."

"I may be down, but we'll be tearing 'em apart in the Series final tomorrow," Cochrane declared from his hospital bed. But one writer's description of him after Game 6 belied Mickey's thoughts. The writer described Mickey in these words, giving perhaps the ultimate measure of how it indeed is tough to catch: "Cochrane hobbled into the dressing room. He slammed his mask against a trunk. He removed both shin guards and hurled them likewise. He sat silently for a moment, then started to remove his uniform. It was a tough job. He was aching all over and his face plainly revealed it."

With Cochrane in the hospital overnight for observation and rest, leadership to charge up the Tigers was missing. When he returned, it was the player and not the manager. The headline on page one of the *Detroit Free Press* said it all, "Our Stricken Leader."

Cochrane insisted he would play in Game 7, but the Tigers were demoralized and they self-destructed. Dizzy Dean took the fourth Cardinal win in a 11–0 romp, making good a pre-Series promise that "Me 'n Paul'd win four games."

"Nobody was saying much in the clubhouse," it was reported. "Not even Cochrane."

Some say that Cochrane was saying before the game, "At least we'll go down swinging."

Dean scored the first run of the 11–0 onslaught, and as he crossed home plate, he said to Cochrane: "Well, Mickey, this does it. This is the ballgame." And Dean was amazed that Cochrane's reply was, "I know it."

Auker didn't last through the 3rd as the Cardinals scored seven runs in that frame. Cochrane tried to pull out all the stops to win Game 7, using all his ace pitchers in relief of Auker. It didn't help. Rowe, who had pitched only the day before in Game 6, lasted only two batters. Hogsett, who had pitched good relief earlier in the Series, couldn't get any of four batters out. Bridges finally put out the third inning fire, but he was pitching on one day's rest from Game 5 and needed help from Marberry and Crowder at the end.

In all, St. Louis collected 17 hits off the beleaguered Detroit pitching staff in Game 7. By the end even Cochrane's fatigue gave in as he replaced himself with Hayworth in the 9th, the only inning of World Series play that Mickey would ever miss.

Medwick, the Cardinal hitting leader for the Series at .379, had only one hit in Game 7, but it would lead to one of the most memorable moments in World Series history. In the 6th, Medwick tripled with Detroit already down 7–0 to score two more runs. When Medwick came into third base, he slid hard into Marv Owen or Owen kicked him, no one is sure which is the true saga, and an altercation began on the field.

The Detroit fans were already frustrated at blowing the Series when it seemingly was within their grasp. They were not amused, and in the bottom of the 6th, they pelted Medwick in left field with bottles, vegetables, and anything they could get their hands on. Those additional bleachers in left field that Navin had installed held an army of angry Tiger fans. Cochrane participated in the conference with Landis concerning the play and probably said to Landis something to the effect of "Do anything. Let's get the damn game over with."

Commissioner Landis ordered Medwick removed from the game for his own safety. It didn't phase the Cardinals hitting, as his replacement Charlie Fullis singled in the 9th.

At that point it made no difference to Cochrane. Not even the $3,354 check as the loser's share, the $10,000 bonus from Navin, or the MVP Award would soothe over the disappointment of failure in the 1934 World Series.

- 17 -

Top of the Hill in a Depression

Detroit started very slowly in the 1935 season. It hardly looked as if the Tigers would capture another pennant when they plummeted into last place on April 26 after losing six in a row.

"I was willing to bet my last pair of socks we'd win the pennant by about five games," Mike reminded critics of his preseason prediction of another pennant. "I'll bet I won't have to eat those words."

Cochrane pulled the Tigers together and moved up into fifth place a month later, but they were still hardly pennant material. Detroit was barely over the .500 mark at Memorial Day in fourth place. Bridges was pitching well, but Rowe was quite inconsistent. Cochrane started slowly as well, finally reaching the .300 mark at the plate by early June, although he had only 13 RBI's.

Mickey's problems didn't dampen his attitude when he, Rowe, and White participated in Herald Baseball School Day at Fenway Park on May 25, a clinic for youngsters who clipped a coupon from that day's *Boston Herald* newspaper. "I brought my catcher's mitt," Eddie Barry, a 65 year old remembered in a 1988 retrospective. "Meeting Mickey Cochrane was such a wonderful thrill. He instructed me in respect to catching. It was wonderful. That particular kind of thing you never forget."

By the All-Star break, the Tigers crawled up into second place, three games behind the first place Yankees as the White Sox, the hot team in the early going, faded.

"Cochrane won a pennant in 1934 by inspired leadership; he is winning one in 1935 by expert managership," Salsinger wrote in the *Detroit News* in a September review of the Tiger season that year.

> The situation called for more than leadership; it demanded managerial skill and a deep knowledge of baseball. Cochrane began shifting his lineup almost daily. He experimented with individuals and combinations. He

Cochrane at the plate during spring training with the Tigers in Lakeland, Florida (National Baseball Library & Archive, Cooperstown, New York).

used all the psychology he knew. He pleaded and cajoled. He tried all the tricks at his command.

Cochrane's main work, of course, has been with the pitchers. There was never a catcher who handled pitchers better. There probably never was one who equalled Cochrane's performance this year when he took a staff that was unable to win anything but very loose games and developed it into the strongest in either major league.

Cochrane is the No. 1 catcher of baseball today. He is a great catcher because (1) he is one of the finest mechanical performers of all time, (2) because he is an outstanding strategist, (3) because he has the ability to get the maximum amount of work out of his pitchers, (4) because he is a steadying influence on them, (5) because he knows their individual peculiarities and works them accordingly, (6) because he gives them confidence.

Because Detroit had captured the pennant the previous year, Cochrane was named manager of the 1935 American League All-Star team. In 1935 the practice of fan voting was abolished, and the managers were empowered to select all the players for the team. Mike, however, polled his manager peers to put together the American League squad, which included Bridges, Rowe, and Gehringer from the Tigers along with Cochrane himself and tabbed old teammates Grove, Foxx, Simmons, and Cramer to fill out almost half of the American League team.

17. Top of the Hill in a Depression

Almost unbelievably, Cochrane did not choose Greenberg for the American League team, even though the first baseman had 25 home runs and 103 RBI's at the All-Star break.

"Players for the All-Star Game were picked on their performances in World Series and All-Star games. The league wanted players who could stand up under high pressure," Cochrane said before the July 8 game at Cleveland's Municipal Stadium, which he had helped christen three years earlier.

With two veteran first basemen in Gehrig and Foxx, Greenberg would need to wait his chance for All-Star selection. Greenberg carried the Tigers through 1935, hammering 36 home runs and banging in 170 RBI's, both league-leading statistics. Greenberg had over 50 more RBI's than the next closest slugger, Gehrig with 119. Greenberg easily copped the American League MVP Award in 1935.

Dickey and Ferrell were picked by Cochrane as the other catchers for the American League. When Dickey was injured, Cochrane replaced him with Rollie Hemsley of the Browns, whom Mickey surprisingly chose to start the game. The American League won 4–1 on the strength of Foxx's 2-run home run and RBI single. Cochrane didn't play himself in the game.

The turning point of the 1935 season for Cochrane's Tigers would come two weeks after the All-Star Game, when Detroit took on first place New York at Yankee Stadium for a five-game series.

Cochrane announced several days ahead of the Yankee series that he planned to pitch Rowe twice in New York, with two days' rest between starts.

"The Yanks have only beaten him once since he came into the league and it took 11 innings to do it," Cochrane said, as he explained the Rowe strategy from Boston, where the Tigers had just tied the Yankees for first place. "I'm going to throw him twice against them next week. And when we leave New York next Thursday we'll be out in front and there will be nothing left of the pennant race but the shouting."

It turned out that the brashness that Mickey espoused became true, but not because of the Rowe strategy. The first and last games of the series were rained out, but the Tigers still won two games in the abbreviated three-game series to overtake the Yankees and vault into first place for the remainder of the 1935 season.

Both teams split a doubleheader on July 23. The Yankees took the opener 7–5 as Johnny Allen bested the touted Rowe. Cochrane homered in the top of the first inning, which combined with a Greenberg homer gave Detroit a 2–0 lead.

"So tumultuous was the acclaim which greeted Cochrane's homer that one wondered whether the battle was being waged at Yankee Stadium or Navin Field, there were more than just a few Tiger fans," the *New York Times* reported.

Unfortunately, Rowe wasn't up to his 1934 standards, and he couldn't hold the lead, walking four of the last eight batters he faced. "Cochrane looked as though he was about to go out there and bite his Mr. Rowe on the ankles," Kieran wrote. Sorrell defeated Gomez 3–1 in the second game, however, for a Detroit victory.

The next day, July 24, Detroit beat New York 4–0 to take over first place by half a game, as Crowder hurled a 4-hitter to best Ruffing. Detroit wrapped up the game early as White homered in the 1st and the Tigers put together a 3-run rally in the 3rd. Cochrane contributed an RBI-single to ignite the scoring binge.

Cochrane was so pumped up to take over first place that he waived the Tiger infield to the side of the diamond in the fifth inning to ensure that he would have no interference to catch Ruffing's pop up, which he snagged on the pitcher's mound.

"The admiration that Detroit showed for Cochrane in 1934 turned to unabashed idolatry in 1935. While Cochrane was torturing his soul and forcing the best from his players, Detroit was reveling in the excitement of championship baseball," Jack Newcombe wrote in a 1960 piece on Cochrane.

Mickey caught only 110 games on the way to his second Tiger pennant, worrying, fuming, and pushing himself as far as he could each game as the strain of managing persisted.

"When I was a player I worried only about myself. Good money and easy work," Cochrane said. "Now I have to worry about everybody. I have to see that they're in shape and stay in shape. If one of them eats something that makes him sick, it makes me sick too."

John Kieran of "Sports of the Times" column fame put it thusly: "When Cochrane has lost a fight he hates to call it a closed incident. He prefers to regard it as unfinished business until he can get to bat again."

Cochrane was regarded as a civic savior, even though he had nothing to do with the city's economic improvements. His name blared out over radio loudspeakers in the factories that had reopened. He was listed in *Who's Who in Detroit*. He was on the cover of *Time* magazine in October prior to the World Series, with a story that noted: "Cochrane's arrival in Detroit coincided roughly with the revival of the automobile industry and the first signs of revised prosperity. His determined jolly face soon came to represent the picture of what a dynamic Detroiter ought to look like."

Adults across America saw advertisements using Cochrane's words and his picture in sales pitches, especially for cigarettes. A Chesterfield cigarette ad read, "We don't know what MR. COCHRANE smokes and he's not endorsing our cigarette but he is an outstanding man in the baseball world and has won his place on merit." Chesterfield didn't want to admit that Mike smoked Camel cigarettes. A Camel ad proclaimed Cochrane as saying: "One thing the team agrees on is their choice of cigarettes—Camels. 19 of 22 regulars smoke Camels. The Tigers say they can smoke Camels all they

17. Top of the Hill in a Depression

want because Camels are so mild they don't get their wind or upset their nerves."

Children were collecting Cochrane baseball cards issued by the Goudey Gum Company. Its 1935 card pictured on the front Cochrane in one corner, with Gehringer, Bridges, and Rogell in the other corners. On the back was a puzzle piece to make one of nine different pictures, one of which was an interesting photo of Cochrane in full catcher's gear shot from above as if a ball was coming into his mitt.

Even Mike's family entered the spotlight. Gordon Jr. was pictured in the newspapers playing football and baseball for Detroit Country Day School, a private school that Cochrane could afford for his children now. He was quoted as saying Greenberg was his idol. A crowd of 100,000 jammed downtown Detroit to see daughter Joan unfurl a banner outside Hudson's department store.

The Tigers were hitting the ball fine, as Cochrane related in New York, "We got the hitting and the Yanks got the pitching and that's how it looks." Cochrane's biggest challenge was the pitching staff management, with only seven healthy arms in late July. He picked up Roxie Lawson from Toledo, who won three key games for the Tigers.

The Tigers had a hot August at Navin Field, as season attendance moved over 1,000,000. They won 22 of 29 games to solidify their first place lead, which reached nine games over the Yankees. Detroit then took three of four games at Yankee Stadium during September 12–14, as Auker, Rowe, and Lawson overpowered the Yankees and made the Tigers tough to catch to prevent a second consecutive pennant.

The Tigers came to Boston's Fenway Park on September 16 carrying an 89–49 record with a 9 1/2-game lead over second place New York. Fifty years later on June 24, 1985, Mickey Cochrane Night would be held at Fenway Park to celebrate his memory.

After Detroit took the opener of the four-game series with a 5–3 victory, the Tigers dropped the next three, starting a season-ending slide as Cochrane's troops relaxed down the stretch run with the flag virtually locked up. On September 17, the day of the Cochrane testimonial in Bridgewater, the Red Sox defeated the Tigers 5–4.

Before 500 people crowded in to Bridgewater's Boyden Gym, Malcolm Bingay, editor of the *Detroit Free Press*, told of the explosion that would rock Detroit when the Tigers returned home victorious in the World Series, saying that Cochrane wouldn't be licked or yell quits. "His spirit has done much to pull Detroit out of the despondency it slipped into a few years ago."

After all the adulation, Cochrane took the podium and said slowly:

> It's not easy to get up here and talk tonight after such a demonstration. It sort of chokes me up. I played, went swimming and even had boyhood fights with some of you and those are days none of us ever forgets. The

wonderful tribute you have paid me tonight will always be one of my dearest memories.

A year ago they said our ball club was lucky and that's all right with me. I'd rather be lucky than smart. We're a different club now. Last year the jump from fifth place to a pennant was pretty sudden and our young club was naturally nervous in the series. But they know what's it's like now and they'll be that much better for it. We want to meet the Cardinals again, because we want to prove we can beat them, but if we play the Giants or the Cubs I'll be just as sure we'll win.

Cochrane didn't seem to be concerned that the Tigers were loose down the stretch, he undoubtedly encouraged it so his players wouldn't be as tight in the World Series as they had been in 1934. When in Washington in early September, the Tigers visited FBI headquarters and were pictured in the newspaper under the headline "Number One G-Man Shows Mickey's G-Men How It's Done." Cochrane and FBI head J. Edgar Hoover were shown with machine guns along with Tiger G-stars Gehringer, Goslin, and Greenberg.

The Tigers clinched the pennant on September 21 with a doubleheader victory over the St. Louis Browns; Bridges and Auker were the pitching victors. Auker's 18–7 record for the season gave him the league's highest winning percentage at .720.

Auker attributed much of his pitching success to Cochrane. "He was such an inspiration to me, when I was pitching. His drive and desire to win was so overwhelming that it would carry me through my troubles. He made me a good pitcher, he gave me confidence and strength, like no other catcher did. I was not the same pitcher without him behind the plate."

Detroit's nine-game margin eventually dwindled to three games by season's end, as the Tigers got ready for the World Series. Cochrane even left the team on September 24 from a game in Cleveland to take the train to New York to watch the Louis-Baer heavyweight boxing title fight at Yankee Stadium.

Mickey finished with a .319 batting average, the eighth time in 11 seasons that he had hit higher than .300, assisted by hitting almost .400 in July and wading out 25 walks that month. He would finish fifth in the A.L. in walks with a 96 total and third in the league in on-base percentage with a .452 average.

After letting the 1934 World Series slip away, Cochrane was even more motivated than usual to win when the 1935 Series opened at Navin Field on October 2. Detroit's opponent was the Chicago Cubs, who had taken the National League pennant on the strength of a 21-game September winning streak to overtake the Giants and the Cardinals.

In a "Sports of the Times" column before the Series, John Kieran pinpointed a key factor for Detroit, the application of BTU energy. Only he wasn't talking about the British Thermal Unit, but rather the Bridgewater Thermal Unit — Cochrane.

17. Top of the Hill in a Depression

Detroit was badly at rest in September, while Chicago was in rapid motion. Detroit is looking for Professor Cochrane to find the right force to counter the Chicago inertia. The budding scientist has never disclosed the secret of the product of the BTU. Mack found that it appeared to be a mixture of cold words with hot looks, flavored with a distinct hint that dynamite was about to explode in the immediate vicinity. A possible optical illusion connected with the application of the BTU was that the professor always seemed on the point of walking out to the mound and hitting the occupant with a swift clip on the jaw. He may also apply magnetic force, since he's a positive pole, radiating energy in all directions over a wide field.

Things did not start auspiciously when Lon Warneke shut out the Tigers 3–0 in Game 1. Warneke gave up only four hits and a lot of infield grounders, nine of which Warneke personally fielded.

Cochrane found Warneke particularly frustrating as the Cub pitcher snared three shots off his bat. If Warneke had not raced Mickey to first base for a putout on his fifth inning grounder instead of tossing the ball to first for an assist, Warneke would have set a World Series record for assists by a pitcher rather than tying the mark with his eight assists in Game 1. Warneke had three assists alone in the third inning, including one grounder by Cochrane. Rowe pitched decently after a shaky first inning in which the Cubs scored two runs. Support for Schoolboy was iffy, though, with three Tiger errors and even a passed ball by Cochrane.

"You'll go a long time until you see better pitching than that Warneke tossed at us this afternoon," Cochrane told writers, who reported he was the only one to break the silence of the morguelike dressing quarters of the Tigers. "It's likely to be a different story tomorrow when those Cubs get a look at Tommy Bridges."

Detroit tied the Series 1–1 the next day before heading to Chicago as Bridges won Game 2 in frigid weather 8–3. Cochrane helped to start things rolling early off Cub starter Charlie Root, who departed without retiring a batter after yielding hits to the first four Tiger batters in Detroit's 4-run, first inning uprising. Mickey doubled to right off Root to score White, who had opened the inning with a single. It would be Cochrane's only RBI in the Series.

Following the game, Cochrane learned that Greenberg, who had hit that day what would be the Tigers' only home run of the Series, had broken his wrist and would be lost for the rest of the Series. Mike's first thought was to take over first base himself and have Hayworth catch the remaining Series games. This would get more bat in the lineup to compensate for the loss of Greenberg, but would leave Detroit vulnerable in the field at first base, a position Cochrane hadn't played since college.

After discussions between Navin and Cochrane, the light-hitting Owen was moved from third to first base and even lighter-hitting "Flea" Clifton was installed at third base to maximize the Tiger defense and hope that the remaining troops could pull through on offense.

Game 3 at Wrigley Field was a classic dogfight, which the Tigers eventually won 6–5 in 11 innings. The Cubs took a 3–0 lead after five innings against Auker. After the Tigers came back with one run in the 6th and a 4-run rally in the 8th to gain a 5–3 lead, Cochrane sent his Game 1 pitcher Rowe out to the mound to hold the Game 3 lead for what Mickey expected to be two innings of relief. It turned out to be four innings because the Cubs tied the game with two runs in the 9th to send the game into extra innings.

Pressing too much to compensate for Greenberg's missing bat, Cochrane was 0 for 5 in Game 3. He had popped out to shortstop in the Tigers' 4-run 8th, fouled out to third base in the 10th, and fouled out to Hartnett to end the Tiger rally in the 11th after White's single put Detroit ahead to stay 6–5.

"Well, the Tigers finally showed folks they are a money ball club," Cochrane wrote in his syndicated column. "They had to be great to defeat a game, fighting club like the Cubs."

At this point in Mike's career, his newspaper column was undoubtedly ghostwritten by someone in Christy Walsh's syndicate, which handled Babe Ruth, Knute Rockne, and many other star athletes and coaches. "The ghostwritten sports story became such a staple that a sportswriter covering a World Series entered the press box and said it reminded him of a haunted house." Walsh had his writers do stories that at least agreed with the notions of the alleged author and roughly fit his temperament. "But nowadays those old essays seem full of slangy, false heartiness, and empty of content."

Detroit charged to a 3–1 Series lead with a 2–1 victory in Game 4, as Crowder pitched a masterful 5-hitter. Still pressing, Cochrane tried to extend Detroit's 1-run rally in the 3rd off Jim Carleton on Pete Fox's grounder to first baseman Phil Cavarretta, but was thrown out at the plate trying to score.

The Cubs put together a rally in the bottom of the 9th, getting the tying run on second base and the winning run at first with just one out.

Cochrane ran out to the mound to check on Crowder. "How's the arm? Getting tired? Do you want relief?" Crowder reported a wired Cochrane asked him. The unworried Crowder proceeded to induce the next batter to hit into a double play to end the game.

"The old general just about pitched us into the world's championship today," Cochrane wrote in his column. "A fellow named Cochrane was up there twice with men on base when a hit would have meant runs, so I guess I better not say anything about those men left on base."

Cochrane sent Rowe back to the mound for Game 5 to nail down the Series against Warneke for the Cubs, but Chicago didn't cooperate. Chuck Klein, part of the 1933 Philadelphia Triple Crown team with Foxx, hit a 2-run home run in the 3d to solidify a 3–1 victory and send the Series back to Detroit.

17. Top of the Hill in a Depression

Mickey singled twice in the game but was twice stranded at third base waiting for his teammates to produce an RBI hit.

Perhaps it was only fitting that the first Detroit World Series championship should be captured on home turf. As Cochrane wrote in his column, "If everything breaks right the World Series will end in Navin Field tomorrow and the Tigers will be world's champions."

Game 6 was another classic battle. Cochrane got Detroit on the scoreboard in the 1st when he scored on Fox's double after opening the rally with a single, one of three base hits in Game 6. The Cubs tied it in the 3rd, in the 4th Detroit went back ahead 2–1, before Chicago retaliated with two runs in the 5th to move in front 3–2. In the 6th the Tigers tied the game 3–3 on Owen's only hit of the Series, and that's the way it stood until the fateful ninth inning, Bridges and Larry French battling it out on the mound all the way.

After Cochrane and Bridges held the Cubs at bay in the top of the 9th, stranding Hack at third following his inning-opening triple, Mickey followed with his one-out single to begin the Detroit rally. Then came Gehringer's smash down the first base line that Cavarretta somehow knocked down, although Cochrane managed to advance to second base.

"Well, I tied into one and thought for sure I'd got myself a two-base hit," Gehringer recalled later in life. "But Cavarretta had never moved away from the bag. He should have gotten off the minute the ball was pitched, since I'm more apt to hit one to his right than to his left. But for some reason he stayed there and I hit it like a shot at him."

"It was one of those instances when you see a man swing a bat and a split second later there's a line drive exploding right on top of you," Cavarretta remembered. "More in self-protection than anything else I threw up my gloved hand."

With the Navin Field crowd going wild, Goslin proceeded to put French's second serve into right center field to score Cochrane and give the 1935 World Series to Detroit. Goslin explained in *The Glory of Their Times* that he told the plate umpire as he went into the batter's box, "If they pitch that ball over this plate, you can take that monkey suit off."

As Cochrane crossed home plate with the winning run, Detroit sprang into bedlam which lasted all night until dawn broke over the waters of Lake St. Clair. Escaping the maelstrom of victory which was engulfing the grassy surface of Navin Field, Cochrane headed after coach Cy Perkins, who was leading the Tiger procession of sweating, swearing ballplayers to the locker room to celebrate victory.

Goslin was mauled by his teammates, who tore his jersey off and began hauling him on their shoulders around the dressing room. A photographer captured Cochrane's merriment as a player in a picture that was printed nationwide the next day showing Cochrane kissing Goslin with Bridges smooching at Goose from the other side.

Soon the radio and print reporters descended upon the celebrants, and Cochrane needed to alternate his dual roles as both labor and management.

"I'm the happiest guy in the world," Cochrane said from his player's perspective with a broad grin on his face. "When I raced home with that run it was the happiest moment of my life."

Then switching gears to his manager role, he beamed with pride when he said: "Bridges was wonderful. He gave us the gamest exhibition of pitching I ever saw in the ninth inning after Hack's triple. But he's all heart, Bridges. He broke over six of the greatest curve balls I ever saw in my life getting out of that hole. What a man! He's 150 pounds of courage."

Bridges hadn't seen Goslin hit in the winning run, ironically. He was in the runway from the dugout smoking a cigarette when shortstop Rogell came down the steps on top of him shouting, "World Champions!"

With his father and brother Bert in tow, Cochrane made his way to the manager's office to cool down from the excitement. Before long though, Commissioner Landis pushed his way through the gathering outside Cochrane's office to congratulate him. With characteristic aplomb, he accepted the Commissioner's words by saying, "It was a tough game for the Cubs to lose."

"I am not only happy but proud, because those Tigers certainly came through to win the sixth game," Cochrane wrote in his syndicated column the next day. "Every man played his part. Every man in the lineup contributed his share. It's great to be champions."

The syndicated series stopped the following day with these words from Cochrane, "It was the greatest series in which I ever played. I thought I had experienced all the thrills one can wring out of baseball. I knew the thrill of my first major league game, my first World's Series. I thought they were tops until I stepped on the plate in the ninth inning of the sixth game and knew that the Tigers had won their first World's Series."

"The city went crazy. But it was good clean fun, everybody happy and nothing vicious," Rogell recalled later in life. "I was in Detroit in 1984 when they won the Series. By then kids were acting like a bunch of wild animals. Where the hell do they get a kick out of tipping someone's car over?"

At a team testimonial on October 8 at the Book-Cadillac Hotel, Cochrane thanked Detroit rooters in front of a Tiger ice sculpture. "We have already taken care of the Cubs and now I'm looking for bears," Mike said as he departed for Wyoming the next day for a four-week hunting trip with Tris Speaker, Del Baker, and some Detroit businessmen at the Valley, Wyoming, ranch of Max Wilde.

Cochrane had played 1411 regular season games through the 1935 season. He didn't know that he would play only 71 more games in his baseball career.

- 18 -

Watch Out for That Bump

Tiger owner Frank Navin died just five weeks after the 1935 World Series, and with his passing it seemed Cochrane's success also ceased to have life thereafter. Walter Briggs bought his partner Navin's shares, and the Briggs family controlled the ball club for the next 20 years. One of Briggs' first acts was to promote Tiger hero Cochrane to vice president in addition to his managerial duties. Not only was Cochrane running the team on the field, he was now in charge of the front office as well, having to deal with contracts and salaries of the players.

This move on Briggs' part was a tonic for disaster, one that caused Cochrane's downfall. Briggs erred in two ways. He failed to realize that Cochrane's leadership strength as manager was his ability to get the players to follow his lead as a player. The players could no longer view him as one of their own if he were in charge of their salaries too. Secondly, Briggs failed to realize that Cochrane's internalizing of his problems would be exacerbated by these additional administrative duties. The signs of the 1931 and 1934 World Series apparently didn't register with Briggs.

Coming off a second place finish in the Major League Ballplayer's Golf Tournament at Sarasota (72-hole total of 316 to Wes Ferrell's 312) and looking to motivate his players towards a third consecutive American League championship in the 1936 season, Cochrane as the new VP of the Tigers offered the players a substantial bonus if Detroit finished in first or second place. A.L. President Will Harridge visited the Tigers' Lakeland, Florida, spring training camp, however, to inform Cochrane that the bonus offer was in violation of league rules.

This first gaffe Cochrane made as Tiger vice president was met by the press with a laugh, "the new vp has more jobs than Mussolini," and the suggestion that Cochrane hadn't yet caught up with that part of his job.

The headaches of the job started early, the first being a Greenberg absence. He was holding out for a $35,000 contract that spring, when he was offered $25,000, a raise of $10,000 from 1935. Cochrane's initial response was a baseball

Executive Cochrane at December 1936 American League Meeting with Washington owner Clark Griffith (left) and the man who was responsible for trading him to Detroit, Connie Mack (right) (Urban Archives, Temple University, Philadelphia, Pennsylvania).

move, acquiring young Rudy York from the Indians to show Greenberg he had a replacement slugger waiting to take over the first base position. Greenberg finally signed the $25,000 contract in late March after a heated negotiating session with Briggs and Cochrane in the owner's Lakeland hotel suite.

"During the discussion Mickey was very annoyed," Greenberg recalled. "He had played eleven years and in five World Series and was now a player/manager and he claimed that I was asking for more money than he was getting."

Cochrane's second headache was also a Greenberg absence. On April 29 while fielding a throw at first base, Greenberg collided with base runner Jake Powell, rookie outfielder with the Senators, and broke his wrist. Greenberg would be lost for the 1936 season.

Rather than go with rookie York at first base, a ploy Greenberg had earlier known was a bad bluff, Cochrane traded ace reliever Chief Hogsett to the Browns for veteran first baseman Jack Burns. York would, unfortunately for Cochrane, play an important role with the Tigers in the 1937 season.

"I was disappointed in being traded," Hogsett said, recalling that move

18. Watch Out for That Bump

by Cochrane, the fan favorite. "When he did something wrong [though], he heard it from the fans — same as all of us."

The strain was already showing on Cochrane in April before the loss of Greenberg. Mickey missed the Navin Field opener when he was injured in the Tigers' second game at Cleveland, where he was hit on the thumb on a foul tip by Bill Knickerbocker. Later in April he missed two games because of eye strain and managed in civilian clothes à la Connie Mack with his prescription glasses.

This was too much for his competitive spirit. Cochrane declared, "It's easier to catch with one eye than to sit on the bench biting ten-penny nails," and he proceeded to catch Auker's 10–0 shutout of the Browns on April 23. He was wearing glasses off the field but not on.

Then the day after Greenberg's collision with Powell, Cochrane took a foul tip off Powell's bat on the left instep. He laughed it off, "I'd rather have tough luck now than later."

The Tigers went on an 8-game winning streak in May, but only Bridges was pitching well this year. Bridges' curve was too good sometimes, so one day Cochrane rolled the ball back to Tommy on the mound. Briggs tracked down Cochrane after the game to ask why. "Well, I had to do something to try to get the chewing gum off the ball," Mike replied to a taken-aback Briggs.

Rowe had a sore shoulder, and Auker and Crowder were just not pitching well. Pete Fox was battling lumbago, while newly acquired Al Simmons, whom Cochrane paid the White Sox $75,000 to obtain to reunite the former A's mates again, was struggling with a sprained ankle.

Bringing in old friend Simmons was a big mistake on Cochrane's part. Simmons disliked Cochrane's authoritarian airs as Detroit VP as well as catcher. Cochrane was annoyed with Simmons for assuming he was entitled to special treatment based on their friendship. And many Tigers resented the way Cochrane just handed right field to Simmons and benched Fox.

It all came to a head at Shibe Park in a June 4 game with the A's, who now hardly resembled the squad from Cochrane's days with Mack. Shibe Park also had been changed, with the recently installed "spite fence" in right field. Mack erected a 20-foot extension atop the old 12-foot fence to prevent onlookers from viewing the game from houses on 20th Street. The neighbors had won the legal battles to put bleachers atop their houses, so Mack prevented them from seeing the games from those bleachers. It hardly mattered anymore, though. No one wanted to watch the A's after Mack disassembled the team from its heyday when Cochrane wore the flannels with the blue Gothic A.

After Mickey legged out a bases-loaded, inside-the-park home run in the Tiger 10-run third inning on June 4, he left the game and collapsed in the clubhouse. Cochrane had been fretting for many weeks about the team's pitching woes and other assorted problems, spending many a sleepless night. It was leading to a nervous breakdown. Friends in Philadelphia urged him to seek medical attention, but he refused and left with the team to go to Washington on the next leg of the road trip. But he did turn over the catching duties to Ray Hayworth and Frank Reiber for the games with the Senators.

Things did not get any better for Cochrane by the time the Tigers reached Boston for their series with the Red Sox. The added pressure of his now-proximate parents finally caused Cochrane to leave the team and head back to Detroit for a complete check-up. He left Boston on June 9 to enter Henry Ford Hospital for a 10-day stay for observation and treatment of what Red Sox physician Edward J. O'Brien termed an oversecretion in the thyroid gland.

"They're counting the Tigers out a bit early," Cochrane declared before leaving Boston. "They didn't think we had much of a chance a year ago when we trailed the Yankees by seven games going into the last week of June."

"It seems as if the Yanks have to hole a six inch putt to win, but you can rest assured that the Tigers aren't going to concede the putt," Cochrane used a golf analogy. "Those Yankees will have to hole out. We'll be in there battling for our third straight [pennant]."

Doctors simply advised Cochrane to take some time off to convalesce, to get away from it all. He proceeded to spend a two-week period at the Wyoming ranch where he had just spent a vacation following the 1935 World Series championship. In the process Cochrane relinquished the role of American League All-Star team manager, which he had acquired by winning the 1935 pennant. Joe McCarthy took over that role.

"I don't know how long I'll stay this time. I don't suppose I'll be able to start playing right away when I get back," he said before departing on a plane owned by the *Detroit News* headed for Billings, Montana, where he would travel by auto to Wyoming.

Cochrane was beginning to love the rugged terrain of the foot of the Tetons, where he could relax hunting, fishing, and horseback riding completely isolated from world, particularly from worrying about losing baseball games.

When interim manager Del Baker won 13 of 16 games while Cochrane was recovering in Wyoming, rumors started to spread that Briggs would bump Cochrane up to the front office full-time and make Baker manager for the 1937 season. Baker very diplomatically said, "I'm merely filling in for Mike, carrying out his ideas and policies."

On July 15, Cochrane returned to the Tigers for the series with the Yankees at Yankee Stadium, but he was back at Ford Hospital in less than a week, now even experiencing fainting spells. Cochrane just couldn't direct the Tigers in a low-key approach. He fumed over umpire calls, managing from the dugout, arguing constantly over what he considered bad decisions.

Baker was in charge for most of the rest of the 1936 season. Cochrane took in a few games as a spectator in the field boxes, sitting with Briggs, Harridge, Landis, and other dignitaries. He even came back to manage and catch a few

18. Watch Out for That Bump

games in September after the pennant race was conceded to the Yankees, despite the dizziness he still experienced. "You'd better get them Browns out in a hurry," Cochrane once told Auker in the ninth inning of a game against St. Louis. "The batters seem to be coming up three at a time."

Mike bought a farm in Commerce, Michigan, about 30 miles northwest of Detroit, to try to get some of that Wyoming relaxation feeling back home. He liked to brag about his prize-winning steer, but life on the farm was not all that pleasant, particularly when neighbors filed suit against him, seeking to prevent him from fencing off his lake that neighbors had used for years for bass fishing.

But in between the stress of running the Tigers, Mike found time to help others too. The hard-crusted Cochrane that the public knew was all too soft underneath if your case had merit. When former Phillie pitcher Sugar Sweetland wrote Cochrane in 1936 asking for assistance to get into one of Detroit's huge auto factories, Cochrane wrote Briggs. The next day Sweetland was employed at Chrysler, and he worked there 25 years.

Continuing with his prescription for rest, Mike and Mary took an extended trip to Europe after the 1936 season. They then went back to Wyoming for more outdoor life before heading to Florida early for spring training.

Before going to Lakeland, Mike stopped in Washington to testify at a Securities & Exchange Commission hearing in Washington, D.C., regarding W. E. Hutton & Co. and the stock of Atlas Tack.

"A colorful appearance of today's hearing was the appearance of Gordon Stanley (Mickey) Cochrane manager of the Detroit American League baseball team, who admitted that he would rather be behind the plate where 'you know what to look for,'" the *New York Times* reported of Cochrane's investing commentary. "He testified to the purchase of 1,000 shares of Atlas Tack. Jerry McCarthy, customers man in the Detroit office of Hutton took care of his trading, he said."

Auker fondly recalled those winters in Lakeland with Cochrane. "We played golf everyday with Tommy Bridges, Schoolboy Rowe, Al Simmons and others," Auker said. "Mickey was an excellent golfer. He played golf with the same intensity as he played baseball. Always a gentleman, but winning was his only goal. Win or lose, he always had that twinkle in his eye and smile one would never forget."

Over the winter Cochrane announced that he was bringing in three catchers to try for the 1937 season: Birdie Tebbetts, Mike Tresh, and Frank Reiber again. But Cochrane was in the opening day lineup behind the plate.

Cochrane came back as the fiery player-manager that he was. He banned players' wives from spring training, calling them a diversion to the real business of Lakeland. He suspended Rowe from the team because he showed up not in shape to pitch, despite the fact that both he and Bridges had been at Ford Hospital with back problems.

Mickey himself was hitting better, following all that rest in 1936. In the latter part of May, he went on a tear, hitting two doubles in a 3 for 5 effort against Boston on May 22 and following up with 2 for 5 and 4 for 5 games against the Senators on May 23 and 24. After Detroit's 3–1 win on May 24, the *Detroit Free Press* printed a photo of Cochrane sliding into third base in the 7th under the tag of Buddy Lewis with the caption, "Just a stopover for Mickey in his batting spree."

In Rowe's first start of the 1937 season on May 25 at Yankee Stadium, Cochrane tied the game 1–1 in the 3rd with a home run off Bump Hadley. Then in the 5th, Cochrane's life changed forever. With the count at 3 balls 1 strike, he found Hadley's next pitch tough to see in the afternoon sun. As the ball continued at him, Mickey did throw up his right arm to protect himself but it was too late. He slumped to the ground after the pitch struck him in the head.

"I saw the ball roll in front of the plate and then Mickey fell on it, rolled over and cried 'God Almighty!'" Bill Dickey, the catcher that day recalled. The *Detroit Free Press* ran a photo of Cochrane on the ground with Dickey standing over him, stunned, on page one under the headline "Mickey Cochrane's Skull Is Fractured by Pitched Ball in Game with Yankees."

"I was the on-deck hitter when Cochrane got hit by Hadley," Gehringer remembered. "My goodness, he went down like someone had hit him with an ax. The ball bounced right back to the pitcher. Some doctor said that if it'd been an inch lower, he probably would never have awakened."

"Our world came to an end," Auker said. "Schoolboy Rowe and I along with two others carried him on a stretcher from home plate to an ambulance. I was sure he was going to die before he reached the hospital. We cried and prayed."

In one of baseball's most serious hit-batsmen incidents, second only to the 1920 Carl Mays pitch which resulted in Ray Chapman's death, Cochrane hovered between life and death the next 48 hours at New York's St. Elizabeth's Hospital. Mary was summoned from Boston, where she was staying at the time, to be at Mike's side as Dr. Byron Stookey, a leading brain specialist, Dr. Alexander Nicoli, a visiting surgeon at Fordham University, and Dr. Robert Emmett Walsh, the Yankee team physician, all attended to his care.

"After what happened last year and this, well, I guess Mike just fights too hard," Mary said of the beaning at the time.

Mike was conscious, but drowsy, recognizing those at his bedside. Hadley was one of the first callers to check on him at St. Elizabeth's, although he didn't actually get to his bedside. Of the pitch, all Mike could say was, "I lost sight of the ball."

Hadley was shaken, "The ball sailed — I don't know why — it just did."

A helmet might have prevented Mike's injury, but helmets were not used by batters in those days. Helmets wouldn't be in general use for many years, and only in 1971 were they required to be used in the majors.

18. Watch Out for That Bump

The pitch caused a triple fracture of Mike's skull, but his doctors had stabilized him in ten days so that on June 6 a special railroad car could transport him to Ford Hospital back in Detroit.

Was Hadley's pitch a bean ball, meant to be thrown at Cochrane, in retaliation for his homer in the previous at bat? The answer is almost without a doubt, absolutely not. The pitch was thrown on a 3–1 count with a runner on base. A purposely thrown bean ball would have occurred in one of the first few pitches. Hadley was also not known to throw at batters, unlike Mays, who had had a reputation for deliberate bean balls prior to the Chapman incident.

Tiger fans clearly agreed with this conclusion. When Hadley next pitched in Detroit on June 5, the crowd cheered him to express the belief that he hadn't dusted Cochrane.

While Detroit citizens waited anxiously for word on Cochrane's health, United Auto Worker organizers were violently beaten by Ford Motor security workers at the plant in Dearborn the day after Cochrane's accident on the diamond. The incident was referred to as the "Battle of River Rouge." Coverage of this assault eclipsed coverage of Cochrane's hospital watch.

The Detroit economy entered another malaise in 1937 as labor unrest became more widespread. A Supreme Court decision gave workers the right to organize on the job and strike, which combined with federal cutbacks in New Deal programs, contributed to the economy's collapse. Automobile production would fall 48% between 1937 and 1938, no doubt impacting Briggs' finances, as Briggs Manufacturing Company was one of the largest auto body suppliers in the country, making bodies for Ford, Chrysler, Chalmers, Hudson, and Packard. Briggs began taking a renewed interest in his investment in the Detroit Tigers, specifically his highly paid, injured player-manager.

It was almost a month and a half before Cochrane had recovered enough even to attend a Tiger game as a spectator. On July 18 he and Briggs sat in a box at Navin Field and watched their team defeat the Senators.

"I remember there was a man on first base and I had made up my mind to drive the ball between the first and second basemen," Mike told reporters in a firm voice accompanied with vigorous gestures after the game. "When the pitch was delivered I was all set to meet it. Then I saw that it was going to be a bad pitch and I didn't swing. I thought the ball would go by harmlessly but all of a sudden I lost sight of it. It must have taken a freak turn and smacked me."

Asked about returning to the diamond, Cochrane responded, "Frankly I don't know if the old confidence will come back. I'm no sissy, but I keep thinking of those x-ray plates of my head. The old bean looks like a road map." May 25, 1937, would indeed be Cochrane's last major league game.

As one writer had written earlier, "Mickey's injury came at a time when

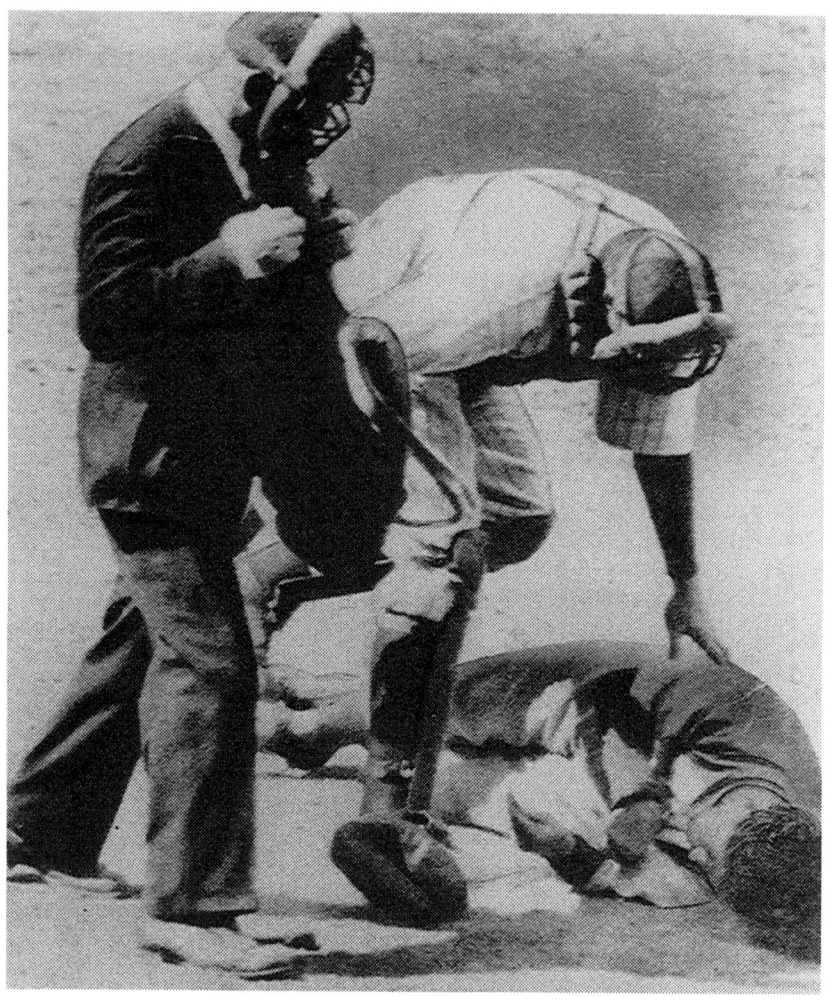

Cochrane felled by Bump Hadley's pitch on May 25, 1937. Yankee catcher Bill Dickey and umpire Steve Basil hurry to lend assistance (Urban Archives, Temple University, Philadelphia, Pennsylvania).

it looked as if he had finally rid himself of the last traces of the ailments that kept him out of uniform the greater part of last season."

York, Cochrane's budding future first baseman, replaced Cochrane as the regular Tiger catcher for the rest of the 1937 season and proceeded to hit a record 18 homers in August as interim-manager Baker led Detroit on a late season assault on the pennant-winning Yankees.

Once again the pundits were saying that Briggs would push Cochrane into the front office and install Baker firmly at the manager position. Briggs continued to deny these rumors. To demonstrate his confidence in Cochrane, Briggs even gave Cochrane a new two-year contract after he returned from another restful European excursion aboard the ocean liner *Conte di Savoia* to visit Naples, Florence, Paris, Berlin, and London. Briggs, though, would not honor the entire contract.

- 19 -

All Fired Up

Cochrane hit the banquet circuit once again after returning from Europe. He also did some hunting in upstate Michigan and took in a few college football games before starting to rebuild the Tigers for the 1938 season.

To shore up the Tigers' ailing pitching staff, Cochrane thought he needed to obtain a front line pitcher for 1938. He thought he had one in Vern Kennedy of the White Sox, for whom he traded away Gee Walker, Marv Owen, and Mike Tresh. It was not a popular move for Detroit fans.

"I hated to let Walker go. I didn't like the idea of giving up Owen, but we had to make some sacrifices," Cochrane said at the time. "If this business doesn't turn out to benefit the Tigers, I'll take the rap."

Cochrane also wanted to make a comeback as a catcher, a move that was not popular with Briggs, who wanted to move forward and remake the Tigers from their prior Navin image. Briggs enlarged the stadium by 20,000 seats permanently to make room for more fans and renamed Navin Field to be Briggs Stadium for 1938. He also wanted Cochrane to find a younger catcher and to handle only the manager chores on the field. Cochrane had different ideas.

The Tigers didn't respond to Cochrane in 1938 though. As a nonplaying manager, he didn't inspire the same confidence that he had with the Tigers in 1934 and 1935 when he was a field leader. He tried too hard to be an authority figure, and it didn't work.

"The day he was hit in the head, he was not the same man, because he couldn't play," Rogell recalled. "Something happened. The club was not the same. Why? Hard to explain — we lost our Leader."

Mike just couldn't handle the transition from playing manager to bench manager. He was not a "do-as-I-say" kind of leader. Many equated him to Ty Cobb, "a great player in his day, but he fails as a bench manager because he has no patience with those whose abilities and ambition are not equal to his own." Some of the Tigers called him Grumpy Cochrane.

"When Mickey was managing the Tigers from behind the plate I can't remember him ever fouling up anything. Seemed like he made snap judgments that always worked out well," Gehringer said after his player career ended. "After he became a bench manager it seemed like he weighted everything a little more, and you can't do that in baseball — in politics maybe, but not baseball — you've got to jump into things or you miss your chance. And after Mickey got hit in the head, it seems like we missed more chances."

Salsinger described Cochrane during the 1938 season in this way: "When the Tigers were losing, he'd pace up and down the dugout raging like an angry lion. This naturally made his players, particularly the younger men, jittery with the result that they fell into slumps."

Mike was indeed frustrated with his younger players. He was hypercritical, especially of his young pitchers, and too impatient to give them the opportunity to make good. He also frequently bewailed the club's lack of talent. It was rumored that one vindictive player once heaved a ball at Cochrane's legs during batting practice in retaliation for Mike's comments.

In late June in a series at Shibe Park against the A's, Cochrane blew up in the clubhouse, charging certain players with laxity on the field and carelessness toward training rules. He fined Boots Poffenberger $100 for violating both counts and warned of further fines, suspensions, and releases.

Cochrane issued an early to bed, early to rise edict, hoping to motivate the team as he had back in 1934, but the Tigers were mired in fifth place at the All-Star break.

On July 13, Dixie Walker missed a hit-and-run signal, and Cochrane fined him $25. "They'll learn to protect the runner even if they have to pay to learn," Cochrane announced.

The Tiger players may have disliked Cochrane's tactics, but the Detroit fans still adored him. After a dismal July road trip, 10,000 loyal fans welcomed Cochrane and the team at the train station. Detroit still loved Mickey.

Briggs, however, increasingly didn't like his Tiger manager. He sensed that Cochrane had lost his effectiveness of leadership when forced to work from the sidelines. He had seen the players respond to Baker as interim manager during 1936 and 1937 when Cochrane was incapacitated and it was vastly different from the current 1938 situation.

On Saturday August 6, the Tigers lost 14–8 to the Red Sox at Briggs Stadium, Detroit's fourth consecutive defeat, which moved them 17 games out of first place. The team had a 47–51 record in fifth place.

After the game Cochrane and Briggs discussed the team in Briggs' office.

"What's the alibi for today?" Briggs inquired as a greeting.

"To tell you the plain truth, you haven't got the players to win," Cochrane replied.

When Briggs suggested that the team's disappointing results were Cochrane's fault as manager, Cochrane suggested that if he thought so, he should get another manager.

Briggs then reportedly turned to his secretary and said, "Make out a check to Mr. Cochrane for the balance of the season." With that, Briggs fired Cochrane and issued a terse announcement:

> Mickey Cochrane and I had a conference today at which it was agreed that he would no longer continue his connection with the Detroit Baseball Club. He will be paid through the end of the 1938 season.
> I regret sincerely the termination of our baseball relationship both from a personal standpoint and because of the contribution which Mickey Cochrane made to Detroit and the club when he came here as manager and catcher five years ago, but it seems apparent to both of us that for the good of the club and in justice to the sporting fans, a change should be made.

The hero of 1935 was a bum by 1938, according to Briggs.

"Mickey did more for baseball in four years here then Briggs can do in a lifetime," Lefty Grove, in town with the Red Sox, was quoted as saying. "Just look at the stadium, that's the stadium that Mickey Cochrane built."

Cochrane kept silent at the time, although a reporter did track him down that evening at his 18110 Muirland Street residence. "No, I haven't anything to say," Mike said from the den in his house, fidgeting in his chair, as the reporter noted. "I might say something I would regret. It was just as much a surprise to me as it was to you."

Told that there were other baseball towns, Mike quickly shot back, "But not like this one, buddy."

Salsinger wrote a lengthy story in the August 8 edition of the *Detroit News* entitled "Mike, Magnetic Leader, Idol of City for Two Years" in which he paid homage to Cochrane, the man he had talked Navin into hiring in the fall of 1933.

"Two strikes meant nothing to Cochrane. To other players it generally means a slight change in grip or stance. Two strikes never handicapped Cochrane, never caused him to offer at a bad pitch to keep from striking out. Pitchers had to make the 'big one' good for Cochrane," Salsinger said in praise of Cochrane.

It was a bitter end for Mike. It was somewhat embarrassing that *The Sporting News* had just a week earlier pictured on its front page his wife Mary and daughter Joan.

Mary Cochrane kept photocopies of John Kieran's "Sports of the Times" column of August 9, 1938, entitled "The Cochrane Case," which sympathized with Mike's supporters: "Cochrane is out. Baker is in. The King is dead; long live the King! Sic transit gloria." Kieran's Latin phrase translates to Thus Passes Glory or roughly, There Go the Tigers.

Most thought Cochrane would have no trouble hooking onto another managership. "One of the most popular figures in baseball, Cochrane should not have much difficulty making a new connection."

But he did. And the failure to make a new connection led to a life filled with an awkward relationship with baseball.

"You would have thought that somebody with Mickey's record would find a place in the Tiger organization," Gehringer remarked years later. "Of course, Mickey was pretty quick on the draw with his temper, as was Briggs, and I guess Briggs and Cochrane had a word fest that didn't help matters."

Cochrane decided to leave Detroit almost immediately to fly out to Wyoming, where he would soon buy a ranch in Montana with Detroit businessman Frank Book. At the air field, Detroit lawyer John Watkins was said to have put his arms around Mike's shoulders and with tears sliding down his face, said, "We'll never forget what you did here."

Watkins spoke for all of Detroit and a good part of the USA. The *Detroit Free Press* put it in perspective 25 years later:

> Had he come to it at another time, he might be remembered as a colorful, fiery playing manager who led the Tigers to two pennants and a World Series win — and nothing more.
>
> But there was an alchemy of era and man. To a Depression ridden Detroit, Cochrane's baseball leadership brought an interest, an enthusiasm, an elan that somehow kept hearts high and grins going despite life's daily disappointments.
>
> It has been said that Mickey Cochrane licked the Depression in Detroit. That's overstating it, naturally. But the man had a magic about him that made it easier for Detroit to ride out those early 1930's.
>
> With the Tigers under Cochrane, Detroit talked, thought, and lived baseball, and in so doing was at least partly able to forget its travail.

The stadium was never renamed after Cochrane, as Grove had hinted, but the citizens of Detroit did rename a street behind left field Cochrane Place after their fallen hero.

But reality was that removing Cochrane as manager was a necessary move for the Detroit baseball team. Baker did lift the team again, and Detroit went on in 1940 to win another American League pennant. That wouldn't have occurred had Briggs acceded to sentiment to keep Cochrane in the manager's seat. But Briggs could have handled the situation much more diplomatically than he did.

"He wasn't the same Cochrane," Rogell noted. "He was canned for his own good. Otherwise, the poor guy might've died, he was so high strung."

There were persistent rumors during the next few years that Mike was under consideration for this or that managerial position, particularly with the Red Sox and the Dodgers. But none ever panned out. Cochrane's reputation as a "caged lion" bench manager unfortunately preceded him wherever he went.

As part of the Detroit dismissal, Cochrane seemingly agreed with Briggs to forego his contractual right to a $36,000 salary for 1939. Briggs appears to have taken advantage of Cochrane's shock when he was fired to take back his financial obligation to Cochrane. He then cleverly credited Cochrane publicly as being magnanimous in giving up his pay for a job he wouldn't be performing in 1939.

"The generous gesture was expensive, but sporting," Bob Broeg wrote of Cochrane's situation, "because at the time he died Mickey's resources had been pared by illness and reverses to the point he'd wondered why baseball at least didn't pension Hall of Famer members among its old-timers."

Cochrane's income had been rather significant in Detroit. He was baseball's highest paid player in 1937 according to the 1939 release of a corporation salary report by the Treasury Department to the House Ways and Means Committee of Congress. Cochrane had earned $45,000 in 1937, $36,000 in salary with a $9,000 bonus, to top the paychecks of Lou Gehrig and Dizzy Dean, who were the next highest. Mike had also earned $45,000 in each of the preceding two years in a combination of salary and bonus, while collecting $40,000 in his initial 1934 season.

While the economic slump of 1938 may have been a factor for Briggs, his apparent dislike for Cochrane's style manifested itself when he dismissed Cochrane as Tiger manager. Briggs took a different attitude toward Cochrane than Navin had as owner; perhaps the fact that Briggs had fronted the $100,000 purchase price for Cochrane's services made his expectations of him even higher than the two American League championships that Cochrane did deliver.

Some say Briggs was not an easy man to work for. Briggs one day asked Cochrane what his players did nights on road trips. When Mike replied that he didn't know or care, Briggs handed him a detective's report showing where the players had spent their off-field hours during a full month of traveling.

Although Cochrane was ostensibly in charge of player movements as general manager, Briggs often mingled in these affairs. Perhaps the die was cast when Cochrane one day in 1938 asked for Poffenberger to warm up on the sideline to pitch, only to be told that he wasn't with the team anymore. Briggs had sent him to Toledo. And Briggs installed his son "Spike" Briggs as the team's treasurer. Cochrane and the younger Briggs often had words too.

To replace his income, Mike became a manufacturer's representative, selling steel, wire, and rubber goods to Detroit firms, using the contacts and reputation he had built there with the Tigers.

"I sit around for thirty minutes or an hour or two in the offices of purchasing agents waiting for them to see me," Cochrane told *Public Ledger* writer Bill Duncan in November 1938 when he visited Mike in Detroit. "I have to hustle and the work isn't easy, but I like it and have absolutely no intention of returning to baseball. I believe I could play ball for a few years, but then what? I cannot see anything smart in my returning to the game. I see a future in being a manufacturer's agent."

As one writer put it, however, "Out of baseball, to which he had given everything but his life, he was completely unhappy."

While baseball was in his blood, so was flying planes, as Mike's nephew

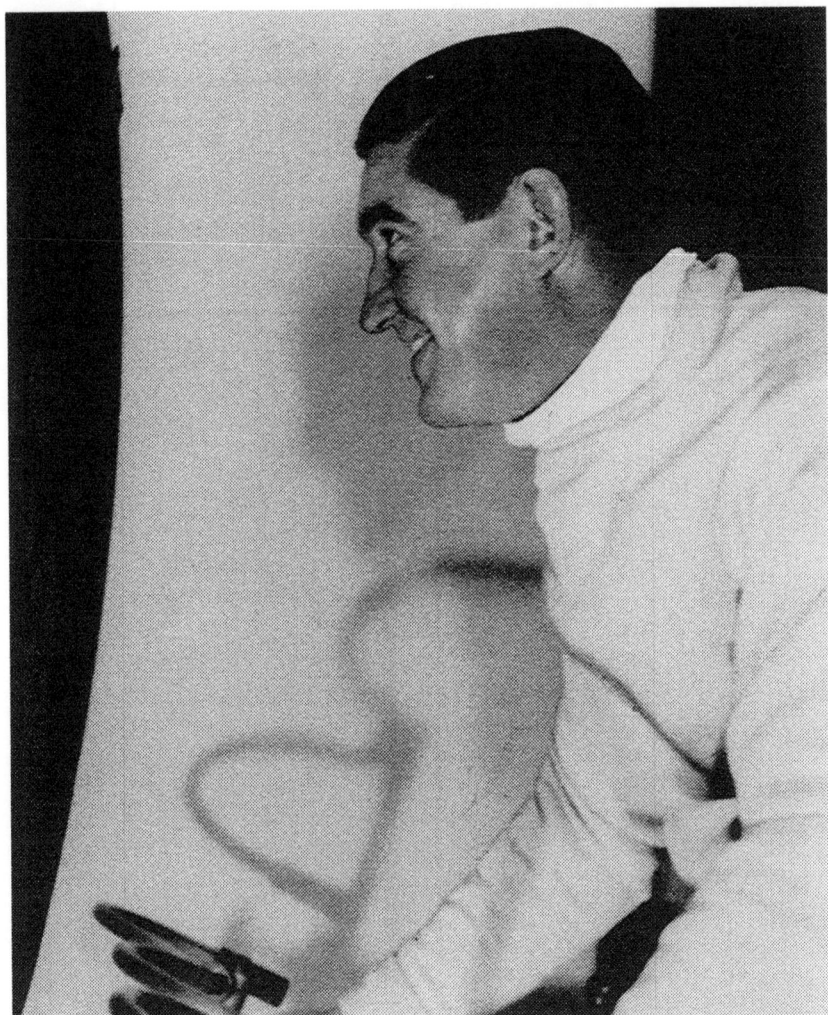

Cochrane exercising on stationary bicycle at Philadelphia Health Club in 1939 (Urban Archives, Temple University, Philadelphia, Pennsylvania).

Al Cochrane recalled. "I got my first airplane ride through Uncle Mike. He took me to the Cleveland Air Races just before the war started. That was quite a thrill for a kid of 9 or 10."

Mike wrote a baseball book that was published in 1938 entitled *Baseball The Fan's Game*, which focused on playing fundamentals. "He autographed a copy for me 'To young Bert from Uncle Mike' and because Tris Speaker happened to be at his house when I got the book, Uncle Mike had him sign it too," Al Cochrane recalled.

Mike was spotted at the 1940 World Series sitting with Cobb, and a reporter noted, "He was all over his seat, twitched on every pitch, lurched with every catch and left the ball yard exhausted." It was obvious that Cochrane missed baseball.

- 20 -

Battling Japan on the Diamond — Part II

The Japanese attack on Pearl Harbor on December 7, 1941, plunged America into World War II and hung a dark cloud over the country. But there was a silver lining — Cochrane was back in baseball. He had met the Japanese on friendly terms on tour in 1931. Ironically, Japan's attack in 1941 presented the opportunity for Mike to return to big-time baseball.

In January 1942, Cochrane was accepted into the U.S. Navy as a lieutenant under Lt. Commander Gene Tunney; Cochrane was to be in charge of the baseball program at the Great Lakes Naval Training Center about 40 miles north of Chicago near the Wisconsin border.

"Cochrane never liked sitting on the sidelines," *The Sporting News* commented. "Mike is one of the thousands of Americans who is making sacrifices to help us win the big war."

Cochrane had actually begun the wheels turning with the Navy months before Pearl Harbor, but at age 38, with only his college ROTC experience for military background, the bureaucratic wheels moved too slowly for the congenitally impatient Cochrane. He turned to one of his high-level Detroit contacts for assistance with Washington.

"Harry Bennett got Mike in the Navy," Mary Cochrane said, referring to Henry Ford's top assistant at Ford Motor Company. "Harry pulled a lot of strings. Mike might not have gotten in otherwise. He was too old."

One of Cochrane's first recruiting challenges was Red Sox star Ted Williams, who had batted .406 the past season in what would turn out to be the last time an everyday player would hit .400 over a season. Williams had been taking a lot of heat in the press to enlist after his 1-A draft classification was rescinded and changed back to a 3-A status, based on his claim that he was the sole support for his mother. The press was painting Williams as un-American for not joining up to fight the war.

Red Sox manager Joe Cronin arranged for Williams to meet with Cochrane on March 5 at Great Lakes, to see what could be worked out for Williams to continue playing ball, but in the Navy.

"Cochrane had a new car, a Lincoln Continental with pushbutton doors, and he drove me around the Great Lakes Center," Williams recounted in his autobiography. "There were 10,000 guys there and Cochrane's all decked out in his Navy uniform, buttons shining like mad, and he gave me the big pitch. I met a few of the guys and I'm weakening. I'm about to enlist right now. Then he says 'Gee, it's going to be awful tough to play ball. You try to play ball this summer, they'll boo you out of every park in the big leagues.'"

Mike thought he was clinching the sale, but it backfired. The very next day Williams announced that he was going to play for the Red Sox in 1942.

As one writer noted it was a "touchy subject, this question of how to deal with the ballplayers turned serviceman. True, it was not a 'powder puff war' but soldiers and sailors did have a need for entertainment, so why not let it be provided by those comrades in arms who had a special skill? And who better could run the military's conditioning programs than professional athletes, assigned, naturally, as recreation specialists?"

A fair number of major league ball players did find their way to the Great Lakes Bluejackets team run by Cochrane even though Williams didn't. Mike was able to command a team that compiled a 63–14 record against collegiate, minor, and major league competition during the 1942 season.

Johnny Rigney of the White Sox was the ace pitcher, with Frankie Pytlak of the Red Sox behind the plate. Second baseman Benny McCoy of the Philadelphia A's was the team's dominant player. Two ex–St. Louis Brown players stood out for the Bluejackets, outfielder Joe Grace and shortstop Johnny Lucadello, as did outfielders Don Padgett from the St. Louis Cardinals and Frank Baumholz of the Cincinnati Reds minor league system. Two other minor leaguers rounded out Cochrane's infield, first baseman Chet Hajduk of the White Sox system and third baseman Ernie Andres of the Red Sox system.

These players weren't household names from the big leagues, but they were the first wave of servicemen. Cochrane was able to use his baseball talents to mold the squad into a cohesive team.

The Bluejackets won 17 straight games in May against college and minor league teams after dropping their opening game versus major league competition to the Cubs. The Bluejackets were logging a lot of mileage to take on all comers. On May 27 in a prelude to the Cubs-Reds game for Army-Navy relief at Wrigley Field, Great Lakes defeated Camp Grant 4–1. The next day they traveled to Indianapolis and defeated the American Association team 15–1 in the opener to the Indianapolis-Kansas City game for Navy relief. Then two days later they went to Owensboro, Kentucky, to play the Army's Fort Knox squad.

Then in mid–June the Navy restricted travel for sports events "due to the possibility of disruption of normal training schedules of personnel involved." This was Navy double talk to curb extended tours by teams and individuals,

20. Battling Japan on the Diamond — Part II

Cochrane as manager of the Great Lakes Naval Training team during World War II, demonstrates the art of bunting (*The Sporting News* Archive, St. Louis, Missouri).

particularly the Great Lakes team, because Cochrane's competitive spirit to find the best baseball opponents was too obviously putting baseball first and the Navy second.

In addition to managing the team, Cochrane occasionally put himself into the game for a little action. In the July 4 game at Briggs Stadium against the Army's Fort Custer, he struck out as a pinch hitter in Great Lakes' 5–0 victory.

And Cochrane hadn't lost his touch at bench jockeying, which first gained him fame with his "serving tea" comment in the 1929 World Series. Elliot Baker pitched for the University of Indiana before entering the service, and he faced Great Lakes in one of his pitching stints that he recounted in a 1991 magazine article. "He kept up the nice, clean all-American chatter as I got ready to throw," Baker said, describing Cochrane's tone of voice from the third base coach's box. "Then my great boyhood idol started on me."

"What we got out there?" Cochrane called out to Baker on the mound. "Hey beanpole, get your ass back to your dancing class."

"How's your old lady, beanpole? I hear she's a terrific lay!" Cochrane yelled as Baker's first pitch went into the screen behind home plate.

Cochrane was still out to win, no matter what the competition.

"You got any sisters, kid? They whorin' aroun' too?" Cochrane called out as Baker's pitch hit the dirt in front of the catcher.

After walking the first four Great Lakes batters on 16 pitches, "I got a smattering of applause and some boos as I went to our bench," Baker wrote upon being lifted from the game by his coach. "But Cochrane's high voice cut through them. He was already starting on the next pitcher's mother."

Cochrane's leadership yielded phenomenal success for the 1942 Bluejackets, and he was named to manage the combined Army-Navy service all-star team that was to take on the winner of the major league All-Star Game. This "second" All-Star Game was held on July 7 at Cleveland's Municipal Stadium, all proceeds going towards military relief.

The American League under Joe McCarthy's direction had defeated the National League 3–1 at the Polo Grounds on July 6 and then traveled to Cleveland to take on the military all-stars. Before 62,000 spectators Cochrane's squad bowed 5–0, unable to stop McCarthy's big bats in Joe DiMaggio and Ted Williams. (Chief Boatswain's Mate Bob Feller lasted only one inning.)

"As for the servicemen, they lost but their training had been for a bigger game! Their victory will come later," *The Sporting News* reported of Cochrane's last major baseball appearance. Although Mike would manage at Great Lakes two more years, the war became increasingly more high profile, and the baseball program diminished quite a bit from its 1942 heights.

This line wasn't all wartime rhetoric. Following the completion of the Bluejackets' 63–14 season, the players began training recruits and were given companies of men to march, drill, and coach in the fundamentals of seamanship. Hajduk and Eddie Pellagrini were given commendations for their work in training.

As for Cochrane, he was scheduled to be assistant football coach at Great Lakes for the fall of 1942. In one of the early sessions, however, Cochrane suffered a ballooned finger after catching a football off the end of his fingers. He recalled to reporters that he had caught over 1500 games in baseball and never seriously banged up a finger.

Since Great Lakes was a naval training station, it was its nature to see servicemen pass through for short stretches and then go on to more permanent duty elsewhere. Therefore Cochrane started virtually from scratch each year. For 1943 he had only three players left from the previous season, although he picked up power-hitting Johnny Mize of the New York Giants as a first baseman. Vern Olsen from the Cubs became Mike's top pitcher in 1943, winning ten games as Great Lakes compiled a 52–10–1 record that year.

Great Lakes defeated its major league competition more consistently in 1943 than it had in 1942, not surprisingly, since more players departed from the majors for the service to weaken the caliber of major league play. In 1943 the Bluejackets were 4–3 versus major league teams, whereas they were 4–6 the previous year.

Cochrane no doubt enjoyed the power that his position as baseball officer at Great Lakes provided him. It probably reminded him of his heyday as skipper of the Tigers, when he brought two pennants to Detroit.

Lt. Commander Russell Cook, the athletic officer at Great Lakes in 1942

20. Battling Japan on the Diamond — Part II

and 1943, must have enjoyed the political power because it was he who was instrumental in getting the baseball talent to Great Lakes. Tiger pitcher Virgil Trucks, who played for Cochrane in 1944, related how it worked:

> I'd never met Mickey Cochrane, but I liked what I knew and what I had read about him. I wanted to go into the Navy and play ball for him. So I sent him a wire — I was living in Birmingham — and told him I was going into the service and I had chosen the Navy, but that didn't necessarily mean I would be in there. He told me to contact Cook.
>
> Cook sent me a wire back saying to transfer my papers to Chicago Draft Board Number One and they would take over from there. That's exactly what I did. I came to the draft board here in Birmingham and told them I was going to Chicago, I had a job there, and I'd like my papers transferred. And they did that. I went immediately afterwards and I'd spent two days in a Chicago hotel when I got a notice that I was drafted to Great Lakes. It was handled by the higher-ups of naval personnel.

Barney McCosky told another tale. "I enlisted, wanted to be a pilot. I went somewhere in Ohio to pre-flight school and hell, I was 25 and there were kids 19 and 20 just out of college. I couldn't keep up with those guys. So I called Great Lakes and said, 'Mickey, get me out of this end of it. Get me over there, I'll be a sailor.' About a week later I was in Great Lakes."

Cochrane's team compiled a 48–2 record in 1944 and by many accounts probably could have won either the American or National League pennant that season. Great Lakes beat 11 of its 12 major league opponents that season, losing only to the Brooklyn Dodgers.

Trucks was a mainstay of the team, posting a 10–0 record with 161 strikeouts and an 0.88 earned run average. He threw 2-hitters against the Red Sox and White Sox and 3-hitters against the Browns and the Giants.

Jim Trexler had a 14–1 pitching record for Cochrane after playing in Indianapolis previously, and Pittsburgh Pirate Bob Klinger finished with a 9–0 mark.

The second loss that season came at the hands of a semipro team comprised of Ford Motor Company employees in Dearborn, Michigan. It was a defeat that the fiery Cochrane didn't take lightly. A loss was a loss to Mickey, whether it was to the Cardinals in the World Series or to the Ford All-Stars in a wartime exhibition game.

Schoolboy Rowe was reunited with Mike at Great Lakes in 1944 and played mostly outfield for Cochrane, since outfielders were in short supply that year. Rowe actually led the team in hitting in 1944 with his .446 average.

For the Dearborn game, Mickey decided a touch of nostalgia was in order, and the former Tiger duo teamed up again as a battery, Rowe on the mound and Cochrane behind the plate.

The Ford squad managed to hold onto a 1–1 tie going into the bottom of the 9th, when Rowe decided to experiment with a blooper pitch, a delivery made famous during the war by Pittsburgh hurler Rip Sewell. Rowe experienced considerably less success with his serve, however, as a Ford player by the name of Gene Malish promptly waited on it and smashed it 400 feet in the open field for an inside-the-park home run to win the game 2–1.

"When we got on the bus, I thought Cochrane was gonna give Rowe a dishonorable discharge, he was so mad at him," Trucks said because Cochrane had called for a fast ball and Rowe had ignored him.

"If I call for a fast ball, or whatever pitch I call for, you better throw it. You'd better not throw the opposite pitch or I'll have you shipped out so far you'll never get back," Cochrane screamed at Rowe on the bus.

Rowe ditched the blooper pitch for the rest of 1944, which turned out to be Cochrane's final season at Great Lakes. Bob Feller was brought in to coach Great Lakes in 1945.

After Mike saw that his only son, Gordon Jr., had enlisted in the Army while away at Georgia Military Academy and was under fire in Europe, he pushed to get into the action too. While he succeeded in getting shipped to the Marianas, he sat out a good part of the rest of the war on a recaptured island in the Pacific carving mementos out of Japanese "zero" airplane parts.

"When he was in the Navy at Guam he wrote letters that really thrilled the heart of a kid like me," nephew Al Cochrane remembered of his early teen years. "He once sent a small letter opener made from a piece of a Japanese zero wing."

While he himself was serving in relatively safe positions, Mike expressed his concern for his son's safety in a letter to Ed Pollock of the *Public Ledger*, who printed this passage in his February 28, 1945, column: "The boy has been in some heavy action in Belgium. So far he's come out all right. He went back from the lines for some rest, probably is up there again by now and I have my fingers crossed."

"Like millions of fathers all over the world, Mickey Cochrane is worried about his son," said columnist Pollack.

Private First Class Gordon Cochrane, Jr., had already been killed in action while in a farmhouse in Holland that month, before the column appeared in the newspaper. It wasn't until mid–March that Mary Cochrane was notified by the War Department at their home in Lake Forest, Illinois, about the death of their son.

"That affected Mike, no doubt about it. Nice kid, too, damn it," Billy Rogell remembered. "Gordon Jr. played with my son Billy."

"He wasn't a hard driving guy like his father. He was more easy going," Doc Cramer recalled. "That killed Mike. That hurt him something terrible, the mother too."

"Gordon never should have seen active duty," Mike's daughter Sara declared, "with his hearing loss due to mastoid problems as a child."

It was tough to catch Mike's feelings as he faced his only son's death. He was hard on the outside, but inside he was hurting.

"I always thought that Mike suffered from a form of guilt," Eldon Auker believed. "His traveling 50% of summer and his responsibilities as manager left little time to spend with his son. I think he wished he could live those years over, but it was too late. His heart was crushed."

"Many years later Mike met a soldier from Gordon's unit," Mary Cochrane said. "He said that Gordon hadn't suffered, that he died instantly. That helped us out."

Gordon Jr. was buried beside Mike's mother, who had died of leukemia on November 12, 1942, at age 72, in the family plot in Mt. Prospect Cemetery back in Bridgewater, Massachusetts. The cemetery is just a few hundred yards from where Mike had grown up, on the road where he had practiced his sprinting, a hopeful Olympian at the time.

- 21 -

Ranch Dressing in Salad Days

On July 21, 1947, Cochrane was enshrined among the game's great players at a Hall of Fame induction ceremony in Cooperstown.

As a matter of fact, Mike wasn't even there. Nor were the other 3 electees, nor 10 of the 11 appointed inductees. Only Big Ed Walsh appeared at the 1947 ceremony.

Today the culmination of a player's career is induction to the Hall of Fame, which takes place before thousands of spectators in a big media event each summer in Cooperstown. To ignore one's induction would now be quite a snub. But things were different back in 1947. The Hall hadn't yet obtained the somewhat larger-than-life status it now enjoys.

"It didn't seem important to Mike," Mary Cochrane remembered. "We were out West at the ranch at the time."

According to nephew Jack Thompson, "Uncle Mike never got snobbish about being a celebrity ballplayer. He seemed happy being just plain old Mike Cochrane. I never heard him say one word to anyone about being in the Hall of Fame."

"He never really talked about the Hall of Fame," Mike's daughter Sara said. "I think he thought it was the kiss of death to be in the Hall of Fame. A lot of those players fell on hard times after their playing days were over."

"Daddy never wanted the spotlight," Sara believed. "The Detroit fans, they wanted too much of their hero."

Deep down inside, Hall of Fame status probably did have meaning to Mike. The only outward sign was a trip Mary says Mike took to Cooperstown in the 1950s with his father. Perhaps it was Mike's way of showing his father that he had indeed achieved success.

Mike's father outlived him by almost five years, dying in 1967 at the age of 96. Ironically, a John Cochrane obituary was headlined "Father of Ball Player," noting his son's deeds rather than his own. John Cochrane was buried back in Bridgewater with his wife and grandson.

Cochrane was one of four Hall of Famers elected by the Baseball Writers

21. Ranch Dressing in Salad Days

Author at age 11 intrigued with Cochrane's Hall of Fame plaque during summer of 1965 (author's collection).

Association of America in balloting announced on January 22, 1947. He was named on 128 of 161 ballots, sufficiently above the 75% required for election. Former A's teammate Lefty Grove joined Cochrane in the Hall that year with 123 votes. Carl Hubbell topped the voting with 140 votes, and World Series archrival Frank Frisch finished second with 136 votes.

Only 14 ballplayers had previously been elected to the Hall, so this first postwar group was still a pretty select crew in baseball circles. This point has been lost to baseball history as the total population of the Hall has now grown to over 160.

Admittedly, Cochrane's election in 1947 was assisted by a rule change implemented in December 1946 that called for members of the Hall of Fame to be chosen from the ranks of players who were active during the 25-year period preceding the election. Only one player, Rogers Hornsby, had been elected between 1939 and 1947 under the 75% standard because votes were split among a logjam of potential candidates spanning back to the beginning of the game. Twenty-one "old-timers" were selected in 1945 and 1946 to help remedy this situation.

Cochrane and Grove were the first stars from the great Athletics teams of

1929–31 to be enshrined at Cooperstown. Foxx would enter four years later in 1951, and Simmons in 1953. Mack of course had preceded them all, being named in 1937.

Cochrane was the first catcher to be elected to the Hall. Three other backstops were chosen by veteran committees prior to Cochrane's election: Buck Ewing in 1939 and King Kelly and Roger Bresnahan in 1945.

No contemporary of Cochrane was chosen prior to his election in 1947. Bill Dickey was elected in 1954 and Gabby Hartnett in 1955. Rick Ferrell was named by the veteran's committee in 1984 and Ernie Lombardi in 1986. Josh Gibson was enshrined in 1972 based on his Negro League playing career of that era. From an earlier era, Ray Schalk was named by the veteran's committee in 1955.

Only three catchers who have played in the fifty years since Cochrane's career ended with that Bump Hadley pitch in May 1937 have been selected to the Hall: Yogi Berra in 1971, Roy Campanella in 1969, and Johnny Bench in 1989. It would appear that Carlton Fisk will be a fourth catching selection by the end of this century.

Cochrane was named on Hall of Fame ballots all the way back to the initial election in 1936 when the original immortal quintet was chosen: Ty Cobb, Babe Ruth, Honus Wagner, Christy Mathewson, and Walter Johnson. Cochrane finished tenth in that voting, being named on 80 of 226 ballots. Cochrane finished ninth in the 1942 voting (88 of 233 ballots), seventh in 1945 (125 of 247), and ninth again in 1946 (65 of 263) before achieving election in 1947.

There are three exhibits at the Hall of Fame where the memory of Cochrane is continued. The 1933 leaping tag picture is there in the Philadelphia A's 1929–31 exhibit, along with his glove in the Detroit Tigers 1934–35 exhibit and his mask and chest protector in the catcher's equipment display.

Mickey Cochrane had been the only major league ball player with that surname until 1986, when Dave Cochrane broke in with the White Sox as an infielder-outfielder. He was later a catcher with the Seattle Mariners.

"I'm not related, but I wish I could have his career," the modern day Cochrane remarked about the forerunner Cochrane.

The late 1940s were perhaps the best years for Mike, who was running the 4K Ranch spread in Dean, Montana, as a dude ranch during the summers. He escaped the hustle and bustle of postwar America out west, working hard but also getting in lots of outdoor activity. He also could spend more family time with Mary and their two daughters, Joan, now a teenager, and Sara, who was born in 1939, along with his partner Frank Book and his family. Also nearby were Mike's father and two brothers Bert and Archie, who had moved out to Montana permanently.

Situated on a plateau above the Stillwater River valley, the 4K Ranch abutted the Absaroka Wilderness about 60 miles southwest of the city of Billings. The 4K was a climb from the Yellowstone River valley outside Billings

21. Ranch Dressing in Salad Days

Top: Cochrane relaxing at his cattle ranch in Montana, with his father John Cochrane (left) and Mary Jane Book (right), daughter of partner Frank Book. *Bottom:* Babe Ruth and his wife visit the 4K ranch, shortly before Ruth's death in 1948 (Cochrane family collection).

into the foothills of the Beartooth Range of the Rocky Mountains, which contains the highest peaks in Montana.

"That was God's country, 360 acres of it," Mike's daughter Sara fondly remembers of her summers at the ranch. "Daddy could relax out there."

The name 4K stood for Keen's Kozy Kountry Klub. As one wag put it, "either the offbeat spelling or the 62-mile gravel road from Billings spelled its failure as a golf club and made it available for purchase."

Mike and Frank Book were partners in the 4K, which they bought in 1939 along with a nearby cattle ranch. The cattle portion was sold during the war when they were able to find trustworthy managers. They operated the ranch up through the late 1950s. Nephew Jack Thompson, who spent a summer on the ranch during school break in 1949, recalled:

> Uncle Mike worked my tail off on the ranch, it was no vacation. One afternoon after a particularly tough day, Uncle Mike told me to saddle up a couple of horses and the two of us headed up into the hills. Climbing up the trail was no picnic either, as the horses struggled to keep their footing in places.
>
> Well, I'm thinking, he worked my butt off during the day and now he was working my butt off again, what's with this guy. Then we reached this spot with a view of the mountains that was spectacular. Just an unbelievable sight. We simply sat there, the two of us alone, and admired it.
>
> That was Uncle Mike. You worked hard and your reward would come. He was tough on the outside, but inside he was an old softy.

Mike could really unwind at the 4K too. Loads of friends would always stop by, including Babe Ruth, who made a visit before he died in 1948. There would be lots of socializing at night, some imbibing and lots of dancing.

"Everyone met around the bar in the lodge at 5 o'clock," Sara recalled. "Daddy really loved that time to talk and tell stories and have a few drinks."

Near the bar were a few round tables with chairs, where Mary and the other ladies usually gravitated. Upstairs in the dining room was the piano. "Daddy loved to hear the piano. Anyone who could play would be pressed into service at the keyboard after dinner. We sang and danced," Sara remembered. "But Daddy couldn't play it. He could play the clarinet and saxophone, but not piano. He spent a lot of money on piano lessons for me, to little avail."

"Uncle Mike loved to dance, particularly with Joan who was in her late teens then. Uncle Mike adored Joan," Jack Thompson recalled of his cousin, who as a five year-old was the darling of Detroit during her father's heyday as manager of the Detroit Tigers.

"Daddy was a great dancer," Sara recalled. "He taught Joan and I to follow the lead, rather than specific steps. That way we could dance with anyone. Our friends would marvel at how fast we'd pick up different dance steps. Heck, we were just following the lead and having a great time!"

21. Ranch Dressing in Salad Days

Sunday dinner at the 4K ranch. From left to right: Mary Cochrane, Frank Book carving the meat, Joan Cochrane, and Mike (Cochrane family collection).

"To this day I still love Big Band music," Sara said of the 40s music that typically came out of the phonograph in the 4K lodge.

There was a swimming pool in front of the lodge, "melted snow which never warmed up," according to Sara, beaver ponds below the ranch, and a lake above it which was popular for trout fishing and swimming.

"Daddy pretty much gave up big game hunting after he shot his trophy moose in 1928. The moose and a large trophy elk hung on the wall of the lodge," Sara said. "But he liked to fish. He taught me how to cast a fly rod and how to troll. He also taught me how to clean the catch."

"The rule was 'you catch it, you clean it and if you use my rod, you clean mine too!' I probably would have enjoyed fishing more if not for that rule," Sara mused.

Horseback riding was another interest Mike shared with his children. "Daddy's favorite was a smooth gaited Quarter Horse named Shorty," Sara recalled.

Billings was becoming Cochrane territory in the late 1940s. Mike's brother Archie wanted to buy the Ford dealership in Billings and move his family out of Detroit. That sounded good to brother Bert too. Fortunately, Mike's connections to the Ford family helped his brothers achieve their goal.

"Mike was friendly with Edsel Ford," Mary has said of their neighbors back in Grosse Pointe, Michigan, where Cochrane had established his primary residence at the end of the war. Edsel was president of Ford Motor Company while Mike was with the Tigers in the 30s, but he died in 1943. Edsel's son Henry Ford II returned from the Navy then and soon assumed his father's job. He brought Ford Motor back to profitability. Mike was no doubt helped by his connections to the Ford family to get the dealership in Billings.

"Uncle Archie wrote to Daddy during the War requesting a loan to purchase the Ford dealership," Sara related. "Ford didn't want to separate the Ford part from the Lincoln-Mercury side, so Daddy and Bert bought the Lincoln-Mercury portion and Archie got his Ford dealership."

Bert ran the day-to-day operation of Yellowstone Motors until it was sold several years later. Archie Cochrane Ford is still a thriving business, although with new ownership since Archie's death.

"Mary said she wished everyone Mike loaned money to repaid him as Archie did," Archie's wife Roz commented. "Daddy loaned money out of the goodness of his heart, not for the payback," Sara believed. "He took some business risks that didn't pay off too well, like investing in a new concept, canned soda pop, when Coke and Pepsi were still in bottles. Right idea, wrong company."

Mike also got involved with the civic life of Billings. Along with his brother Archie, who was president, he was a director of the Billings Mustangs, a baseball farm club in the Pioneer League. Mike was a member of the Shriners as well.

With most of his children putting down roots in Billings, John Cochrane soon joined the move west. Now a widower, he busied himself working around Archie's dealership and making new friends.

After two summers of retreat in Montana, Mike's baseball restlessness resurfaced following his induction into the Hall of Fame. In July 1948, Cochrane left Montana to head east to talk to Phillies' president Bob Carpenter about a manager or general manager position with the team, which now was a tenant at Shibe Park, Mike's old haunt with the A's.

Mike also made time on August 21, 1949, to attend an old-timers game at a Connie Mack Day celebration in New York. He donned the catcher's gear once again to catch the two-inning game, which saw the Yankees old-timers defeat the A's 3–2 before 66,132 fans at Yankee Stadium. Mike struck out in his one plate appearance, facing Lefty Gomez who growled, "Ya Bum, you never did anything like that when we were playing for keeps."

At that old-timers game, Mack offered Cochrane a chance to return to major league baseball as a coach for the 1950 Athletics. It was the break Mike was seeking, and in November 1949 it was announced that Cochrane would have a role with the 1950 A's as bullpen coach. It was a reunion of sorts because Bing Miller and Jimmy Dykes were to be coaches as well.

"I'm tickled to be with the A's again," Cochrane told the press at the announcement. "Mary will be glad to return to Philadelphia. She had

21. Ranch Dressing in Salad Days

Cochrane with the family at Grosse Pointe, Michigan, in December 1949, just before returning to the A's as coach, then general manager. From left, Joan, Mike, Sara, and Mary. (Cochrane Family Collection)

a good time when I was there with the A's. The only trouble is my two daughters Joan, 19, and Sara, 10, are going to [stay at] my ranch in Montana [for the summer.]"

In February 1950, Mike quit as a director of the Billings Mustangs and took his family to the A's spring training in West Palm Beach, Florida. He caught batting practice in one of the early sessions, winding up a mass of aches and pains, and he even pinch hit in an intrasquad game, tagging a single.

"How stupid can a guy get?" Mike joked at the time. "Twenty-five years ago I came to the A's and caught batting practice. Here I am still catching batting practice. Is this progress?"

The World Series returned to Shibe Park in 1950 after an absence of nearly 20 years, but it was the Phillies not the A's who were in the Series spotlight, engaging the Yankees for the 1950 World Series title after their first National League pennant since 1915.

As the aging Mack, now 87, struggled to maintain control of the franchise, Cochrane was elevated to general manager on May 6, 1950. It was a short-lived executive lifestyle for Cochrane though, as he wasn't even around for the October classic.

Cochrane was caught in the middle of the war among members of the Mack family. Connie had tried to pass control to his sons from his first marriage, Roy and Earle, with shares to Mrs. Mack and son Connie Jr. from his second marriage. Connie's second wife, however, wanted their five daughters included also. There were also the Shibe heirs to contend with, who sided with Connie Jr. and his mother to control 60% of the shares. They pushed for Cochrane's promotion to general manager, in order to lessen the almost senile Connie Mack's control of the ballclub.

As the Mack family feuded, Mike grieved over the lack of talent in the A's farm system. "If I had the pick of players from the 24 teams in the three Triple A leagues, I couldn't put together an outfit that would get us out of the hole this year," Mike lamented two months into the job.

Most of the moves that Mike wanted to make to improve the team were thwarted by one or the other Mack faction, so he soon became general manager in name only.

"Cochrane's restless temperament was anything but suited to the general manager's office," one writer noted. "In 13 big league seasons, Cochrane made only 111 errors. In one inning Cochrane the desk-bound executive had reached for the wrong phone, fumbled the receiver, twiddled the wrong switch key for at least two dozen boots."

The Mack family feud became nasty and public during the summer of 1950. Earle and Roy were eventually given the opportunity to buy out the other shareholders. To come up with the $1.75 million needed, they were forced to mortgage Shibe Park. With the debt, the Mack brothers, never strong business managers, struggled with the A's franchise and were forced to sell the club in 1954 to Arnold Johnson. He moved the team to Kansas City.

With the Shibes and Connie Jr. being bought-out, Cochrane was expendable and he was out as general manager by September 2. It was his last meaningful association with major league baseball.

"Well, it's back to the ranch," Mike said of his departure. But he was disgusted and bitter at getting caught in the Mack feud and not getting a real opportunity to be a baseball executive. Happenings at the 4K ranch didn't make him any happier.

The decision to take the job with Connie Mack was one Mike would always regret, for if he had been at the ranch, he might have been able to stop his 19-year-old daughter Joan from eloping with rodeo cowboy John Cobb.

"Joan eloped," her sister Sara sheepishly recalled. "John was a charming, handsome guy. Rodeo life sounded much more romantic and exciting than returning to Grosse Pointe with us."

Mike had lost his only son to the war and had now "lost" one of his daughters to a stranger.

"That really hurt Uncle Mike," nephew Jack Thompson believed. "John

21. Ranch Dressing in Salad Days

Cochrane dancing with daughter Sara at her wedding, June 10, 1960, at the officer's Club, Great Lakes Naval Base. It was their last dance together (Cochrane family collection).

Cobb was a wild seed. Uncle Mike and Aunt Mary had to help out a lot." Cobb (no relation to Ty Cobb) seemingly had a tough time trying to settle down.

As the last child, Sara felt a lot of pressure to succeed. She didn't want to disappoint her father either. "Everything he did, he did 100%. That intensity is a legacy which has a positive and a negative side," Sara has said. "As a teen, all I saw was what he had accomplished. I didn't know about the hours he spent learning to catch pop flys. It was years after his death that I realized that it was *not trying* that was unacceptable, not *failing*."

"Daddy always told me 'Be the best at whatever you do. Even if you're a street sweeper, be the world's best street sweeper,'" Sara recalled. "While I know he was proud of my honors in high school and college, I also know he was disappointed when I left college to marry Ken. He always hoped his children would earn their college degrees. He dropped out just months short of his to play with the Portland team."

"You needed to measure up if he was in charge," Mike's nephew Jack said. "He wasn't much on compliments, but if you did the job, he was very gentle with you."

Cochrane still enjoying plane flight in the late 1950s following his induction into the Boston University Athletic Hall of Fame (Boston University Photo Services, Boston, Massachusetts).

The 1950s were a tough decade for Mike. Baseball didn't seem to have a place for him. His connections in Detroit had eroded to the point that returning to being a manufacturer's rep wasn't an option. With more friends than paying customers at the 4K, it became necessary for Mike to drop out of that partnership with Frank Book. Book's health was declining, so the ranch was sold in the early 1960s. Mike tried various short-term careers, including a local TV show in Chicago.

"Having reached his goal at an early age, what else did he have to accomplish in life? Perhaps this was the proverbial kiss of death Daddy meant about being in the Hall of Fame," daughter Sara mused.

But Mike was back in uniform again in 1955 as a scout and training camp coach for the New York Yankees at their St. Petersburg, Florida, spring training site. Yankee general manager George Weiss had hired Mike to scout players in Michigan and southern Ontario. "It's funny when you think of it," Mike said about being in Yankee pinstripes. "I used to hate the Yankees."

Sara went down to visit with her father during her school break in March. "I was 16 at the time and all these boys on the team I could meet," she remembered. "Well, Daddy had different ideas. I found out they were instructed to say no more than hello to me. I was walking through the dining room at the hotel to meet my father and heard him shout out to the players, 'Eyes Right!'" Mike had understandably become a little overprotective with his youngest daughter.

21. Ranch Dressing in Salad Days

In an old-timers game at Yankee Stadium that summer celebrating Joe DiMaggio's Hall of Fame induction, Cochrane got one of his team's three hits, a single off Red Ruffing. Cochrane batted third and played third base, leaving the catching chores to another 1955 inductee, Gabby Hartnett. Much more playful in his later years, Mike switched positions with Jimmie Foxx in the second inning to play right field while Foxx patrolled third base.

The scouting job lasted just one season. "I got tired of seeing so much bush league baseball and so few ballplayers," Mike said of his departure. He was really sour on the game at this point. "There is a different class in the game. They're all big business now," Mike complained, admitting that he preferred watching Chicago Bear and Northwestern University football than seeing — and suffering through — baseball.

"Daddy had a tough time handling the changes in the game of baseball," Sara believed. "He enjoyed the game for the game's sake."

"Maybe it was getting fired," nephew Jack speculated about Mike's bitterness towards the game. "Why did he blame baseball?"

"Cochrane thought the game had turned its back on him," his Tiger first baseman Hank Greenberg believed. "He never got over being let out as manager by Mr. Briggs. Baseball is funny that way, especially for the great ones like Cochrane. He never got over the hurt. And this wasn't getting hit on the head by Bump Hadley. Mike's hurt was his heart, not his head."

Mike drifted through life the next few years after holding the Yankee scouting position. "I'm eating regular, but I'm not doing much of anything now and could use a job," he said in early 1958, angling for a position as a batting or catching coach. "All the work I've done in the last three years has been a little in radio and TV. I really want to get back into baseball."

Cochrane was not on the financial upswing in the 1950s, but just how far he had fallen from wealth is tough to judge. One 1984 biographer of Ty Cobb wrote: "Mickey Cochrane had suffered a frightful beaning in 1937. He never fully recovered from his head injury and was down on his luck by the 1950's when Cobb began sending him regular checks." An earlier 1975 Cobb biographer was more subtle: "A Hall of Fame member beaned by a pitched ball and enfeebled came under Cobb's wing for years."

Al Stump's 1994 book *Cobb* generated the most controversy. It included this passage: "Each month he [Cobb] mailed support checks to some three dozen men who had faced his spikes and not backed away. Their names were kept confidential. Another beneficiary was Mickey Cochrane, a future Hall of Fame catcher. Near-fatally beaned by a pitch in 1937, Cochrane afterward could not function. The Cobb fund helped support him for the rest of his life."

Stump's book was the basis for the movie *Cobb*, which began to perpetuate this story more broadly than the earlier biographies of Cobb, with no stated attribution for the statement, ever did. Movie reviewers picked it up also, as illustrated by a line from a *Boston Globe* review: "There is an episode where he [Cobb] anonymously subsidizes tapped-out one-time teammate Mickey Cochrane."

Cochrane's family denies this allegation, which appears to have started with Stump's interviews with Cobb during the last months of his life in 1960. "Stump admitted that Cobb was on heavy medication at the time and that a lot of things he said were not true. But he never made any effort to check out the statements about Cochrane with his family," daughter Sara has reported. "My father provided me with a college education, paying the University of Colorado's high out-of-state tuition. He paid cash for his cars, homes, everything. I would hardly call that indigent."

Then there was Ty Cobb's phone call to Mike in 1960. "Cobb wanted to tell Daddy that Coca-Cola stock was about to split and that he should buy the stock. He took the advice. The stock has since grown and split several times and has been a big help to my mother's financial security," Sara has related. "The point is, Daddy had the money to buy the stock and to pay for my wedding all in the same summer. Does that sound like an indigent old ballplayer getting by on Ty Cobb's handouts?"

Says Mary Cochrane, "Mike was too proud, he'd never take a handout."

"What Stump wrote is pure B.S.," Sara has concluded.

Friends of Cochrane tried to pull whatever strings they could to get Cochrane a job back in baseball. Cochrane's former Tiger shortstop Billy Rogell, then a Detroit city councilman, told a story about getting a phone call while in bed.

> It's Cochrane. He's up at this bar and says to come over. My wife says, "You can't go out now, it's too late." And I'm putting on my pants and saying, "It's Mickey. I gotta go." Well, he's there with this other guy and he wants me to go to the Tigers and see if I can get Mickey the job of general manager. I said, "Hell, what do I know about the Tigers anymore?" I've been away from it 15, 20 years and I'm not going to tell those people how to run their business.
>
> Well, he gets up, this guy, and says, "You little shit, you mean you're not going to help Mickey." Now I'm mad because I love Mickey and nobody is going to call me that. I get up and he takes one swing and misses. I hit him once. That's all. Once. See this? [holds out his right hand and points to the knuckle, which is also swollen and out of place]. I guess I busted it pretty good. But he went flying. He's out cold.

Mike didn't get the Tiger general manager job when the Briggs family gave up control of the Tigers in the late 1950s. But new Tiger general manager Bill DeWitt did bring Cochrane back into the Tiger fold in 1960.

"What Musial is to St. Louis or DiMaggio to New York—Cochrane was to Detroit," DeWitt said. "So I brought him back and put him on as a scout of minor league players."

Cochrane's health was deteriorating at this point, so the role was mostly

21. Ranch Dressing in Salad Days

an honorary one, but a class move on DeWitt's part. Mike had been hospitalized in 1958 because of difficulty in breathing. It was the beginning effects of the lymphatic cancer that he would eventually succumb to in 1962, the same disease that claimed his mother in 1942.

Mike attended another old-timers game in Detroit on June 28, 1958. Sara went along with him. "All these kids came up to Daddy for his autograph," she remembered. "There was one kid whose mouth was open, just in awe. That's when it hit me about my father's baseball career. Daddy enjoyed it, saying 'Whose autograph did you want?' and the kid kept gaping at him."

The entire starting lineup for the 1935 World Series champs was there for the old-timers game, along with Ty Cobb. Cochrane caught both innings of the game, receiving pitches from Bridges, Rowe, Auker, Crowder, and Sorrell from his earlier playing days.

"It was lighthitting Jo Jo White from the 1934–35 pennant winners who provided the big thrill in the short game," the *Boston Herald* reported of the game, which preceded the Tigers-Red Sox regular game. "White belted one of Grove's offerings on a line into the lower right field seats. He trotted around the bases shaking hands with Red Sox and umpires alike as he went."

Although he was having difficulty getting around, Mike went to spring training in 1961. He also met his internally imposed obligation to attend Ty Cobb's funeral that year as well. The baseball establishment spurned Cobb at his death, but Cochrane and Ray Schalk both made the journey from Chicago to Royston, Georgia, on July 19 to pay their last respects to Cobb, two of only three baseball figures to do so.

Cochrane maintained his intensity and high standards to the end. "Daddy played golf in the summer of 1961 with my husband Ken, who was new to the game," Sara recalled. "The cancer had set in and his eye sight was failing, yet he still managed to shoot 85." Sara reported that a disgruntled Cochrane told her husband: "That's my last round. If you can't play the game right, you shouldn't play it at all."

"As a beginner, Ken would have been ecstatic to shoot an 85," Sara laughed.

The last baseball game Mike saw in person was at Tampa in April 1962 as a guest of DeWitt, who was then with the Cincinnati Reds. He sat through four innings in a wheelchair but was too tired to stay longer.

Cochrane died at the age of 59 at 6:35 A.M. on June 28, 1962, in Lake Forest Hospital, just south of his home in Lake Bluff, Illinois, near the Great Lakes Naval Training Center. The cause of death was listed as lympho-sarcoma on his certificate of death, which also showed his occupation as baseball scout.

Cochrane's death generated a flurry of effusive obituaries honoring the man who was a Baseball Hall of Famer and was also a Great Depression hero to many in America. Memorial services were held in a packed Lake Forest Presbyterian Church, where just two years earlier Mike had walked his youngest daughter down the aisle on her wedding day. As he wished, his body was cremated and the ashes scattered in a nearby cemetery, making it impossibly tough to catch a glimpse of any earthly monument to mark his passing.

Even in death, the fiery spirit of Gordon Stanley Cochrane was impossible to confine.

- 22 -

Greatest Receiver, TV or Radio Days

Cochrane pictured with Dennis Eckersley and Warren Spahn on the mound? In a special 1992 issue of *Sports Illustrated* magazine, this drawing was part of an illustration depicting a baseball dream team, with Cochrane as the catcher, Eckersley as the relief pitcher, and Spahn as the top left-handed pitcher.

Many *Sports Illustrated* readers undoubtedly said with a quizzical look, "Mickey who?" when viewing that picture. The legendary qualities of Cochrane have endured into the 1990s only among the most die-hard baseball fans.

When the A's departed Philadelphia for Kansas City after the 1954 season, they became frozen in time. "The passage of time, with its insidious process of selection, has cast them [Simmons, Cochrane, Foxx] in a dimming haze, at least in comparison with their contemporaries Ruth, Gehrig and Hornsby," Donald Honig has written. "Because of the paucity of multitalented catchers, Cochrane retains a certain luster.... Lefty Grove alone maintains a unique and solitary grandeur among the crème de la crème of baseball hierarchy."

No one talks about breaking a certain 1930 Athletics record or exceeding some Athletics standard set by Foxx, as happens with Yankee or Red Sox history. It's as if the A's of Philadelphia have no history. There is no easy way to perpetuate A's lore if there is no current team to use as a platform. It seems as if the Oakland Athletics just dropped onto the planet in 1968. A *Sports Illustrated* retrospective on the 1929 A's recounts:

> The A's were victims of the Yankee mystique. Perhaps the 1927 Yankees were the greatest team of all time. But if there was a close second, perhaps an equal, it was those A's. They are the most over-looked team in baseball.
>
> The A's of 1929 to 1931 left a generation of Philadelphians with memories of what it was like to have a team that ate the great Yankees for dinner. Of course New York won the battle for urban supremacy. The A's were Philadelphia's last illusion of ascendancy. The poignant aftermath to all this was that the Yankees led the lobby that drove the A's out of Philadelphia and into Kansas City for the 1955 season. Like conquered slaves the

Kansas City A's became a sort of farm team for the Yankees and helped feed New York players such as Roger Maris.

Although Mickey did play four years with the Tigers, who were pennant winners in two of those years, Cochrane's reputation has to survive to a large extent on his accomplishments with the A's over 60 years ago.

Whether Cochrane is the greatest catcher in the history of baseball is of course subject to intense debate. There is no definitive way to compare players of different generations, especially under different playing conditions. For instance, Cochrane never played a night game, and he played only on grass and only against members of the Caucasian race.

There is no question that Cochrane is one of the game's best catchers, but the likes of Bill Dickey, Yogi Berra, or Roy Campanella many times take honors in all-time or dream-team selections today.

The 1992 *Sports Illustrated* dream team is just one of a vast number of all-time, all-star teams created by an equally vast number of so-called experts. Cochrane has been named to numerous such squads and has been selected by many pundits as the top catcher of all time.

As early as 1930, famed sportswriter Grantland Rice was touting Cochrane as "a young fellow who may finish his career as the greatest catcher that ever lived." At the time, Rice was comparing Cochrane to nineteenth-century catchers Buck Ewing and King Kelly, as well as Roger Bresnahan, Ray Schalk, and Johnny Kling.

In 1952 the Baseball Writers of America selected Cochrane as a catcher on their Team of the Half Century. Contrary to his monument on the Bridgewater town common, it wasn't an exclusive selection as the greatest catcher. Dickey was also chosen to the 17-man team.

A national fan poll conducted in 1969 as part of baseball's celebration of its first 100 years of professional play selected Cochrane as its all-time catcher, providing at least a glimpse of how the average fan viewed Cochrane's exploits in light of the old-time catchers that Rice had as a standard, Cochrane's contemporary Dickey, and the more modern catchers such as Berra and Campanella. The 1969 Centennial All-Star Team was honored at a banquet at the Sheraton Park Hotel in Washington and a reception at the White House prior to the All-Star Game that year.

"That reception, where I met President Nixon, was my fondest memory," said Mary Cochrane, recalling her husband's baseball career. A picture of her accepting the award on behalf of her then-late husband graced the wall of her home in the early 1990s.

Cochrane is without a doubt one of the 13 best catchers in the history of the game, as only 13 catchers are enshrined in the Hall of Fame in Cooperstown.

Comparison with 3 of the 13 is very difficult: Josh Gibson played in the Negro Leagues, and Ewing and Kelly played in the nineteenth century, when

Baseball fields renamed in Cochrane's hometown in 1997 (author's collection).

the game was very different from the twentieth-century version. (Kelly actually played more games as an outfielder than as a catcher and is often listed among Hall of Fame outfielders.) Four others were not elected to the Hall but were selected by veteran committees — Bresnahan, Schalk, Rick Ferrell, and Ernie Lombardi — putting these catchers a slight notch below those honored by election.

Any discussion of who was the greatest catcher seemingly boils down to the six receivers who have been elected to the Hall of Fame. By this standard, Cochrane is one of the top six catchers in the game, along with Dickey, Berra, Campanella, Gabby Hartnett, and Johnny Bench.

While it cannot be conclusively proven that Cochrane is baseball's best all-time catcher among these six great catchers, the arguments for why Mickey Cochrane, rather than one of the other five Hall of Fame electees, is the greatest catcher can be fashioned two ways: quantitatively and qualitatively.

Cochrane was a complete ballplayer. As Connie Mack wrote in 1950: "The baseball world will probably never see a greater catcher than Mickey Cochrane. A great hitter, fast on the bases, a throwing arm like a bolt of lightning, and a true American sportsman."

Not only did Mickey have the attributes expected of a great catcher — mastery of calling pitches, good arm, defensive capabilities — he also had the attributes expected of any great ballplayer. He could hit for average, had above-average speed on the base paths, and when needed, could hit for power.

Hitting for power — home runs — is the category in which Cochrane falls up short against the likes of Berra, Campanella, Bench, and even Dickey. Mickey hit just 119 homers in his major league career, while the aforementioned catchers all hit over 200 career roundtrippers. (Berra had the most at 358.)

Cochrane didn't need to hit home runs in his days with Connie Mack, who had Foxx and Simmons for that job. When the A's faltered in 1932, though, Cochrane stepped up to hit 23 homers.

Lost in the discussion of power-hitting among catchers is the fact that among Hall of Fame catchers who played in the twentieth century, Cochrane leads in career triples with 64. Triples combine the skills of both power and speed and are perhaps more indicative of greatness among catchers.

While Cochrane didn't hit home runs in excess, his ability to launch doubles and triples does land him in the game's top 100 in slugging percentage. He ranks in position number 96 with a .478 slugging average, according to the 1995 edition of *Total Baseball* (the source for all statistics noted in this chapter). Despite Berra's homers, his career slugging average is only four points higher than Cochrane's at .482, with Hartnett and Dickey only slightly higher at .489 and .486 respectively.

Cochrane did achieve superiority among catchers with his .320 lifetime batting average over his 13-season career, the highest among all catchers in the history of the game and 47th highest among all players.

22. Greatest Receiver, TV or Radio Days

Memorial to Cochrane in his hometown, dedicated April 1997 (author's collection).

Mickey topped his closest competition, Dickey's .313 average, by 7 points. The only other catchers to hit over .300 lifetime were Lombardi at .306 and Spud Davis, a 16-year National League veteran and contemporary of Cochrane who played from 1928 to 1945. (Davis was backup to Cardinal rookie Bill DeLancey in the 1934 World Series against Cochrane's Tigers.)

Batting average as a measure of greatness does have its detractors. Thorn and Palmer in *The Hidden Game of Baseball* call it "that venerable, uncannily durable fraud, the batting average. A two-out bunt single in the 9th with no one on base and your team trailing by six runs counts the same as Bobby Thompson's 'shot heard round the world.'" Its most glaring weakness is that it does not indicate value to the team. The latter type of approach makes Cochrane stand out even further upon more in-depth analysis.

Cochrane also leads catchers in lifetime on-base percentage with his .419 average, taking into account Mickey's patience in waiting out pitchers as translated into his 857 career walks. Cochrane has the 17th highest on-base average among all players, combining his 47th highest batting average with the added distinction of having the 49th highest walk percentage, once every 14.22 plate appearances. (Incidentally, Mickey also has the 31st best ratio at not striking out, as he struck out only once every 23.8 plate appearances, or less than once a week.) No other Hall of Fame catcher is even close.

While statistical measures like batting, slugging, and on-base percentages are helpful in showing that Cochrane excelled among catchers, a more complex statistic known as "runs created" furthers the traditional measures to get closer to what baseball is all about — team wins and losses, not individual statistics.

The concept of runs created is that wins and losses are proportional in some way to runs scored and runs allowed and that runs in turn are proportional to the events that go into their making. Historical research has shown that the number of runs required to turn a loss into a win in the final standings is around 10.

Through the complex formulation of Bill James that uses a variety of batting and baserunning events, Cochrane is credited with 1079 runs created in his career. Dividing this total by the 1482 games Mickey played in his career and then seasonally adjusting this by multiplying by 150 as a proxy for a complete season yields an average of 109.2 runs created by Cochrane per season. This is the highest among Hall of Fame catchers, excluding Ewing and Kelly, for whom not all input data was available for comparability. Dickey was 9 runs per season behind Cochrane with his 100.1 average.

An extension of runs created is provided by the Total Player Rating statistic, which uses a linear weights system that "takes every offensive event and treats it in terms of its impact upon the team."

Computer analysis of game results was used to determine appropriate run values for each variable in the formula. For instance, they found that a single created .46 runs on average, while a home run created not four times the singles value but rather 1.40 runs. "The linear progression, the sum, of the various offensive results (batting, fielding, and base running) when weighted by their accurately predicted run values, will total the runs contributed by that batter beyond the league average."

In this light Cochrane at a 3.18 Total Player Rating of that many team victories per 150-game season is second to only Ewing at 3.25, while Hartnett at 3.02 and Dickey at 2.97 are runners-up. Cochrane's Total Player Rating is 40th highest among all players, with Babe Ruth on top at 6.45.

The minibiography of Cochrane in *Total Baseball* (1991 edition) written by John Holway and Bob Carroll notes that in arguments over who was the greatest catcher, "when Mickey gets the edge, it's usually on 'leadership,' which is measured as easily as the distance to Oz."

Indeed, words speak louder than statistics on the leadership front. "Grove and Foxx were glamour boys, but Cochrane held it together with his leadership. They took orders from Mack but their inspiration came from the man behind the plate," one writer put it. "With Cochrane on the ball club, nobody ever took it easy. Nobody dared. Mickey wouldn't stand for it."

"He showed us how to get a man on first, move him over to third and then get him in. We needed somebody to take charge and show us how to win and that's what Mickey did," Hank Greenberg said. "He was an inspirational leader. He'd been on three pennant winners and winning was a way of life with him, a winning spirit that was really infectious. He was the greatest fighting spirit on the ball field, he'd go through a brick wall to catch a ball."

"Cochrane was a great inspirational leader," Charlie Gehringer remembered. "Boy, he was a hard loser, the hardest loser I think I ever saw. He wouldn't stand for any tomfoolery. He wanted everybody to put out as hard as they could and he set the example himself. Always hustling, always battling. Cochrane was in charge out there."

Cochrane's 1928 and 1934 Most Valuable Player Awards are a testament to his leadership. Both years his playing statistics didn't propel him to the MVP Award, as Cochrane wasn't ranked high in any category either year (unless you count his .428 on base percentage in 1934, which was fourth best in the league).

Cochrane's winning spirit and leadership in those two seasons led to his MVP Awards. In 1928 the A's made a late charge at the Yankees for the pennant and fell just short, 2 1 games out despite 98 victories. Mickey's .293 average, 10 homers, and 57 RBI's were not indicative of his contribution to the A's effort.

Similarly, in 1934 player-manager Cochrane led the Tigers to an American League pennant, personally leading the charge to victory, Detroit's first championship in 25 years. To Great Depression-weary inhabitants of Detroit, Cochrane was almost a god.

Cochrane helped Lefty Grove and Schoolboy Rowe tie the American League record for consecutive pitching victories in 1931 and 1934 respectively.

Mickey was the catcher calling the pitches for Grove and Rowe to achieve that success of 16 straight wins on the mound. Characteristically, Mike downplayed his role in these two streaks. "By a freakish coincidence I caught most of the games which both of them pitched to tie the American League record of consecutive victories," he once wrote.

Of course, both pitchers needed to possess the pitching skill to throw the pitches Cochrane called for, but Mickey's ability to know his pitchers and to recognize the most appropriate pitch to throw and the place to spot that throw in the crucial situations was critical to Grove's and Rowe's achievements.

"Greatest catcher of them all, Cochrane was," Grove has said. "Hardly ever shook him off. If Mickey was living today, he'd tell you I only shook him off about five or six times all the years he caught me. Funny, before I'd even look at him, I had in my mind what I was going to pitch and I'd look up and there'd be Mickey's signal, just what I was thinking. Like he was reading my mind. That's the kind of catcher he was."

Assisting Rowe was Cochrane's insatiable desire to win, as Rowe once related:

> Cochrane gave me the knockdown signal, as one of the Cleveland players was killing Detroit with his bat. I shook him off. Cochrane gave it again and I shook him off again. So he comes to the mound and says "Whatsa matter?" I told him I can't throw at this guy, he's a good friend. Cochrane snooted and said "Schoolie, my boy, I don't care if this guy is your twin brother. If he doesn't go down on the next pitch and bounce when he hits the ground, you're fined $250." Need I say more?

Leadership was perhaps best exhibited by where Cochrane considered himself among the all-time catchers. A handwritten note by Mike in a file at the National Baseball Library shows that on the Cochrane-picked all-time team, Hartnett and Dickey are Mike's choice for the catcher position.

It's not tough to catch Mike's drift on that choice. The team always came before himself in whatever Gordon Stanley Cochrane was involved with.

All in all, he was baseball's greatest catcher.

Notes

Interviews

Mary Cochrane, Scottsdale, Arizona, 24 April 1991.
Jack Thompson, Canton, Massachusetts, 1 October 1992.
Sara Cochrane Bollman, Scottsdale, Arizona, 2 March 1996
(including letter from Auker, 9 September 1995).

Abbreviations Used

Newspapers

Boston Globe	BG	*New York Times*	NYT
Boston Herald	BH	*Philadelphia Bulletin*	PHB
Boston Post	BP	*Philadelphia Inquirer*	PHI
Brockton (Mass.) *Enterprise*	BE	Philadelphia *Public Ledger*	PL
Detroit Free Press	DFP	Portland *Oregonian*	OR
Detroit News	DN	*Providence* (RI) *Journal*	PRJ
Fort Myers (Florida) *News-Press*	FMNP	*The Sporting News*	TSN
New York Herald Tribune	NYHT		

Clipping Files

National Baseball Hall of Fame Library, Cooperstown, New York	NBL
Urban Archives, Temple University, Philadelphia	UA

Chapter 1

Page

5   Ten more pitches. DFP, 8 October 1935. Accounts vary as to which of the ten pitches was not a strike. The DFP version of events was selected over New York newspaper accounts as the most credible of contemporary versions because of the local angle. The DFP writers had more incentive for accuracy at this level of detail because it had more meaning to its readers.

6   "There was only one thing." Cochrane, *Baseball*, p. 128.

Notes—Chapter 2

Page

6   "When I think back." Honig, *Baseball When the Grass Was Real*, p. 144.

8   "Yea, Goose." NYHT, 8 October 1935.
"World Series money tickled Cochrane's feet." NYHT, 8 October 1935.
"Damn, that was so frustrating ." Honig, *Baseball When the Grass Was Real*, p. 144.

8–9   "It was something to see." DFP, 8 October 1935.

9   Cochrane is one of those three. Author's analysis of World Series eligibles in World Series records. The other two were Tiger teammate Goose Goslin and Baltimore Oriole pitcher Jim Palmer, who played in six Series from 1966 to 1983.

Chapter 2

Page

10   "Mickey Cochrane, ace pilot." BE, "Tribute to Mickey."

11   "Automobile horns." Dudgeon, "Bridgewater Citizens."
The hero ... was born. Massachusetts Registry of Vital Records. Most other genealogical information on the family comes from either the Registry or the Massachusetts Archives, Birth, Marriage & Death Records.

11–12   John Cochrane was born. State of Montana Certificate of Death 67–1493 and Federal Archives naturalization record dated 19 October 1892.

12   "This Scottish surname." Brian de Breffny, *Irish Family Names* (New York: W. W. Norton, 1983).
The Cochranes were ... from County Tyronne. Massachusetts Registry, Certificate of Death of James Cochrane, 1920-27-377.
"Grampa had this mix." Sara Bollman interview.
John Cochrane came to the United States in 1888. 1920 U.S. Census, reel 95–27, sheet 8.
John ... became a naturalized citizen. Federal Archives naturalization record dated 19 October 1892.
father bought a 16-acre farm. Registry of Deeds, Plymouth County Massachusetts, book 1003 page 431.

13   "I'd get to that wall." Dooly, "How Cochrane Became."
"That stretch of road." Ibid.
"Mike used to borrow our hunting dogs." Mary Cochrane interview.
"The Kid's love." *Standard-Times*, "Conquering Hero."
"A lot of kids." Graham, "Cochrane Story."

14   Flora Stuart ... foresaw that as well. Dudgeon, "Bridgewater Citizens."
Mike remembered his transition ... into pro baseball. NBL clipping, 15 June 1933.
"Cochrane's Folks in Bridgewater." BG, 28 December 1924.
"Thoughts wandered." BE, "Tribute to Mickey."
"I suppose we'll have to take the kid." Cochrane, *Baseball*, prologue.
"Put the kid in!" BE, 29 June 1962.
"I had experienced." Cochrane, *Baseball*, p. 1.

15   "the High School team." BE, 19 May 1917.
"Cochrane tried his hand." BE, 25 May 1918.

15–16   "Cochrane went to the box." BE, 25 May 1919.

16	"While Cochrane was hit hard." BE, 15 June 1919.
	"Cochrane at quarterback." BE, 29 November 1918.
17	"From the first kickoff." BE, 9 October 1919.
	"Cochrane, the clever high school player." BE, 14 February 1920.
	"At first he wanted to do all the scoring." BE, "Tribute to Mickey."
	"The Bridgewater Club." *Standard-Times*, "Conquering Hero."
	"We used to go to Hayes." Mary Cochrane interview.
18	"One thing at Charlie's store." *Standard-Times*, "Conquering Hero."
	"Charlie Hayes, former confectioner." Ibid.
	"Mike wanted to play." Mary Cochrane interview.
	"With two strikes." BE, 16 August 1920.
19	Stanley Iron Works. Brundidge, "Backstop Job."

Chapter 3

Page

20	"My parents liked Mike." Mary Cochrane interview.
21	"The team had a coach." Newcombe, "Black Mike."
	"Wendell used the Harvard system." Dooly, "How Cochrane Became."
	"Whalen shifted me." Ibid.
	"the punting of Cochrane." BH, 16 October 1921.
	pictured ... in a Boston newspaper. BH, 6 November 1921.
22	transferred to Georgetown University. BE, 23 January 1922.
	"They never played him where he'd stand out." Mary Cochrane interview.
	"Cochrane, protected." BH, 8 October 1922.
	"Cochrane Returns." BH, 22 October 1922.
24	"Cochrane was all over the field." BH, 5 November 1922.
	"He did all the work." Newcombe, "Black Mike."
	"I worked until four." NBL clipping, 15 June 1933.
	numerous long runs by the Kid. PRJ, 21 October 1923.
	"He is a normal young man." PHB, 19 December 1924.
25	"most versatile athlete." BE, "Tribute to Mickey."
	"I know that Cochrane is a great baseball player." Dudgeon, "Bridgewater Citizens."
	Original Celtics game: BE, 30 March 1921.
	"Cochrane heard about the vacancy." PHB, 19 December 1924.
	"We were fighting." Newcombe, "Black Mike."
	"If Mickey had ever landed." NBL clipping, 27 May 1937.
25–26	"on the steel runners." PHB, 19 December 1924.
26	Burrill ... fell through the thin ice. BE, 29 January 1923.
	"See those lucky stiffs." NBL clipping, 27 October 1928.
	"the lure of security." Cochrane, *Baseball*, p. 1.
	"They couldn't decide." Ibid.
27	"Cochrane was nipped." BH, 23 April 1922.
	"The catcher got hurt." Kieran, "Iron Mask."
	Cochrane was the catcher. BH, 23 May 1923.
28	playing minor league baseball. NBL box score of 26 May 1923, Dover game vs. Milford.

Chapter 4

Page

29 Cochrane was almost always silent. Brundidge, "Backstop Job."
"Hall of Famers." James H. Ellis, "Cape Cod League a Talent Showcase," *Baseball Research Journal*, 1986.
There was not a Cochrane. Ibid.

30 "Cochrane once played for Dirty Dan." Author's interview with Tony Lupien, former major league player, in Norwich, Vermont, 9 November 1991.
"a coach's dream." BE, "Tribute to Mickey."
"There's no truth." Mary Cochrane interview.
"I don't want to catch." Dooly, "How Cochrane Became."
"I didn't want to be a catcher." Kieran, "Iron Mask."
"It was the one position." Brundidge, "Backstop Job."

31 "My mother thought it was odd." Mary Cochrane interview.
"I was fast." Cochrane, *Baseball*, p. 2.
"I was terrible." Dooly, "How Cochrane Became."
Donohue played in the majors. Kieran, "Iron Mask."
"In payment for warming him up." Cochrane, *Baseball*, p. 3.
"Knight has always claimed." Dooly, "How Cochrane Became."

32 The Dover Dobbins won. TSN, 20 September 1923.
Coming into the final weekend. Brundidge, "Backstop Job."
"We're about to start." Ibid.
"The series was marred." TSN, 13 September 1923.
"The ump called me out." NBL clipping, 15 June 1933.

32–33 "It was one of the darkest chapters." NBL clipping, undated.

33 "Portland Baseball Club signs catcher Gordon Cochrane." Original copy of contract in Cochrane's early scrapbook, reviewed during Mary Cochrane interview.
"I couldn't turn it down." Newcombe, "Black Mike."
"Mike never got his degree." Mary Cochrane interview.
"Do you want to be a good ballplayer?" Lane, "All the World."
"Tell you what." Cochrane, *Baseball*, p. 6.

34 implied "for two" aspect. Ibid, p 7.
"We couldn't get married in Massachusetts." Mary Cochrane interview.
"Mickey Cochrane led the onslaught." OR, 2 April 1924.
"Manager Kenworthy is working Mickey." TSN, 12 June 1924.

35 "has given ample demonstration." TSN, 7 August 1924.
"taught the youngster." BG, 28 December 1924.
"I was on my way out." BE, "Tribute to Mickey."
"They had silver showers." NBL clipping, 15 June 1933.
"in the fifth inning Cochrane doubled." OR, 18 August 1924.

36 "When I found out." Dooly, "How Cochrane Became."

37 "I got Mickey Cochrane." Mack, *My 66 Years*.
"Worth it!" *Cross and Crescent*, "Black Mike."
"While Mack has every confidence." TSN, 19 February 1925.

Chapter 5

Page

38   "Headlines like 'Mack Keen About Kid Catchers.'" TSN, 5 March 1925.
"Fox [sic] and Cochrane." FMNP, 27 March 1925.
The cocky Cochrane demanded. TSN, 19 & 26 February 1925.
"I understand Connie." UA clipping, 20 February 1925.
"Cochrane propelled Stokes' first pitch." PHB, 24 February 1925.

39   "I liked him on the train." PL, 8 June 1937.
"I couldn't convince Mack." Graham, "Cochrane Story."
"One morning I found him." PL, 8 June 1937.
"When I first saw him." Broeg, "Full of Fight."
Cochrane always told the story. Cochrane, *Baseball*, p. 12.
Mack sent Cochrane up. BH, 15 April 1925.

39–40   "It hurt me to hear." Graham, "Cochrane Story."

40   Foxx remembered. UA clipping, 1935.

41   rookie Tom Glass. Charlie Bevis, "Major League Short Stories," *Baseball Quarterly Reviews*, Fall 1987.
apartment at 2736 North 22nd Street. Mary Cochrane interview.
Al Simmons, like many. Kuklick, *Shibe Park*.
"Now a catcher." Harron, "What Home Town Thinks."

42   SABR poll. Lyle Spatz, "SABR Picks 1900–1948 Rookies of the Year," *Baseball Research Journal*, 1986.
As Grantland Rice wrote. *Collier's*, 10 October 1925.

Chapter 6

Page

43   Cochrane had kept in physical shape. NBL clipping of BG, 1925.
"a six hour drive." FMNP, 16 March 1925.

45   "With Cochrane hurt." TSN, 29 July 1926.
"It's no wonder." Broeg, "Full of Fight."

46   "The way it worked out." Cochrane, *Baseball*, p. 11.
"I taught him." Povich, "Perkins Votes."
"Mastering it protected my fingers." Cochrane, *Baseball*, p. 12
"One of the New York papers." Curran, *Mitts*.
"My uncle gave it to me." Cataneo, *Peanuts and Crackerjack*.
"Grove had speed." Graham, "Cochrane Story."
"Rommel had a knuckler." Ibid.

47   "When those zeros change." Newcombe, "Black Mike."
"What would be tough." Kieran, "Iron Mask."
"I used to call all the pitches." Mack, *My 66 Years*.
"Ty Cobb was endowed by nature." Lane, "King of Catchers."
"Cobb was like a father." Mary Cochrane interview.
"He was a little crusty." Lane, "All the World."

47–48   "some like Mickey Cochrane worshipped him." McCallum, *The Tiger Wore Spikes*, p. 205.

48   Mike was one of but three. Alexander, *Ty Cobb*, p. 235.

Page

48   "As a rival." Ty Cobb, "The Boss Tiger," NBL clipping [1936].
      "Cobb was probably the first." Gallico, *Golden People*.
      A Cobb biographer wrote. McCallum, *The Tiger Wore Spikes*, p. 103.
      Cobb also picked up patterns. Ibid.
49   Mike would move his family. Mary Cochrane interview.
      "Crowder had apparently been concentrating." TSN, 28 April 1927.
      "Simmons, Lamar, Hale." TSN, 5 May 1927.
      "Were the Athletics not provided with two top rank catchers." TSN, 16 June 1927.
      using a two-week streak. Author's analysis of NBL day-by-day records of Cochrane.
50   "Get out in front." Cochrane, *Baseball*, p. 90.
      "proceeded to win three pennants." Wilfred Sheed, "Mr. Mack and the Main Chance," *Ultimate Baseball Book* (Boston: Houghton Mifflin, 1984),
      "the best team." NBL, letter from Cochrane to Bob Quinn dated 31 May 1949.

Chapter 7

Page

51   Mike tried to capitalize. UA clipping, 13 November 1927.
      "Cochrane and Foxx are catching." TSN, 5 July 1928.
52   "You yellow-bellied bastards." Broeg, "Full of Fight."
      "There's only one thing." UA clipping, 14 July 1928.
      "with a football tackle." TSN, 6 September 1928.
53   "Yankee-Athletic Ticket Rush." NYT, 7 September 1928.
      "Yes, those Yanks sure did make life miserable." Doerer, "Predicts."
      "We broke their hearts." NYT, 10 September 1928.
54   Cochrane stormed out to the mound. *Cross and Crescent*, "Black Mike."
55   "The direct parental approach." Ibid.
      "inspired great performances." Broeg, "Full of Fight."
      "Sometimes I was a lot madder." NBL clipping, 20 January 1973.
      Soon after the 1928 World Series. BG, 16 October 1928.
56   "I never experienced such a thrill." BG, 1 November 1928.
      The moose meat. BE, 6 November 1928.
57   "It was a great surprise." BG, 2 November 1928.
      "Cochrane was ranked." NYT, October 1928.
      "Cochrane deserves all the honors." BE, 2 November 1928.
      "I feel like a fool." Duncan, "Always a Fighter."
      The broken sax. Ibid.
58   "I have two ambitions." Ibid.
      Mike also wrote a few of his own songs. NBL clipping, undated.

Chapter 8

Page

59   "Those Yanks are going to hit the slide." Doerer, "Predicts."
      "Catching is my business." UA clipping, 7 February 1929.
60   There was some disruption. UA clipping, 27 April 1929.
      "Things never looked better." UA clipping, 20 May 1929.

61	"Facing Cochrane was tough enough." NYT, 22 August 1949.
	"Cochrane looked a little tired." PHB, 5 July 1929.
	"The A's today." PHI, 6 July 1929.
62	"Great stuff, music." PHB, 9 July 1929.
	"These numbers are red hot." Ibid.
	"This is a great place." PHB, 11 July 1929.
	"I won't play until Thursday." PHI, 14 July 1929.
	"birched a solid single." PHI, 15 July 1929.
63	"After an absence." PHI, 15 September 1929.
	"Cochrane was visibly affected." BE, 27 September 1929.
	"All I can say." UA clipping, 28 September 1929.
	"Cochrane is one of the many Mackmen." NBL clipping from PL, 1929.
	"Stock speculation provided a legal spirit." McElvaine, *The Great Depression*.
64	Cochrane was one of the first in line. NYT, 1 October 1929.
	"Is he going to pitch?" Cochrane, *Baseball*, p. 100.
64–65	"the sagacious Connie." NYT, 8 October 1929.
65	"I'll strike this guy out." PL, 9 October 1929.
	"It was an easy game for me." Ibid.
66	"I remember meeting Mickey." NBL clipping, undated.
	"Hurry up, sweetheart." Cochrane, *Baseball*, p. 159.
67	"I'm going to put some of it away." PHB, 15 October 1929.
	"the speculative boom." McElvaine, *The Great Depression*.

Chapter 9

Page

68	"For American fans." Voigt, *American Baseball*.
	"I didn't notice." Mary Cochrane interview.
	house at 723 Kenmare Road. Ibid.
	moose over fireplace. UA clipping, 1930.
	"I like to cook." Ibid.
	"I don't go to baseball games." Ibid.
69	"Mike didn't want me." Mary Cochrane interview.
70	"As far as friendship." Duncan, "Always a Fighter."
	To help out. Povich, "Perkins Votes"; Smith, *Babe Ruth's America*.
	"Mickey the Mauler." Duncan, "Always a Fighter."
	"Just forget it." Ibid.
	"I'll stick to catching." UA clipping, 19 December 1929.
	"I'm ready to catch anytime." TSN, 30 January 1930.
71	"It was nobody's fault." PL, 20 May 1930.
	Mickey batted at a .457 clip. Author's analysis of NBL day-by-day records.
	"If he could own a plane." UA clipping, 1930.
	"Gee, what a funny sensation." PHI, 1 July 1930.
73	"Confidence is a favorite theme." Lane, "All the World."
	"Expect every pitch to be a wild pitch." Cochrane, *Baseball*, p. 41.
	"If a catcher wants to squat." Lane, "All the World."
	"A catcher who is on to his job." Cochrane, "Catcher's Mask."
	"The greatest catcher that ever lived." Lane, "King of Catchers."
74	"Cochrane is the most important man." Ibid.

Page

74   "his position seemed." Jones, *Golf Is My Game.*
        "I just told him." NYHT, 2 October 1930.
75   "Cochrane collected revenge." NYT, 2 October 1930.
        Grimes egged on Cochrane. NYHT, 3 October 1930.
        "The sensation evidently pleased him." NYT, 3 October 1930.
        "That ought to teach the Cardinals." NYHT, 3 October 1930.
        "And so it went." NYT, 3 October 1930.
        "What with one witty saying." BE, 7 October 1930.
        "After casting one more disdainful look." NYT, 7 October 1930.
76–77   "The Cardinal taunts and their wisecracks." UA clipping, 16 October 1930.

Chapter 10

Page

78   Mack signed Mike. Lieb, *Connie Mack*, p. 239.
        Mike also took to the basketball courts. UA clipping, 16 January 1931.
        "Baseball's costliest suit of clothes." TSN, 15 January 1931.
        "There haven't been too many changes." Letter from Bob Leibfried to author dated 3 December 1993.
        "She's a good golf type." PHB, 2 April 1931.
79   for a .458 average over the period. Author's analysis of NBL day-by-day records.
81   "You have Grove pitching." Honig, *Baseball When the Grass Was Real*, p. 201.
        "After that game." Ibid, p. 73.
        "No one said a word." Ibid, p. 203.
        "Lefty was really a good-natured fellow." Cochrane, *Baseball*, p. 60.
        "Mike dropped like a sack of cement." PHB, 17 August 1931.
82   "I don't see how." UA clipping, 23 September 1931.
        His own bat model. Letter from Hillerich and Bradsby to author dated 26 September 1996.
        "Before I was even born." Mantle, *The Mick.*
        Mickey Cochran. *Yankee*, September 1995, p. 44.
        William "Mickey" Corcoran. BG, 12 January 1997, p. D8.
        Cornelius "Mickey" Cochrane. Letter to author dated 31 January 1997.

Chapter 11

Page

84   "For the most part." NYT, 2 October 1931.
        "after one of his singles." Smith, "Pepper Martin."
85   "Hafey stole third base." NYT, 2 October 1931.
        "It was Martin who stole third base." NYT, 3 October 1931.
        "Earnshaw may have allowed." Ibid.
        "Cochrane's throw to Williams." Ibid.
        "Folks, we've tried." PHB, 3 October 1931.
        "To be fair to Cochrane." NYT, 5 October 1931.

86	"We gotta win." PHB, 5 October 1931.
	"It may be that at last." PHB, 6 October 1931.
	"On the next pitch." NYT, 7 October 1931.
	"duplicated Frisch's steal." Ibid.
	"Six stolen bases charged." Ibid.
	"Please don't overlook the manner." Ibid.
87	"Cochrane is ill." NYT, 9 October 1931.
	"couldn't find this youngster's weakness." PHB, 8 October 1931.
	"heavily involved in stock." Lieb, "Fireball Cochrane."
88	"At midnight." PL, 6 October 1931.
	"It is understood." TSN, 29 October 1931.
	"These are smart ball players." TSN, 13 August 1931.
	"Mickey is sick at heart." PHI, 8 October 1931.
89	"Grove was so fast." NYT, 10 October 1931.
	Cochrane missed Earnshaw's ... spit into the dirt. Smith, *Babe Ruth's America*.
	"the ball scudding." NYT, 11 October 1931.
90	"Mickey failed in the series." PL, 12 October 1931.
	"I do not see why." PHB, 12 October 1931.
	"A report eddies through the air." PHI, 17 October 1931.
	"Good Night Sweetheart." Graham, "Cochrane Story."
	"I couldn't have shot him." Ibid.
91	"Oh, everybody knows." TSN, 5 October 1944.
	"Pepper was stealing." Honig, *October Heroes*, p. 195.
	"Some of the pitchers felt he wasn't supporting them." Lieb, *Connie Mack*, p. 244.
	"My three championship teams." UA clipping, 27 May 1937.
96	"The fans don't know it was the pitchers." Cochrane, *Baseball*,

Chapter 12

Page

92	"great American team of 1931." Lieb, *Baseball*, p. 201.
93	"What a ride it was!" Frisch, *Fordham Flash*,
	"Hey, Mickey, why didn't you throw out Pepper Martin?" TSN, 12 November 1931.
	"Cochrane is a baseball hustler." TSN, 19 November 1931.
	"Should the major leaguers assembled." Ibid.
94	Cochrane's wry sense of humor. Ibid.
94–95	"Everywhere we were lavishly entertained." FMNP, 10 March 1932.
95	"The Japs can field." UA clipping, 19 April 1932.
	"The fun was how the Japanese handled the situation." Lieb, *Baseball*, pp. 206–7.
96	"The people don't want war." UA clipping, 5 January 1932.

Chapter 13

Page

97	"Trip to Japan Restores Old Zip." TSN, 14 January 1932.
	"After spending the Christmas holidays with his folks." Ibid.
	"The catching mainstay." FMNP, 3 March 1932.

Notes—Chapter 14

Page

97 "Cochrane sprained his left wrist." FMNP, 8 March 1932.
"The foot injury." FMNP, 25 March 1932.
98 "It takes Chapman." UA clipping, 22 April 1932.
Prices on the New York. Klingman, *1929*,
There were 2294 bank failures. Galbraith, *Money*.
99 "Cochrane was one of the first." PL, 7 June 1932.
"Cochrane remained at his post." PHB, 7 June 1932.
"Cochrane is in the worst batting slump." PHB, 10 July 1932.
100 "We were getting nowhere." PHI, 6 August 1932.
101 "With a heavy investment." Mack, *My 66 Years*.
"Having gone through the heartache." Lieb, *Connie Mack*.
"During the four years." Mack, *My 66 Years*.
"In the early 30s." Ibid.
"Rumor was Mack." Sheed, "Mr. Mack."
"Mack believed that .600 baseball was more popular." Kuklick, *Shibe Park*.
102 "temperamental, insolent, pugnacious on the diamond." TSN, 11 August 1932.
Mills Brothers. Newcombe, "Black Mike."
"Miller, who spoke highly of Cochrane's days." BE, "Tribute to Mickey."
"It wasn't daylight." PHB, 29 June 1962.
college football. TSN, 15 January 1931.
"He was very quiet." Mary Cochrane interview.
"We'd go out together." Bak, *Cobb*.
"Farrell and Will Rogers." UA clipping, 1 November 1932.
"I didn't like it." Ibid.

Chapter 14

Page

103 "Whitney, nailed at the plate." PHI, 2 April 1933.
"You didn't have to make a perfect throw." Honig, *Baseball When the Grass Was Real*, p. 201.
104 "It was eerie." Lacey, *Ford*, p. 337.
105 "obtained their physical exertion." FMNP, 1 March 1933.
"Again it looked." FMNP, 10 March 1933.
"Gee, Mike." Shapiro, *The Year They Won the MVP*.
106 "In the summer of '33." Greenberg, *The Celebrant*.
"There was no deviation." TSN, 29 June 1933.
"It's a tragedy that Mickey was slighted." NBL clipping of Bill Dooly, 1933.
107 "which seemed to indicate clearly." NYT, 3 August 1933.
"the mightiest gunners." NYT, 4 August 1933.
108 "Forget it, Frank." PL, 8 June 1937.
"Before he closed the deal." Creamer, *The Babe*.
"Ruth did make several contacts." Lieb, *Tigers*.
108–9 "A newspaperman stepped in." Falls, *Detroit Tigers*, update.
109 "I'd like nothing better." DN, 1 July 1934.
"I saw this was Mickey's chance." PL, 8 June 1937.
"Cochrane Picked Over." UA clipping, 22 December 1933.

109	"I'll be happy." Duncan, "Always a Fighter." "Walberg Saved Cochrane's Life." TSN, 15 December 1933. "All of a sudden." PHB, 29 June 1962.

Chapter 15

Page

110	"I played with the Athletics." TSN, 25 January 1934. "I'm not foolish enough to expect a pennant." TSN, 8 January 1934.
111	"Do you want to be champions?" PHB, 28 September 1934. "When Cochrane joined the Tigers." Bak, *Cobb*. Greenberg said that Sewell. Berkow, *Hank Greenberg*. Sewell said that Greenberg. Honig, *Baseball When the Grass Was Real*, p. 250. "Rip, don't think I feel any less about you." Ibid. "Bucky Harris wouldn't scream at anyone." Bak, *Cobb*.
112	"Nothing doing." Duncan, "Always a Fighter." "I was sick." Povich, "Perkins Votes." Cochrane's face on the cover. *Baseball Magazine*, April 1934. "Every mistake caused Cochrane new agony." Salsinger, "What Price Pennant?" "Cochrane was frantic." Ibid.
113	"You're a better team now." PHB, 28 September 1934. "I don't know what the hell happened." Bak, *Cobb*. "He is strictly unorthodox." DN, 1 July 1934. "Ol' Mick never let you fall asleep." Bak, *Cobb*.
114	"It cost us a ball game." TSN, 12 July 1934. "Cochrane would let you know." Bak, *Cobb*. "My spike caught in the ground." DN, 11 July 1934.
115	this July 13 game. NYT, 14 July 1934. As the second batter. NYHT, 15 July 1934.
116	"I have never believed it effective." Cochrane, *Baseball*, p. 99. "that's about all you can do." Ibid., p. 102.
117	"I've never been able to figure out." NYT, 17 August 1934. "The guy can't say no." Newcombe, "Black Mike." "I've got to win." UA clipping, August 1934.
118	"Streaks put pressure on the pitcher." Cochrane, *Baseball*, p. 130. "Rowe is cold steel." Salsinger, "What Price Pennant?" late September Sunday Rotogravure. DFP, 23 September 1934. "Of course I'm delighted." NYT, 25 September 1934.
119	"Despite the Triple Crown." Robinson, *Iron Horse*.

Chapter 16

Page

120	"That's easy, Rowe." NYT, 21 September 1934. "We'll see about that." Gregory, *Diz*. "The Tigers have been an inspiration." Ibid.

Page

121	"Thank you for these laurel wreaths." Ibid. "Old Master" Ibid. "rolling his eyes." Ibid. "Bring on the Deans." Ibid. "Mickey, the General ain't got nothin." Ibid. "I think he used great judgment." Ibid. "The boys were a little nervous." NYT, 4 October 1934.
122	"They Shall Not Pass" DFP, 5 October 1934. Dean dusted Cochrane. DN, 6 October 1934. "You guys are a great team." Lieb, *Tigers*, p. 208. "Cochrane's tongue-lashing aroused his players." Ibid.
124	"They x-rayed my head." Gregory, *Diz*, "on the theory that Bridges." NYT, 8 October 1934. "Cochrane had a grin." Ibid. "They were a happy pack." Lieb, *Tigers*, p. 210. "What's the matter?" Cochrane, "Fall Guys."
125	"I've been waiting 35 years." Lieb, *Tigers*, p. 43. "Look, I'm not the kind of guy to beef." NYT, 9 October 1934. "Cochrane hobbled into the dressing room." DFP, 9 October 1934. "Our Stricken Leader." Ibid. "Nobody was saying much." Gregory, *Diz*. "At least we'll go down swinging." Ibid. "Well, Mickey, this does it." Ibid.

Chapter 17

Page

127	"I was willing to bet." Newcombe, "Black Mike." "I brought my catcher's mitt." Cataneo, *Peanuts and Crackerjack*.
127–8	"Cochrane won a pennant." DN, 9 September 1935.
129	"Players for the All-Star Game." DN, 8 July 1935. "The Yanks have only beaten him once." NYT, 20 July 1935. "So tumultuous was the acclaim." NYT, 24 July 1935.
129–30	"Cochrane looked as though." Ibid.
130	"The admiration that Detroit showed." Newcombe, "Black Mike." "When I was a player." Ibid. "When Cochrane has lost a fight." Ibid. "Cochrane's arrival in Detroit." *Time*, "Cubs vs. Tigers." Adults across America saw advertisements. BG, 8 October 1935; NYHT, 8 October 1935.
131	A crowd of 100,000 jammed downtown. *Time*, "Cubs vs. Tigers." "We got the hitting." DN, 24 July 1935. "His spirit has done much." BE, "Tribute to Mickey."
131–2	"It's not easy to get up here." Dudgeon, "Bridgewater Citizens."
132	"Number One G-Man." DFP, 12 September 1935. "He was such an inspiration." Sara Bollman interview.
133	"Detroit was badly at rest." NYT, 2 October 1935. "You'll go a long time." NYT, 3 October 1935.

134	"Well, the Tigers finally showed folks." BP, 5 October 1935.
	Christy Walsh's syndicate. Smelser, *The Life That Ruth Built*.
	"How's the arm?" NYT, 6 October 1935.
	"The old general just about pitched us." BP, 6 October 1935.
135	"If everything breaks right." BP, 7 October 1935.
	"Well, I tied into one." Honig, *Baseball When the Grass Was Real*, p. 53.
	"It was one of those instances." Honig, *October Heroes*, p. 222.
	"If they pitch that ball over this plate." Ritter, *Glory*, p. 260.
136	"I'm the happiest guy in the world." NYHT, 8 October 1935.
	"Bridges was wonderful." Ibid.
	"It was a tough game." Ibid.
	"I am not only happy." BP, 8 October 1935.
	"It was the greatest series." BP, 9 October 1935.
	"The city went crazy." Bak, *Cobb*.
	"We have already taken care of the Cubs." DFP, 9 October 1935.

Chapter 18

Page

137	Coming off a second place finish. Gregory, *Diz*,
138	"During the discussion Mickey was very annoyed." Berkow, *Greenberg*.
138–9	"I was disappointed." letter from Hogsett to author, 18 January 1995.
139	"It's easier to catch." TSN, 30 April 1936.
	"I'd rather have tough luck." TSN, 7 May 1936.
	"Well, I had to do something." McCallum, *The Tiger Wore Spikes*, p. 66.
	he left the game and collapsed. TSN, 11 June 1936.
140	"They're counting the Tigers out a bit early." BG, 10 June 1936.
	"I don't know how long." TSN, 25 June 1936.
	"I'm merely filling in." TSN, 16 July 1936.
141	"You'd better get them Browns out." TSN, 1 October 1936.
	Mike bought a farm in Commerce, Michigan. NBL clipping, 15 November 1937.
	The neighbors filed suit against him. UA clipping, 20 October 1936.
	Sweetland wrote Cochrane. TSN, 30 December 1967.
	"A colorful appearance." NYT, 18 February 1937, p. 31.
	"We played golf." Sara Bollman interview.
142	"Just a stopover for Mickey." DFP, 25 May 1937.
	"I saw the ball roll." Falls, *Detroit Tigers*.
	"Mickey's Cochrane's Skull." DFP, 26 May 1937.
	"I was the on-deck hitter." Bak, *Cobb*.
	"Our world came to an end." Sara Bollman interview.
	"After what happened last year." Bak, *Cobb*,
	"I lost sight of the ball." NYT, 26 May 1937.
	"The ball sailed." Ibid.
	Helmets wouldn't be in general use. Thorn and Palmer, *Total Baseball*.
143	"I remember there was a man on first." NYT, 19 July 1937.
	"Frankly I don't know." Ibid.
143–4	"Mickey's injury came at a time." DFP, 26 May 1937.

Chapter 19

Page

146   "I hated to let Walker go." Lieb, *Tigers*, p. 234.
"The day he was hit." Letter from Rogell to author, 12 January 1995.
"a great player in his day." PHB, 8 August 1938.

146–7   "When Mickey was managing." Anthony Connor, *Baseball for the Love of It* (New York: MacMillan, 1982),

147   "When the Tigers were losing." DN, 8 August 1938.
"They'll learn to protect the runner." TSN, 21 July 1938.
"What's the alibi?" Lieb, *Tigers*, p. 234.

148   "Make out a check to Mr. Cochrane." Falls, *Tigers*.
"Mickey Cochrane and I had a conference today." TSN, 11 August 1938.
"Mickey did more for baseball." Newcombe, "Black Mike."
"No, I haven't anything to say." DN, 7 August 1938.
"But not like this one, buddy." Ibid.
"Two strikes meant nothing." DN, 8 August 1938.
Embarrassing that *The Sporting News*. TSN, 28 July 1938.
"Cochrane is out." NYT, 9 August 1938.
"One of the most popular figures." NBL clipping of DFP, August 1938.

149   "You would have thought." Bak, *Cobb*.
"We'll never forget what you did here." Newcombe, "Black Mike."
"Had he come to it at another time." DFP, 29 June 1962.
"He wasn't the same Cochrane." Bak, *Cobb*.

150   "The generous gesture was expensive." Broeg, "Full of Fight."
Cochrane's income. NBL clipping, 7 April 1939.
"I sit around for thirty minutes." PL, 16 November 1938.
"Out of baseball ... he was completely unhappy." Graham, "Cochrane Story."

151   "I got my first airplane ride." Letter from Al Cochrane to author, 8 January 1993.
"He autographed a copy." Ibid.

152   "He was all over his seat." UA clipping, 11 October 1940.

Chapter 20

Page

153   "Cochrane never liked sitting on the sidelines." TSN, 23 April 1942.
"Harry Bennett got Mike in the Navy." Mary Cochrane interview.

154   "Cochrane had a new car." Williams, *My Turn At Bat*, p. 94.
"a touchy subject, this question." Goldstein, *Spartan Seasons*.

155   "He kept up the nice ... chatter." Elliott Baker, "The Road Not Taken," *Gentlemen's Quarterly*, September 1991.

156   "As for the servicemen." TSN, 16 July 1942.

157   "I'd never met Mickey Cochrane." Goldstein, *Spartan Seasons*, p. 227.
"I enlisted." Mead, *Even the Browns*, p. 194.

158   "When we got on the bus." Goldstein, *Spartan Seasons*, p. 233.
"When he was in the Navy." Ibid.

158	"The boy has been in some heavy action." PL, 28 February 1945.
	It wasn't until mid-March. NYT, 20 March 1945.
	"That affected Mike." Bak, *Cobb*.
	"Gordon Jr. played with my son." Ibid.
	"He wasn't a hard driving guy." Ibid.
	"Gordon never should have seen active duty." Sara Bollman interview.
159	"I always thought that Mike suffered ... guilt." Ibid.
	"Many years later." Mary Cochrane interview.
	Gordon Jr. was buried. Bridgewater Cemetery Corp., lot 623.
	Mike's mother, who had died. BE, 16 November 1942.

Chapter 21

Page

160	"It didn't seem important." Mary Cochrane interview.
	"Uncle Mike never got snobbish." Jack Thompson interview.
	"He never really talked about the Hall of Fame." Sara Bollman interview.
	"Daddy never wanted the spotlight." Ibid.
	"Father of Ball Player." BE, 13 March 1967.
162	"I'm not related." Note from Dave Cochrane to author, 21 September 1991.
164	"That was God's country." Sara Bollman interview.
	"either the offbeat spelling." Macht, "Cobb Never."
	"Uncle Mike worked my tail off." Jack Thompson interview.
	"Everyone met around the bar." Sara Bollman interview.
	"Daddy loved to hear the piano." Ibid.
	"Uncle Mike loved to dance." Jack Thompson interview.
	"Daddy was a great dancer." Sara Bollman interview.
165	"Daddy pretty much gave up big game hunting." Ibid.
	"Mike was friendly." Mary Cochrane interview.
166	"Uncle Archie wrote to Daddy." Sara Bollman interview.
	"Mary said she wished." Letter from Roz Cochrane to author, 6 October 1993.
	"Daddy loaned money." Sara Bollman interview.
	After two summers of retreat. UA clipping, 25 July 1948.
	"Ya bum, you never did anything." NYT, 22 August 1949.
166–7	"I'm tickled to be with the A's again." PHB, 1 December 1949.
167	"How stupid can a guy get." NYT, 10 February 1958.
168	"If I had my pick of players." PHB, 9 July 1950.
	"Cochrane's restless temperament." NBL clipping, 1950.
	"In 13 big league seasons." PHB, 9 July 1950.
	"Well, it's back to the ranch." TSN, 13 September 1950.
	"Joan eloped." Sara Bollman interview.
168–9	"That really hurt." Jack Thompson interview.
169	"Everything he did." Sara Bollman interview.
	"You needed to measure up." Jack Thompson interview.
170	"Having reached his goal." Sara Bollman interview.
	"It's funny when you think of it." Graham, "Cochrane Story."
	"I was 16." Sara Bollman interview.
171	In an old-timers game. NYT, 31 July 1955.

Page

| 171 | "I got tired of seeing so much bush league baseball." Newcombe, "Black Mike."
"There is a different class." Ibid.
"Daddy had a tough time." Sara Bollman interview.
"Maybe it was getting fired." Jack Thompson interview.
"Cochrane thought the game had turned its back." Bak, *Cobb*, p. 138.
"I'm eating regular." NYT, 10 February 1958.
"Mickey Cochrane had suffered a frightful beaning." Alexander, *Ty Cobb*, p. 226.
"A Hall of Fame member beaned by a pitched ball." McCallum, *Ty Cobb*, p. 205.
"Each month he mailed support checks." Stump, *Cobb*. |
| 172 | "There is an episode." BG, 6 January 1995.
"Stump admitted that Cobb was on heavy medication." Macht, "Cobb Never."
"Cobb wanted to tell Daddy." Sara Bollman interview.
"Mike was too proud." Mary Cochrane interview.
"What Stump wrote is pure B.S." Sara Bollman interview.
"It's Cochrane." Falls, *Detroit Tigers*.
"What Musial is to St. Louis." TSN, 14 July 1962. |
| 173 | "All these kids came up to Daddy." Sara Bollman interview.
"It was lighthitting." BH, 29 June 1958.
Ty Cobb's funeral. Alexander, *Ty Cobb*, p. 235.
"Daddy played golf." Sara Bollman interview.
The last baseball game Mike saw. TSN, 14 July 1962.
Cochrane died at the age of 59. State of Illinois Medical Certificate of Death, district 497, no. 167. |
| 174 | his body was cremated. Letter from Memorial Park Cemetery to author, 7 March 1995, and Sara Bollman interview. |

Chapter 22

Page

| 175 | "the passage of time." Honig, *Baseball America*, (New York:MacMillan, 1985) p. 174. |
| 175–6 | "The A's were victims." Nack, "Lost in History." |
| 176 | "a young fellow who may finish his career." Rice, "After the Ball Is Over."
"That reception." Mary Cochrane interview. |
| 178 | "The baseball world will probably never see a greater catcher." Mack, *My 66 Years*. |
| 180 | "that venerable, uncannily durable fraud." Thorn, *Hidden Game*.
"takes every offensive event." Ibid. |
| 181 | "when Mickey gets the edge." Thorn, *Total Baseball* (1991 edition),
"Grove and Foxx were glamour boys." Hirshberg, *Baseball's Greatest Catchers*.
"He showed us how to win." Berkow, *Greenberg*.
"Cochrane was a great inspirational leader." Honig, *Baseball When the Grass Was Real*. |
| 182 | "By a freakish coincidence." Cochrane, *Baseball*, p. 130.
"Greatest catcher of them all." Honig, *Baseball When the Grass Was Real*, p. 82.
"Cochrane gave me the knockdown signal." UA clipping, 1 July 1962.
Hartnett and Dickey are Mike's choice. NBL file, undated note from Cochrane. |

Bibliography

Alexander, Charles C. *Ty Cobb*. New York: Oxford University Press, 1984.
Bak, Richard. *Cobb Would Have Caught It*. Detroit: Wayne State University Press, 1991.
Berkow, Ira, ed. *Hank Greenberg: The Story of My Life*. New York: Times Books, 1989.
Brockton Enterprise. "Bridgewater Pays Tribute to Mickey," 18 September 1935.
Broeg, Bob. "Mickey Cochrane: Full of Fight, Ability." *The Sporting News*, 18 April 1970.
Brundidge, Harry T. "Mickey Cochrane, Highest-Salaried Catcher in Majors, Had Backstop Job Forced on Him." *The Sporting News*, 3 September 1931.
Cataneo, David. *Peanuts and Crackerjack*. Nashville, Tenn.: Rutledge Hill, 1996.
Cochrane, Mickey. *Baseball The Fan's Game*. New York: Funk and Wagnalls, 1939.
_____. "Baseball Through a Catcher's Mask." *Baseball Magazine*, June 1932.
_____. "Fall Guys." *Collier's*, 8 October 1938.
Creamer, Robert. *The Babe*. New York: Simon and Schuster, 1974.
Cross and Crescent. "Black Mike." June 1975.
Curran, William. *Mitts*. New York: William Morrow, 1985.
Danzig, Allison, ed. *Sport's Golden Age*. New York: Harper and Brothers, 1948.
Doerer, Tom. "Mickey Cochrane Predicts." *Baseball Magazine*, February 1930.
Dooly, Bill. "How Cochrane, Who Disliked Catching, Became One of Game's Best Backstops." *The Sporting News*, 7 February 1929.
Dudgeon, Phil. "Bridgewater Citizens Laud Mickey Cochrane." *Standard-Times* (New Bedford, Mass.), 18 September 1935.
Duncan, C. William. "Mickey Cochrane, Always a Fighter, Should Bring Back to Detroit Tigers Scrappy Ways of Ty Cobb." *The Sporting News*, 21 December 1933.
Falls, Joe. *Detroit Tigers*. New York: MacMillan, 1975. Update New York: Prentiss Hall, 1989.
Frisch, Frank, and Roy Stockton. *Frank Frisch: The Fordham Flash*. Garden City, N.Y.: Doubleday, 1962.
Galbraith, John Kenneth. *Money: Whence It Came, Where It Went*. Boston: Houghton Mifflin, 1975.
Gallico, Paul. *The Golden People*. Garden City, N.Y.: Doubleday, 1965.
Glass, Joel P. "Mickey Cochrane, Baseball Quarterback." *Literary Digest*, 7 July 1934.
Goldstein, Richard. *Spartan Seasons*. New York: MacMillan, 1980.
Graham, Frank. "The Mickey Cochrane Story." *Sport*, December 1955.
Greenberg, Eric. *The Celebrant*. New York: Everest House, 1983.
Gregory, Robert. *Diz*. New York: Penguin, 1992.
Haag, Irv. "Baseball's All-Time Greatest Catchers." *Baseball Digest*, 1973.
Harron, Robert. "What His Home Town Thinks of 'Mickey' Cochrane." *Baseball Magazine*, June 1926.

Hirshberg, Al. *Baseball's Greatest Catchers*. New York: G. P. Putnam's Sons, 1966.
Honig, Donald. *Baseball When the Grass Was Real*. New York: Coward, McCann & Geoghegan, 1975.
_____. *The October Heroes*. New York: Simon and Schuster, 1979.
Jones, Bobby. *Golf Is My Game*. New York: Doubleday, 1960.
Kieran, John. "The Man in the Iron Mask." *New York Times*, 22 April 1931.
Klingaman, William K. *1929 The Year of the Great Crash*. New York: Harper and Row, 1989.
Kuklick, Bruce. *To Everything a Season: Shibe Park & Urban Philadelphia*. Princeton: Princeton University Press, 1991.
Lacey, Robert. *Ford: The Men and the Machine*. Boston: Little, Brown, 1986.
Lane, F. C. "All the World Calls Him 'Mickey.'" *Baseball Magazine*, August 1929.
_____. "Mickey Cochrane, King of Catchers." *Baseball Magazine*, November 1930.
Lieb, Fred. *Baseball As I Have Known It*. New York: Coward, McCann and Geoghegan, 1977.
_____. *Connie Mack: Grand Old Man of Baseball*. New York: G. P. Putnam's Sons, 1945.
_____. *Detroit Tigers*. New York: G. P. Putnam's Sons, 1946.
_____. "Fireball Cochrane, Led Tigers to Two Flags." *The Sporting News*, 14 July 1962.
McCallum, John D. *The Tiger Wore Spikes*. New York: A. S. Barnes, 1956.
_____. *Ty Cobb*. New York: Praeger, 1975.
McElvaine, Robert S. *The Great Depression*. New York: Times Books, 1984.
Macht, Norman L. "Cobb Never Supported Cochrane." *National Pastime*, 1995.
Mack, Connie. *My 66 Years in the Big Leagues*. Philadelphia: John C. Winston, 1950.
Mantle, Mickey. *The Mick*. New York: Berkley, 1985.
Mead, William. *Even the Browns*. Chicago: Contemporary Books, 1978.
Nack, William. "Lost in History." *Sports Illustrated*, 19 August 1996.
Newcombe, Jack. "Black Mike of the Tigers." *Sport*, April 1960.
Povich, Shirley. "Perkins Votes for Cochrane." *Baseball Digest*, 1949.
Reichler, Joseph L., ed. *Baseball Encyclopedia*. New York: MacMillan, 1985.
Rice, Grantland. "After the Ball Is Over." *Collier's*, 16 August 1930.
Ritter, Lawrence S. *The Glory of Their Times*. New York: MacMillan, 1966.
Robinson, Ray. *Iron Horse*. New York: W. W. Norton, 1990.
Salsinger, H. G. "What Price a Pennant?" *Detroit News*, 26 September 1934.
Shapiro, Milton. *The Year They Won the MVP*. New York: Julian Messner, 1966.
Smelser, Marshall. *The Life That Ruth Built*. New York: Times Book Co., 1975.
Smith, Ken. *Baseball's Hall of Fame*. New York: Grosset & Dunlap, 1952.
Smith, Red. "Pepper Martin vs. Philadelphia, 1931." *The Ultimate Baseball Book*. Boston: Houghton Mifflin, 1984.
Smith, Robert. *Babe Ruth's America*. New York: Thomas Crowell, 1974.
Standard-Times (New Bedford, Mass.). "Mickey Cochrane a Conquering Hero in Bridgewater, His Old Home Town," 16 September 1934.
Stump, Al. *Cobb*. Chapel Hill, N.C.: Algonquin, 1994.
Thorn, John, and Pete Palmer. *The Hidden Game of Baseball*. Garden City, N.Y.: Doubleday, 1984.
_____. *Total Baseball*. New York: Viking, 1995.
Time. "Cubs vs. Tigers." 7 October 1935.
Voigt, David. *American Baseball*, vol 2. Norman, Okla: University of Oklahoma Press, 1970.
Watkins, T. H. *The Great Depression: America in the 1930s*. Boston: Little, Brown, 1993.
Williams, Ted. *My Turn at Bat*. New York: Simon and Schuster, 1969.

Index

Allen, Johnny 129
Andres, Ernie 154
Auker, Eldon: commentary 141, 142, 159; Detroit teammate 116, 131, 132, 139, 173; World Series 123, 125–126, 134
Averill, Earl 100, 114

Baker, Del 8, 35, 136, 140, 144, 147, 148, 149
Barrow, Ed 108
Barry, Dan 52
Baumholz, Frank 154
Bench, Johnny 45, 162, 178
Bengough, Benny 55
Bennett, Harry 153
Berra, Yogi 162, 176, 178
Berry, Charlie 109
Bishop, Max 41, 53, 61, 76, 80, 90, 109
Black, Bill 78
Blackburne, Slats 52
Blaeholder, George 41
Bohr, Mary *see* Cochrane, Mary
Boley, Joe 64
Bollman, Sara *see* Cochrane, Sara
Book, Frank 149, 162, 164, 165, 170
Boston Red Sox 10, 39, 40, 53, 57, 58, 60, 63, 79, 80, 109, 112, 115, 118, 131, 142, 147
Bottomley, Jim 75, 86, 87, 89
Braxton, Garland 60
Braves Field 20, 21, 22, 26, 27, 31, 80
Brazill, Frank 35
Bresnahan, Roger 162, 176, 178
Bridges, Tommy: Detroit teammate 114, 115, 116, 118, 127, 128, 131, 132, 139, 141, 173; opponent of Philadelphia 79; World Series 5, 6, 124, 126, 133, 124, 136
Briggs, Walter 109, 137, 139, 140, 141, 143, 144, 145, 146, 147, 148, 149, 150
Briggs Stadium 146
Brooklyn Dodgers 157
Burns, Denny 37
Burns, Jack 138
Bush, Guy 65
Bush, Joe 55

Campanella, Roy 162, 176, 178
Campbell, Archie 60
Carleton, Jim 134
Cavarretta, Phil 7, 8, 134, 135
Chapman, Ben 98
Chapman, Ray 81, 142, 143
Chicago Cubs 5–8, 64–66, 132–136
Chicago White Sox 50, 52, 62, 80, 99, 109, 115, 116, 127, 157
Cissell, Bill 100
Cleveland Indians 41, 55, 60, 62, 70, 81, 99, 100, 108, 116
Clifton, Flea 6, 7, 114, 124, 133
Cobb, Ty 109, 152; mentor to Cochrane 47–49, 50, 111, 171–172, 173; Philadelphia teammate 49, 51, 52
Cochrane, Al (nephew) 151, 158
Cochrane, Archie (brother) 3, 4, 12, 162, 165, 166
Cochrane, Arthur (brother) 12
Cochrane, Bert (brother) 12, 13, 15, 136, 162, 165, 166
Cochrane, Cornelius 82–83
Cochrane, Dave 162

Cochrane, Edith (sister) 12
Cochrane, Flora (sister) 12
Cochrane, Fred (cousin) 15
Cochrane, Gordon (Mickey): all-star teams, 42, 63, 74, 82, 106, 114, 128–129, 140, 156, 176; amateur baseball 18, 29–30; basketball 14, 16, 17, 25, 78; batting style 54, 62, 82; boxing, 25, 30, 70; catcher, comparison to others 176–178; catcher, doubts as 15, 27, 30–31, 32, 33–34, 36, 37, 39; catching style 34, 45–47, 52, 59, 65, 69, 73, 103, 113, 122, 128, 178, 182; coach 166; college baseball 26–28; dancing 26, 121, 164, 169; death 173–174; earnings 33, 57, 67, 78, 90, 98, 126, 145, 149–150; education 9, 14, 18, 19, 20, 22, 26, 31, 33, 40, 69, 87; endorsements 130–131; fielding 32, 36, 63, 65, 66; finances 48, 50, 58, 63, 66, 68–70, 87–88, 98, 141, 166, 171–172; flying planes 71–73, 92–93, 102, 150–151, 170; football 14, 16–17, 20–24, 26, 33, 156; Frank King name 31, 32, 33; general manager 137, 167–168; golf 51, 72, 74, 78, 94, 97, 105, 107, 137, 141, 173; Great Lakes manager 153–158; Hall of Fame 160–162; heroics off-field 26, 99; hero status 9, 10, 160, 117, 130, 149, 173; high school baseball 15–16, 18; hitting streaks 35, 49–50, 60, 71, 79, 81, 116; hockey 25–26; holdouts 32, 38, 58–59; home runs 16, 27, 35, 36, 38, 40–41, 74–75, 79, 95, 98, 99, 107, 178; hunting 13, 43, 55–56, 68, 77, 109, 136, 140, 146, 165; injuries,21, 22, 24, 45, 52, 61, 70–71, 80, 81, 86–87, 114, 122, 124–125, 139–140; jobs, non-baseball 9, 13, 19, 24, 26, 29, 43, 51, 59, 150, 171; manager style 6, 13–14, 109, 110, 113, 114, 116, 122, 127–128, 133, 137, 141, 146–147, 181; marriage 26, 34; Mickey nickname 12, 22, 33; minor league baseball 30–37; monuments 11, 174, 176, 179; music 62, 102, 164; MVP awards 56–57, 119, 181; old-timers games 166, 171, 173; parades to honor 3, 10, 63, 131–132; pitchers, working with 46–47, 54–55, 73, 84, 118, 132; ranch 149, 162, 164–165, 167; residences 41, 49, 62, 68, 78, 141, 148, 158, 165; running 7, 13, 16, 35, 73, 178; saxophone 26, 57, 164; scout 170, 172–173; signed as pro 33; theatre 12, 26, 57–58; trade to Detroit 109; work, non-baseball 9, 13, 19, 24, 26, 29, 43, 44, 51, 59, 171; worries 58, 87, 112, 117, 130, 137, 139–140, 169; *see also* Detroit Tigers; Philadelphia Athletics
Cochrane, Gordon, Jr. (son) 37, 60, 68, 131, 158–159
Cochrane, James (grandfather) 12
Cochrane, Joan (daughter, Mrs. John Cobb) 68, 131, 148, 162, 164, 165, 167, 168
Cochrane, John (father) 11, 12, 14, 25, 43, 136, 160, 163, 166
Cochrane, Margaret (grandmother) 12
Cochrane, Mary (nee Bohr): girlfriend 13, 17–18, 20, 22, 26, 31; mother 37, 68, 158; wife, 34, 68–69, 76, 77, 78–79, 148, 162, 165, 166–167; widow 176
Cochrane, Sadie (mother) 11, 12, 14, 159
Cochrane, Sara (daughter, Mrs. Kenneth Bollman) 162, 167, 169, 170
Coffman, Dick 81
Collins, Eddie 49, 55, 77, 86, 89
Collins, Joe 122, 124, 125
Combs, Earl 42
Comiskey Park 106
Connally, Sarge 50, 81
Cramer, Doc 81, 90, 102, 103, 105, 107, 128, 158
Cronin, Joe 114, 153
Crowder, Al 49, 116, 120, 126, 134, 139, 173
Cunningham, Bruce 94

Daly, Tom 34, 35, 45, 47
Davis, Spud 123, 180
Dean, Dizzy 114, 120, 121, 123, 124, 125
Dean, Paul 120, 122, 124
DeLancey, Bill 125, 180
Demaree, Frank 8
Dempsey, Jack 20, 30
Derringer, Paul 84
Detroit Tigers: Cochrane as teammate 111–119, 121–126, 127–136, 137–141, 142–144, 146–147; opponent of Philadelphia 50, 52, 55, 60, 70, 71, 108, 109
Dewitt, Bill 172–173

Index

Dickey, Bill 55, 63, 106, 107, 114, 129, 142, 162, 176, 178, 180, 181, 182
Dietrick, Bill 78
DiMaggio, Joe 156, 171
Donahue, Jiggs 30, 31, 32, 35, 45, 47
Dugan, Joe 53
Durham, Ed 80
Durocher, Leo 123
Dykes, Jimmy 61, 66, 70, 76, 85, 90, 97, 100, 106, 116, 166

Earnshaw, George: Philadelphia teammate 51, 63, 74, 82, 85, 86, 89, 90, 109; World Series 64, 65, 66, 75, 76;
Ehmke, Howard 64, 65
Elbing, Doc 61, 71
Ewing, Buck 162, 176, 181

Farrell, Charlie 25, 26, 102
Feller, Bob 156, 158
Fenway Park 26, 40, 79, 80, 112, 127, 131
Ferrell, Rick 100, 106, 107, 129, 162, 178
Ferrell, Wes 137
Finney, Lou 106
Fisk, Carlton 162
Flagstead, Ira 57
Ford Motor Company 117, 121, 143, 153, 157, 166
Fox, Pete 112, 115, 134, 135, 139
Foxx, Jimmie: catcher for A's 38, 49, 51; opponent of Detroit 128, 129; Philadelphia teammate 60, 61, 62, 63, 79, 82, 97, 98, 99, 102, 105, 106, 107, 162, 171, 175, 178, 181; World Series 65, 66, 75, 84, 88
Frankhouse, Fred 114
French, Larry 5, 6, 7, 94, 95, 135
French, Walter 62
Frisch, Frank 123, 161; Japan teammate 93, 94; World Series 74, 75, 86, 89, 120, 122
Fullis, Charlie 126

Galan, Augie 6
Galloway, Chick 45
Gaston, Milt 41, 61
Gehrig, Lou 42, 49, 99, 106, 108, 119, 129, 175; consecutive game streak 95, 115; Japan teammate 93, 94; opponent of Detroit 115; opponent of Philadelphia 45, 79, 107

Gehringer, Charlie: commentary 111, 181; Detroit teammate 111, 113, 115, 118, 119, 128, 131, 132, 142, 149; World Series, 7, 8, 121, 122, 123, 125, 135
Gibson, Josh 162, 176
Glass, Tom 41
Gleason, Kid 45
Gomez, Lefty 61, 80, 116, 118, 119, 130, 166
Goslin, Goose: Detroit teammate 112, 115, 117, 118, 132; World Series 6, 8, 9, 122, 123, 124, 135, 136
Grace, Joe 154
Gray, Sam 40
Great Depression 9, 67, 74, 87, 98, 104–105, 143
Greenberg, Hank: commentary 171, 181; Detroit teammate 111, 113, 117, 129, 131, 132; hold out 137–138; religious issues 111, 118; World Series 6, 123, 125, 133–134
Grimes, Burleigh 74–75, 77, 86, 89, 90, 115
Grimm, Charlie 5, 65
Grove, Lefty: commentary 55, 148, 182; Japan teammate 93, 94; opponent of Detroit 109, 128, 173; Philadelphia teammate 38, 39, 40, 45, 46, 49, 51, 53, 55, 61, 63, 74, 79, 82, 97, 98, 100, 107, 175; 16-game win streak 80, 81, 181–182; World Series 64, 65, 74, 75, 84, 88, 89, 91

Haas, Mule 52, 58, 61, 66, 88, 100
Hack, Stan 5, 6, 135, 136
Hadley, Bump 60, 142, 144, 162
Hafey, Chick 84, 85
Haines, Jesse 75
Hajduk, Chet 154, 156
Hale, Sammy 39, 49, 70
Hallahan, Bill 75–76, 85, 86, 90, 107
Harder, Mel 100, 114, 116
Harridge, Will 137, 140
Harris, Bucky 109, 111
Hartnett, Gabby 7, 42, 134, 162, 171, 178, 181, 182
Hasty, Bob 37
Hauser, Joe 52
Hayes, Charlie 17–18, 63
Hayworth, Ray 106, 112, 114, 115, 118, 126, 133, 140

204 INDEX

Hemsley, Rollie 129
Herman, Billy 6, 7, 8
Heving, John 80, 81, 99, 100
Higgins, Frank 103, 105
High, Andy 89
Hildebrand, Oral 116
Hogsett, Chief 113, 126, 138
Hoover, Herbert 59, 66, 79, 86
Hoover, J. Edgar 132
Hornsby, Rogers 65, 161, 175
Howland, Charley 37
Hoyt, Waite 87, 88
Hubbell, Carl 161
Huggins, Miller 45
Hunter, Herb 92, 93
Huntzinger, Walter 55

Jennings, Hugh 109
Johnson, Bob 103
Johnson, Hank 79
Johnson, Walter 40, 41, 44, 80, 102
Jones, Bobby 20, 74
Jones, Johnny 100
Jones, Sam 55
Judge, Joe 56
Jurges, Billy 5, 8

Kallio, Rudy 35, 39
Kamm, Willie 94
Kelly, George 94
Kelly, King 162, 176
Kennedy, Vern 146
Kenworthy, Duke 34, 35
King, Frank 31, 32
Klein, Chuck 134
Klem, Bill 65
Kline, Bob 80
Kling, Johnny 176
Knickerbocker, Bill 139
Knight, Frank 31
Krausse, Lew 99, 105

Lazzeri, Tony 56
Lamar, Bill 49, 50
Landis, Judge 38, 66, 126, 136, 140
Lawson, Roxie 131
League Park 99
Lee, Hal 103
Lewis, Buddy 142
Lewis, Duffy 36
Lindsey, Jim 76

Lombardi, Ernie 162, 178
Lucadello, Johnny 154
Lyons, Ted 50, 52

Mack, Connie 138, 162; all-star game manager 105–106; developing Cochrane 39, 45; Philadelphia manager 39, 40, 45, 47, 50, 51, 53, 60–61, 62, 63, 70, 99, 100, 166; Philadelphia owner 37, 78, 88, 100–101, 105, 108–109, 112, 167–168; signing Cochrane 32, 36–37; World Series 64, 88
Mack, Connie, Jr. 168
Mack, Earle 32, 101, 168
Mack, Roy 101, 168
Madjeski, Ed 99
Malone, Pat 65, 66
Mancuso, Al 74
Mantle, Mickey 82
Manush, Heinie 56
Maranville, Rabbit 94
Marberry, Fred 60, 112, 115, 116, 126
Martin, Pepper 82, 84–87, 89–91, 92, 93, 97, 98, 123
Mays, Carl 81, 142, 143
McCann, Emmett 36
McCarthy, Joe 64, 108, 115, 116, 156
McCosky, Barney 157
McCoy, Benny 154
McGowan, Bill 85
McGraw, John 106
McMillan, Norm 65
McNair, Eric 86, 99
McNamara, John 46
Medwick, Joe 122, 123, 124, 126
Melillo, Oscar 81
Meusel, Bob 53
Miller, Bing 52, 61, 66, 76, 80, 90, 97, 100, 102, 109, 166
Milligan, John 78
Mize, Johnny 156
Moore, Jim 81
Morris, Ed 57
Municipal Stadium 100, 129, 156
Myer, Buddy 59

Navin, Frank 108–109, 125, 132, 133, 135, 137, 150
Navin Field 8, 79, 114, 117, 124, 131, 135, 146
New York Giants 43, 120, 132

New York Yankees: opponents of Detroit 112, 114, 116, 118, 129–130, 131, 132, 140, 142; opponents of Philadelphia 44–45, 49, 51–55, 59–61, 71, 79–80, 98, 107, 175–176

O'Doul, Lefty 36, 94
Oliver, Tom 94
Olsen, Vern 156
Onslow, Jack 35
Orsatti, Ernie 89, 124, 125
Orwoll, Ossie 52
Owen, Marv 6, 7, 112, 113, 115, 126, 133, 135, 146

Padgett, Don, 154
Palmisano, Joe 91
Pasek, Johnny 109
Pearson, Monte 116
Pellagrini, Eddie 156
Perkins, Cy: Detroit coach 112, 117, 124, 135; financial help, 70, 88; Philadelphia teammate 38, 39, 40, 49, 50, 51, 61, 62, 76, 77, 80; teaching Cochrane 45–46, 47, 73
Philadelphia Athletics: Cochrane as teammate 38–41, 43–45, 49–50, 51–55, 59–66, 70–73, 74–76, 79–82, 84–91, 97–100, 107–108, 175; opponents of Detroit 113, 139
Philadelphia Phillies 43, 62, 103
Phillips, Red 116
Picinich, Val 40
Pipgras, George 53, 80
Poffenberger, Boots 147, 150
Polo Grounds 114, 156
Poole, Jim 36, 39
Powell, Jack 138, 139
Pytlak, Frank 154

Query, Wray 34
Quinn, Jack 46–47, 53
Quinn, John 103

Reiber, Frank 140, 141
Rhem, Flint 75
Riconda, Harry 37
Rigney, Johnny 154
Roettger, Wally 89
Rogell, Billy: commentary 111, 146, 149, 158, 172; Detroit teammate 111, 113, 115, 118, 131; opponent of Philadelphia 39; World Series 123, 136
Rolfe, Red 29, 115
Rommel, Ed 40, 44, 46, 53, 64, 97, 99
Root, Charlie 64, 133
Rowe, Schoolboy: commentary 182; Detroit teammate 112, 114, 118, 119, 127, 128, 129–130, 131, 139, 141, 142, 173; Great Lakes teammate 157–158; 16-game win streak 115–116, 117–118, 181–182; World Series 120, 121, 122, 124, 126, 134
Ruel, Muddy 42, 66, 93
Ruffing, Red 79, 98, 107, 115, 116, 130, 171
Ruppert, Jake 108
Russell, Joe 30
Ruth, Babe 20, 49, 92, 98, 106, 175, 181; Cochrane's ranch 163, 164; Detroit manager job 108, 109; opponent of Detroit 115; opponent of Philadelphia 53, 59, 79, 107

St. Louis Browns 40, 41, 48, 52, 59, 61, 70, 73, 81, 100, 118, 132, 139, 141, 157
St. Louis Cardinals 32, 74–76, 82, 84–91, 97, 120–126, 132
Schalk, Ray 162, 173, 176, 178
Schang, Wally 70, 71, 80
Schulte, Fred 81
Sewell, Joe 62
Sewell, Luke 100, 106
Sewell, Rip 111, 157
Shawkey, Bob 74
Sherid, Roy 78
Sherling, Ed 37
Shibe Park, 38, 40, 43, 49, 64, 74, 79, 86, 98, 100, 102, 104, 108, 139, 166, 167, 168
Shinners, Ralph 94
Shires, Art 70
Shocker, Urban 45
Simmons, Al: Detroit teammate 139, 141; Japan teammate 93, 94, 96; opponent of Detroit 100, 102, 106, 128; Philadelphia teammate 38, 41, 49, 53, 61, 62, 63, 71, 73, 76, 79, 80, 81, 82, 98, 99, 162, 175, 178; World Series 65, 75, 84, 88
Sorrell, Vic 115, 116, 130, 173
Speaker, Tris 51, 52, 77, 136, 151

Sportsman's Park 75, 84, 124
Street, Gabby 77
Stokes, Art 38
Sullivan, Dan 29, 30
Sunday baseball 85, 99–100
Sweetland, Sugar 141

Tebbetts, Birdie 141
Thomas, Ira 29, 30
Thompson, Jack (nephew) 164
Tolson, Chick 65
Tresh, Mike 141, 146
Trexler, Jim 157
Trucks, Virgil 157, 158
Turner, Tom 33, 36, 38

Van Atta, Russ 115
Vance, Dazzy 123
Vosmik, Joe 100

Walberg, Rube 46, 53, 54, 55, 59, 65, 80, 97, 109
Walker, Bill 123
Walker, Dixie 147
Walker, Gee 5, 112, 114, 115, 121, 146
Walters, Bucky 78

Warneke, Lon 133
Washington Senators 41, 53, 59, 60, 71, 73, 79, 107, 117, 142
Watkins, George 89
Whalen, Charles 21, 24–25, 33
Wheat, Zack 49
White, JoJo 114, 121, 123, 124, 127, 133, 134, 173
Whitehill, Earl 50
Whitney, Pinky 103, 104
Williams, Dib 85, 90
Williams, Ted 153–154, 156
Wilson, Hack 66
Wilson, Jim 82, 85
Wingfield, Ted 39
Wood, Joe 80
World Series: 1929 64–66; 1930 74–76; 1931 84–91; 1934 121–126; 1935 5–9, 132–136
Wrigley Field 64, 134, 154

Yankee Stadium 24, 49, 53, 79, 116, 131, 142, 171
York, Rudy 138, 144

Zinn, Jimmy 62

www.ingramcontent.com/pod-product-compliance
Ingram Content Group UK Ltd.
Pitfield, Milton Keynes, MK11 3LW, UK
UKHW042002140426
5217IPUK00015B/944